*Like a gourmet chef, Lynda Hunter Bjorklund has prepared a bountiful feast for all whose hearts are hungry to really know God in a deeper way. I invite you to come and partake of these soul-satisfying truths and leave filled with the knowledge of how to have an intimate, passionate, and committed relationship with the Lord.*

—**Cynthia Heald,** on staff with The Navigators, conference speaker, and author of *Becoming a Woman Who Loves*

*From the first time I met Lynda, years ago, I loved this woman. She had a heart for God. It was evident that nothing—no circumstance of life—would deter her from pursuing him. This is the kind of woman I want to learn from.*

—**Kay Arthur,** CEO and cofounder of Precept Ministries International and author of *Trusting God in Times of Adversity*

*Dr. Lynda Hunter Bjorklund is an articulate communicator and a gifted writer. Her message grabs the attention of her listeners and effectively speaks truth to her readers.* The Hungry Heart *is filled with biblical principles, captivating illustrations, and practical applications. This book will create a desire within the reader to "go deeper" with God. Don't miss it!*

—**Carol Kent,** president of Speak Up Speaker Services and international speaker and author

Satisfy Your Desire
to Know God
in Deeper Ways

# THE *Hungry Heart*

## LYNDA HUNTER BJORKLUND

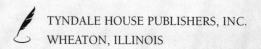

TYNDALE HOUSE PUBLISHERS, INC.
WHEATON, ILLINOIS

Visit Tyndale's exciting Web site at www.tyndale.com

*The Hungry Heart: Satisfy Your Desire to Know God in Deeper Ways*

Designed by Beth Sparkman

Edited by Susan Taylor

Published in association with the literary agency of Alive Communications, Inc., 7680 Goddard Street, Suite 200, Colorado Springs, CO 80920.

The names of some of the people mentioned in this book have been changed to protect their privacy.

**Library of Congress Cataloging-in-Publication Data**

Bjorklund, Lynda Hunter.
   The hungry heart : satisfy your desire to know God in deeper ways / Lynda Hunter Bjorklund
    p. cm.
Includes bibliographical references.
   ISBN 0-8423-7938-X (sc)
   1. Spiritual life—Christianity. 2. Christian life.   I. Title.
BV4501.3 .B52 2004
248.4—dc22                                     2003019276

Printed in the United States of America

10  09  08  07  06  05  04
7   6   5   4   3   2   1

# DEDICATION

*To my mother, Audrey, who whetted my appetite
for the deeper things of God when I was a little girl.
We didn't have great wealth, but she gave me riches
stored in secret places (Isaiah 45:3).
And now to my children,
Angie, Susan, Matt, Ashley, Courtney, and Clint,
I pray my life has somehow fed your insatiable desire
for intimacy with the Almighty.*

# CONTENTS

# ACKNOWLEDGMENTS

Every book written about the Christian walk comes together as a result of what 1 Corinthians 12 calls the spiritual gifts and the body ministry. Thanks to all those people in the body who shared their gifts and helped to make *The Hungry Heart* a reality:

- Dave Bjorklund, my husband, who encouraged me with every word;
- Countless people who expressed to me their stories of wanting to know God in deeper ways;
- Tyndale House Publishers' team: Tammy Faxel, who embraced this book in her tireless work to broaden and deepen Tyndale's excellent ministry to women; Susan Taylor, who used her wonderful editing skills to help me look good; and countless other Tyndale people who, from cover design to shipping, worked together to bring this book to you.

As all of us carefully prepare our favorite dishes to bring to potluck meals, so the body ministry has done to create this book. May each who comes to eat at the table be blessed by the message of *The Hungry Heart*. And may its reading stimulate your insatiable appetite to know God more and more.

> *Your words were found, and I ate them.*
> Jeremiah 15:16

# Introduction

At some point in my childhood, I heard the Bible story about Elijah's asking Elisha what he could do for him before he left for heaven. Elisha's response to his predecessor and mentor was clear and certain: "Please let a double portion of your spirit be upon me" (2 Kings 2:9).

I don't remember how old I was the day I prayed for a double portion of the intimate relationship my mother had with God. Something about the way she trusted him fascinated me. Something about the way she engaged in conversation with him enticed me. Something about the way she really knew him intrigued me.

Mom's journey began in early fall when I was about six months old, the second of what would be a brood of eight children. Her eighteen-year-old sister, Joan, was dying of a rheumatic heart, and the family had given Joan an early Christmas and an early graduation from high school. My grandfather, Mom's dad, heard of a man who prayed for the sick and they were healed. Out of other options, my grandfather persevered through ignorance of all spiritual things and the opposition of family members. He carried Joan's swollen body into the stranger's tent revival the following Friday night. By Tuesday my aunt was completely healed. Joan lived to see not only that Christmas but more than fifty Christmases since.

As great as Joan's miracle was, the greater miracle was the conversion of my mom and dad and many extended family members to Christ. My mother said, "I want to know this Lord who would heal my little sister."

Mom wasn't content with just becoming acquainted with Christ. She wanted to know everything about him. She scoured the Bible to learn all she could. I saw her turn the pages of Scripture as she stirred pots on the stove. I heard her in our furnace room—the only place she could find to be alone, away from all her kids—crying out to the One with whom she had fallen in love.

That's how I grew up, watching my mother get to know the Lord intimately. I realized more was available than just a perfunctory Sunday morning walk with God. I got a glimpse of a Lord who cared about everything in our lives, and he talked to my parents and showed them the way to go. God knew them, and they knew God. Somehow our problems found solutions, and our needs were met.

## FROM THEIRS TO MINE

Throughout my teen years I continued to enjoy this intimate fellowship with God vicariously through my parents' relationship with him, especially my mother's. When I was in my early twenties, I sat beside my dad in church one Sunday morning, singing a hymn I'd never heard before:

> Learning to lean.
> Learning to lean.
> I'm learning to lean on Jesus.
> Finding more power than I ever dreamed.
> I'm learning to lean on Jesus.[1]

As I look back, I realize that morning signaled a new direction for me, one that would take me on a new journey. No longer would it be enough for me to lean on my mom and dad, who'd learned to lean on the Lord. The time would come for me to learn to lean for myself.

In the years that followed, I graduated from college, took my first teaching job, got married, and had two little girls. When I was thirty-three and pregnant with my third child, I watched my dad grow ill with pancreatic cancer. Then my husband left and ended our marriage. It was in September 1985, in the midst of all those circumstances, that I tucked a Bible under my arm, walked to the field behind our home, and surrendered my hungry heart to Christ. I prayed, "I give you not just these situations. I give you my life." My surrender that day marked the beginning of my own relationship with God.

I will never forget the years that followed and the experiences I had as I found a God who was not distant but instead came through in the middle of the night when I felt that everyone slept but me. I'll never forget the time my children and I prayed about a bill we couldn't pay, and that night we watched as five hundred dollars came to us out of nowhere. I'll never forget how God warned me that one of my children would go through some hard times. She did. And God held me and guided me—and my daughter. I'll never forget the times I dragged my finger across Bible verses that promised me safe passage through to the other side of a trial, and I always arrived safely and with a sense of victory. All these things and many, many more, I will never forget.

Through it all, I have gotten to know God as my mother did, yet differently, uniquely. My friendship with God was designed just for me. I sometimes questioned how he could love me so much, but I knew he did. I wondered how he could be so patient with me, but I knew he was. I wondered how he kept from getting aggravated with my lack of trust, but I knew he wasn't. With gentleness he kept me going on the right track. I learned I could talk with him, laugh with him, rejoice with him—even brag to him, and I knew I was his delight.

## FROM MINE TO YOURS

I had to write this book. I pray that I can begin to convey the depths of God that I have only begun to know. I hope that I can stir in you the longing for adventure and friendship with God that has been inside you since the day you were born. My greatest desire is to whet your appetite for the incredible, indescribable, unutterable, undeniable sweet things of God, just as the aroma of cinnamon rolls fresh from the oven whets your physical appetite.

This book is about getting to know God. Many books and sermons have been devoted to this subject, and their treatment, depth, and explanations are as varied as the people who created them. The more I study what it means to know Christ, the more I'm convinced we still don't really understand all it involves. Paul said in 1 Corinthians 2:9: "Eye has not seen, nor ear heard, nor have entered into the heart of man the things which God has prepared for those who love Him."

But between coming to Christ and going to be with him in heaven, between the eye, ear, and mind's gearing up for the incredible surprise that awaits us on the day we finally see, hear, and understand what all that means, God offers each of us the opportunity to really know him.

Divided into three parts, this book bases your growth in knowing the depths of God on three verses from the Scriptures. Part 1, "From the Outside Looking In," is based on John 14:9: "Have I been with you so long, and yet you have not *known* Me?" Part 2, "A View from the Inside," is based on Philippians 3:10: "That I may *know* Him." Part 3, "Taking the Inside Out," is based on Daniel 11:32: "The people who *know* their God shall be strong, and carry out great exploits."[2]

During those early years Mom got to know God in the furnace room. Now she kneels on a little rug at the end of her couch. After more than fourteen years as a widow, Mom talked to me recently by phone about the sale of their home, about her relocation, about her struggle to feel at home, and about where she should live. "Like I have done for more than fifty years, I look in his Word before I get up in the morning," she said, "and today, Lynda, this is what I read from Psalm 104: 'He sends the springs into the valleys; they flow among the hills. They give drink to every beast of the field; the wild donkeys quench their thirst. By them the birds of the heavens have their home'" (vv. 10-12).

God provides for the animals, and he reminds my mom through his Word that he continues to provide for her too. Once more Mom received her daily direction and peace from the One she has gotten to know, trust, and love with all her might.

God has something in store for you that is sweet and deep and unique. So come with me. Wipe your feet and step inside to the place where really knowing the Almighty and having your own hungry heart filled is only a decision away. The decision is yours.

—Lynda Hunter Bjorklund

# PART ONE

## FROM THE OUTSIDE LOOKING IN

Have I been with you so long, and
yet you have not *known* Me?*

*John 14:9*

*emphasis added

# 1

# What Does It Mean to Know God?

For a long time I have had a recurring dream in which a special room is attached to my home. Filled with magnificent antiques, it's a place few people get to see because it seems too special and unique to make available to those who wouldn't appreciate its splendor. Beauty is in the eye of the beholder, so I invite inside only those beholders who ask to see its beauty.

I thought of that dream recently as I took a walk with a friend. She said, "My prayer every day for two years has been that I would come to know God. Really know him."

*To know God.* After many years in ministry and living life in general, I have probably heard women express this desire more than any other. These women I encounter possess an insatiable thirst for spiritual things. They long to see the beauty and the mystery places, such as the one in my dream.

No words more accurately sum up the essence, purpose, and meaning of life, both now and in eternity to come, than the words *to know God.* No words provide more concise direction for navigating our way through decisions. No words better guide us through life's storms. No words illustrate a greater miracle than that the all-sufficient, all-powerful, all-glorious God of the universe would offer individual people like you and me relationship with himself. Author and theologian J. I. Packer writes, "What matters supremely . . . is not, in the last analysis, the fact that I know God, but the larger fact which underlies it—the fact that *he knows me*. I am graven on the palms of his hands. I am never out of his mind. All my knowledge of him depends on his sustained initiative in knowing me. I know him because he first knew me, and continues to know me. He knows me as a friend, one who loves me; and there is no moment when his eye is off me, or his attention distracted from me, and no moment, therefore, when his care falters."[1]

When we open the Bible, we read at the beginning how God walked in the cool of the day with the first man he created. They talked together. God knew him, and he knew God. We turn to the end of the Book of Life's story, and we find that as Christians we will someday live with God forever, see him face-to-face, and even look like him.

But in between, things happen. Some pages of life's book present joyous events, such as marriage and the births of children. We smile as we sail along on smooth waters. Then just as we're getting accustomed to riding the crest of a wave, we plunge to the depths. We turn another page, and we hear a bad diagnosis. We bury a loved one. We suffer a financial setback.

Life seemed to be sailing along as planned for my thirty-two-year-old niece, Alice. Without any kind of belief in God, she had established herself as an attorney and married her high school sweetheart. Their then eighteen-month-old daughter had become the light of their lives. But one Wednesday changed all that. Alice learned she had cancer and only weeks to live. Suddenly, all that mattered was whether or not she had a relationship with God. She and her husband prayed to receive Christ as their Savior the week they heard the diagnosis. At the writing of this book, it's too early to see whether God will choose to heal Alice and whether she will get the opportunity to know God in a deeper way.

Alice's eternity is secure, but God desires so much more for us.

Knowing God, really knowing him, is an option for every Christian willing to go the extra mile with him, to dig a little deeper, to strive a little more. Just as a cake is still a cake even without the icing, a Christian can still be a Christian and ultimately go to heaven without ever experiencing deep intimacy with God. But so much more is available to us.

Nineteenth-century preacher Charles Spurgeon wrote, "Little faith will bring your souls to heaven, but great faith will bring heaven to your souls." Little saving knowledge of God can get us through the pearly gates, but great knowledge of God brings heaven to our souls right here on earth and sustains us through both the highs and the lows and brings him glory through it all: "The land which you cross over to possess is a land of hills and valleys . . . a land for which the Lord your God cares; the eyes of the Lord your God are always on it, from the beginning of the year to the very end of the year" (Deuteronomy 11:11-12).

Knowing God means we voluntarily embark on the journey to find intimate fellowship with the One who cares and sees all. Knowing God brings us to a place of trust in him, whether we're experiencing the hilltop or the valley. Knowing God allows us to lift our eyes off the hardships and onto the ultimate victory that is to come. Packer writes, "What makes life worthwhile is having a big enough objective, something which catches our imagination and lays hold of our allegiance; and this the Christian has in a way that no other person has. For what higher, more exalted, and compelling goal can there be than to know God?"[2]

Once we realize that our purpose on earth is to find intimate fellowship with God—to really know him—we don't have to concentrate so much on the obstacles we encounter. We gain faith to believe we'll make it through and find level footing once again. Knowing God makes us certain, deep in our hearts, that he knows and cares about everything that concerns us, no matter what happens around us. My mother calls this way of knowing God having it down inside our "knowers." Once that knowledge is there, no circumstance can take it away.

## WHAT DOES *KNOWING* MEAN?

*Roget's* thesaurus says that the word *know* means "to perceive . . . with the intellect" or "to participate in or partake of personally." Synonyms include *apprehend, comprehend, fathom, grasp,* or *understand.*[3]

In Western thought, we say we know in one of two ways: (1) *We know things.* "I know my address and my phone number." This knowledge consists of cognitive facts and data that we possess and file in the brain. It does not contain an emotional connection. (2) *We know people.* "I know my husband and my friend." This kind of knowing includes emotional bonds, shared interests, common goals, similar outlooks, mutual admiration, time spent together, and interaction at many levels about all kinds of things. Eventually I know you and you know me. This kind of knowing does not take place merely through brain cells. It has an emotive connection that draws us into relationship.

Eastern thought, specifically Hebrew in this case, lends another dimension to *knowing* that connects both the cognitive—or factual—and the emotional elements of the word. It says that *to know* involves experiencing something, not just intellectualizing it. To know someone is to share an intimate relationship with that person. The Hebrew word *yada* means to encounter or experience through life-giving intimacy. A man may "know" a woman through sexual intercourse. We see an example of this kind of knowing in Genesis 4:1: "Adam knew Eve his wife, and she conceived and bore Cain." A woman may "know" a man in the same sense, as in Numbers 31:17: "Now therefore, kill every male among the little ones, and kill every woman who has known a man intimately."

*Yada* involves concern, inner engagement, dedication, or attachment to a person.

We can also *yada* God. Our part in knowing God means walking faithfully in his ways and living out the terms of his covenant. It includes both the internalizing of truth and its outworkings in the affairs of life.

One day I taught the beginnings of *yada*-ing God to one of my daughters after she had said something that muddied her Christian testimony. I knew that my teenage daughter knew what was right. She had her factual knowledge of God down pat. She could recite portions of Scripture and even the theme of last week's sermon at church, but she needed more. So on our way to school I described what someone told me she'd said. "You don't need to respond or explain. I wasn't there and didn't hear the words you spoke," I continued, "but God did. You are responsible to God, now and forever, and your repentance should be directed to him too."

As my daughter was learning, going to church every Sunday and attending Christian school isn't enough. Graduating from seminary or reading the Bible from cover to cover will not of itself bring personal relationship with the Father. We can't know anyone by compiling a spreadsheet of characteristics. We can't read, study, and attend church and when we've gathered enough information, assume that we know God. If that's all it took, God would be nothing more than a mere man, and our relationship with him would be dependent on how much information we had about him. Fact gathering is not relationship.

Knowing God takes place through a day-by-day surrendering of our lives to him, talking with him, and falling in love with him. Yet knowing God is not just an emotional experience either. It doesn't magically happen after we receive a measurable answer to prayer or attend a moving church service. In *The Life God Blesses,* author Gordon MacDonald calls these occurrences "spiritual experiences" that require little discipline of the soul. They become a matter of emotion, last for only a short while, and bring the recipient of the experiences honor or exaltation. But sooner or later, he says, "One has to come down to something that looks like normal. And when that happens, the spiritual experience is over, and the soul remains unconvinced."[4]

Such was the case following the 9/11 terrorist attacks. Every part of U.S. society was left reeling after that fateful Tuesday, and people responded. *Newsweek* reported Gallup poll findings about changing American habits. Of the people surveyed:

- 60 percent attended church
- 70 percent cried more
- 74 percent prayed more
- 82 percent displayed the American flag
- 77 percent showed more affection to others[5]

In addition, Bible sales soared by 28 percent, and liquor sales dropped by 50 percent. Radio stations played "God Bless the USA" 2,605 times the week after the attacks versus 47 times the week before. During the ten days after that dreadful Tuesday, in Houston, Texas, alone four hundred married couples withdrew their divorce applications prior to court proceedings.[6] It appeared people had turned their attention back to God.

I had launched my national radio talk show just three months earlier. During subsequent programs I offered listeners the opportunity to discuss their feelings about the attacks. What I discovered, however, was that they didn't want to talk as much about the terrorist attacks as about the "attacks" in their own lives: divorce, disappointment, disillusionment. The terrorist attacks of 9/11 had exposed the vulnerabilities of individual people throughout the country and forced them to rethink their lives, to reassess their priorities, and to make a stand for what they really believed.

But as the one-year anniversary of the terrorist attacks approached, additional surveys revealed that the new-and-improved way of thinking in America had not continued. Poll after poll indicated that citizens seemed to have returned to the mediocre, complacent, and inactive mind-set of the days before the attacks. By the time we rang in the new year of 2003 fifteen months later, the press had published a list of the twenty events that had affected our society the most that year. Of those events, only one religious event made the list, and it wasn't the fact that people had come to really know God and were sharing their experience with the world. It was the sex scandal involving Catholic priests.

Among other things, 9/11 revealed that many Christians have little experience when it comes to really knowing God. Sure, we have the outer trappings, but these lose their value when life gets turbulent and we find ourselves heading into the valley of difficulties. Author Calvin Miller emphasized this when he wrote, "Things dermal and outward lose their importance when things visceral and inward go wrong. Down where creams and oils cannot penetrate, the body must sometimes reckon with strong judgments. Then the deep issues of life hold final sway over all things surface."[7]

Whether we're dealing with a personal tragedy, such as Alice's cancer diagnosis, or with a global crisis, like terrorist threats, the answer to those difficulties lies in really knowing God.

## KNOWING GOD IN THE OLD TESTAMENT

The Old Testament refers many times to knowing God, but it does so in a somewhat indirect sense. In those days, when God's children wanted to communicate with him, they had to go through the high priest, who offered sacrifices and prayed to God on their behalf. God also used prophets, who went about the countryside telling people about him and performing miracles. When the prophet Elisha sent his servant to ask the Shunammite woman if things were well with her and her family, the woman replied, "It is well," even though her only son had just died and she had come seeking Elisha to raise the child from the dead (see 2 Kings 4:8-37). Despite not having "direct access" to God, this woman had come to know deep down about his faithfulness through what his prophet had taught and the miracles he had performed. Knowing God through Elisha gave her the confidence that all was well, even when things didn't look good.

In Moses' day God proved himself to his people corporately through miracles. He let the Israelites know *about* him through his deeds: "You shall know that I am the Lord your God, who . . ."

- brought you "out from under the burdens of the Egyptians" (Exodus 6:7)
- struck the water of the Nile, "and all the waters that were in the river were turned to blood" (Exodus 7:20)
- got rid of the frogs "from your houses, from your servants, and from your people" (Exodus 8:10-11)
- sent "swarms of flies on [Pharaoh] and [his] servants, on [his] people and into [his] houses" (Exodus 8:21)
- sent the full force of "all My plagues to [Pharaoh's] very heart, and on [his] servants and on [his] people" (Exodus 9:14)
- stopped the thunder and hail (Exodus 9:29)
- "dealt harshly with the Egyptians and . . . performed my signs among them" (Exodus 10:2, NIV)

God used these immediately discernible glimpses into the supernatural as the Israelites' beginning steps in getting to know him. His purpose was to teach those who observed these signs *about* himself: "To you it was shown, that you might know that the Lord Himself is God" (Deuteronomy 4:35).

The Israelites saw, and they believed, at least for the time being. It was the thing to do. If you had asked any of the Israelites then if

God was God, they would probably have said yes. But so would people of other nations who worshiped other gods:

- "The Egyptians will know that I am the Lord when I stretch out my hand against Egypt and bring the Israelites out of it." (Exodus 7:5, NIV)
- "I will gain glory for myself through Pharaoh and all his army, and the Egyptians will know that I am the Lord." (Exodus 14:4, NIV)
- "The Egyptians will know that I am the Lord when I gain glory through Pharaoh, his chariots and his horsemen." (Exodus 14:18, NIV)
- "The Lord will make himself known to the Egyptians, and in that day they will acknowledge the Lord." (Isaiah 19:21, NIV)
- "Now, O Lord our God, deliver us from his hand, so that all kingdoms on earth may know that you alone, O Lord, are God." (Isaiah 37:20, NIV)

Most of the Israelites never got past the level of merely knowing *about* God. That's why in the days after those miracles, when they faced new challenges, they doubted and complained and wondered whether God would ever be faithful to them again.

As a child I watched the movie *The Ten Commandments,* starring Charlton Heston, which depicted the Israelites' doubts following such giant miracles, and I couldn't believe it. How could they wonder about God's sufficiency and wander from his truths after all they had seen? During a recent Easter season, I watched a rerun of that movie classic and again saw the Israelites questioning and doubting God's faithfulness after experiencing his miracles. I see the same scenario played out in the body of Christ. When God's miracles are measurable or we're in a hard place and need him for our very existence, we recognize God as God as we learn *about* him. But how many of us have grown beyond merely knowing *about* God to knowing him personally?

Moses did. He realized that we are made to really know God, and he went beyond a surface relationship with him. He knew that God's people could know a lot *about* the Almighty without having much knowledge *of* him, much like some people who never really get to know their spouse's likes and dislikes, even after years of marriage. Moses realized that God's people could even live outwardly godly lives without an inner knowledge of who God really was. He intentionally expanded his knowledge *about* God to a knowledge *of* God, and he prayed, "'If you are pleased with me, teach me your ways so I may know you and continue to find favor with you.' . . . And the Lord said to Moses, 'I will do the very thing you have asked, because I am pleased with you and I know you by name'"(Exodus 33:13, 17, NIV).

In *Knowing God,* J. I. Packer writes, "A little knowledge *of* God is worth more than a great deal of knowledge *about* Him."[8] Moses realized this, and God revealed himself to Moses and used him for mighty things in delivering the Israelites from Egyptian slavery, establishing them as a nation, and preparing them for entrance into Canaan.

God gave his people the chance to get to know *about* him through the observable so that they would want to know him in deeper ways through a heart relationship with him, and he promised to bring them to that heart relationship: "I will give them a heart to know Me, that I am the Lord; and they shall be My people, and I will be their God, for they shall return to Me with their whole heart" (Jeremiah 24:7).

To know God with all our hearts. That is God's desire for his people, to make the cry of their hearts, *Lord I want to know you. Teach me your ways so I may know You and continue to find favor with you.* When that becomes our desire, God demonstrates his pleasure with us and gives us the things our hearts cry for: he teaches us his ways and deepens our knowledge of him. After all, he knows each of us by name. That's why author J. I. Packer could write, "What matters supremely . . . is not, in the last analysis, the fact that I know God, but the larger fact which underlies it—the fact that *he knows me*."[9]

Knowing God—the purpose of life. He knows us, and we can grow to know him. He wanted it then, and he wants it now.

## KNOWING GOD NOW

Fast-forward to the time when God sent his Son. Four hundred years of "silence" passed between the Old and the New Testaments. No writing of Scripture. No prophets. No miracles. Imagine the panic of people who lived during those centuries and knew only *about* God. They no longer saw immediately observable miracles to sustain their faith. Then along came Jesus, who redefined what it meant to *really know* God intimately.

Depending on the version of the Bible we may be looking at, the book of 1 John uses the word *know* anywhere from twenty to forty times. In 1 John 3:2, we read, "Now we are children of God; and it has not yet been revealed what we shall be, but we know that when He is revealed, we shall be like Him, for we shall see Him as He is."

Our journey to knowing Christ is just that: a journey. We might picture the progression in the following ways:

Salvation ➡ Growth ➡ Eternal Life

Saving Faith ➡ Active Faith ➡ Payoff Faith

Justification ➡ Sanctification ➡ Glorification

Meeting Christ ➡ Getting to Know Christ ➡ Living with Christ

Coming to Christ begins our journey with him, and in the end we will exist for eternity with him. But between that first step and the final one, it's time to grow, and it's only in the *growing* that we gain the *knowing*. All that is required to get into heaven is to take Christ as your Savior, and that's why Jesus could tell the thief crucified beside him, "I tell you the truth, today you will be with me in paradise" (Luke 23:43, NIV).

God wants us to get to know him through relationship. And just as in Moses' day, the people who are willing to do that are few. Most either do not know they have the opportunity to be in that special place, or they have no desire to see it. And the difference between those who do and those who don't lies in the level of satisfaction we settle into. Are we *satisfied* to sit in the same pew every Sunday, do the same things we've always done, and stay at the same level of relationship with Christ we were at five years ago? Or will we *never* be satisfied until we experience 1 John 3:2 and are finally like him? Do we long to look and talk and think and pray and respond a little more like Christ every day of our lives? And will we not be completely satisfied until that day comes?

When we can pray from our hearts the words of Psalm 17:15, "As for me, I will see Your face in righteousness; I shall be satisfied when I awake in Your likeness," we will grow in the active faith and sanctification that God wants for us.

## THE CHALLENGE

In John 14:9, Jesus challenged his disciple Philip to examine his level of satisfaction with where he was in relationship with the Savior.

Like many Christians, Philip was not without godly attributes and achievements. He heard Jesus' teaching and saw his miracles. He brought Nathanael to Christ (John 1:45). He served as a contact man for the Greeks and is known for bringing Gentiles to Jesus (John 12:20-23). In John 6 we read how Jesus crossed the Sea of Galilee and went up on a mountain with his disciples. But the multitudes followed, those who knew *about* Jesus through his miracles. Jesus looked at the five thousand men, plus women and children, and then challenged Philip about whether he really knew Christ or, like the multitude, merely knew *about* him. He asked Philip a rhetorical question: "Where shall we buy bread for these people to eat?" (v. 5, NIV).

Philip's knowing-about-Jesus mentality caused him to answer, "Eight months' wages would not buy enough bread for each one to have a bite!" (v. 7, NIV). He offered a natural answer to a supernatural question. Verse 6 explains that Jesus intended this question as a test for Philip because Jesus already knew what he was going to do about the situation. It's at this point that Jesus performed another miracle and turned a boy's lunch of five barley loaves and two fish into enough food to feed everyone there and still have twelve baskets of food left over. And yet later, Philip, having seen Jesus' miracles and power asked for still more: "Lord, show us the Father and that will be enough for us" (John 14:8, NIV). It was here that Jesus expressed his frustration with Philip: "Don't you know me, Philip, even after I have been among you such a long time?" (John 14:9, NIV).

But in John's Gospel, Jesus gave his early disciples and us hope and offered ways for moving past a head knowledge *about* him to a heart knowledge *of* him:

**Look back; don't worry.** As the people saw what was happening around them, it would have been easy to lose heart and wonder whether God was really aware of what was happening and was involved in it. But Jesus reminded them to "look back," that is, to recall the things they had already experienced with Jesus in the past and remember what they already believed. As they did, they would find comfort in the knowledge of God's power, which was greater than anything they saw happening in the world. "Let not your heart be troubled," Jesus reminded them. "You believe in

God, believe also in Me" (John 14:1). Remembering that we belong to the One who created and rules the universe gives us peace and eases worry.

***Look forward; hope.*** We are tempted to forget that this world is not all there is, especially when we're going through hard times. So Jesus reminds his disciples to look forward and find hope as they focus on the life to come and on the new home he would be building for his people while he was away from them: "In My Father's house are many mansions. . . . I go to prepare a place for you. And if I go and prepare a place for you, I will come again and receive you to Myself; that where I am, there you may be also" (John 14:2-3).

***Look around you; know and do.*** While Jesus is gone, preparing our eternal home, he has given us work to do, and he has equipped us to do it through his power. He explains what a "knowing life" looks like: "I tell you the truth, anyone who has faith in me will do what I have been doing. He will do even greater things than these, because I am going to the Father. And I will do whatever you ask in my name, so that the Son may bring glory to the Father" (John 14:12-13, NIV).

Philip must have thought to himself, *Greater things than Jesus did? Healing? Casting out demons? Raising the dead? How can this be?* Philip lived beneath what Jesus desired for him. He had low expectations and became satisfied with a so-so life. He reduced the "greater things" to only what people could see with their eyes. Though Philip had come to know the Son of the living God, he had not yet found an intimate relationship with him.

That's when the topic of really knowing God came up. The way to know God is to know Jesus: "If you had known Me, you would have known My Father also" (John 14:7). And knowing Jesus comes through the Holy Spirit: "I will pray the Father, and He will give you another Helper, that He may abide with you forever—the Spirit of truth, whom the world cannot receive, because it neither sees Him nor knows Him; but you know Him, for He dwells with you and will be in you" (John 14:16-17).

The Greek word translated "another" in this passage means "one besides, another of the same kind." So Jesus is saying, "one besides me and in addition to me, but one just like me. He will do in my absence what I would do if I were physically present with you." This Helper would continue what Jesus did and taught, and in nine simple words Jesus described his work through this Helper in a person who knows and loves him: "I will love him and manifest Myself to him" (John 14:21).

To manifest something means to reveal, exhibit, or make something visible. It means to present oneself or reveal oneself to another. In this case, Jesus said that he would reveal himself to those who believe in him. In other words, Jesus would allow those who believe in him to "know" him.

God has brought humanity full circle: from the first man and woman's knowing God in the purest sense of the word in the Garden of Eden, to their loss of that intimacy through sin and rebellion, to God's invitation to rediscover him through his Son, Jesus, to the Spirit's coming as the vehicle through which God reveals himself to us.

As we journey toward really knowing Christ, on the hilltops as well as in the valleys, let's stop and ponder what Jesus' words to Philip mean to us today: "Have I been with you so long, and yet you have not known Me?"

Look back; don't worry. Don't be overly concerned about what's happening around you. Remember what you have already experienced and believe about Christ (John 14:1).

Look forward; hope. Jesus is busy preparing a mansion for us, and someday we will get to move in (John 14:2-3).

Look around you; know and do. In the meantime, he wants us doing even greater works than he did. Whatever we ask in his name—that is, according to his will—he will do (John 14:12-13).

These are great promises, and they are as real to us today as they were to the original disciples. But like the first disciples, we must really know God if we are to lay hold of these promises. And really knowing him takes wanting to go into that special place of intimacy that offers a beauty only the eyes of the beholder can see.

---

*LORD, as I begin to discover what really knowing you can mean, I realize that it doesn't describe the relationship I have had with you until now. I have more knowledge about you than knowledge of you. I've been satisfied with where I am, despite the fact that I say I want to know you more. If I had been one of your twelve disciples, you might have asked me why I didn't really know you. As I make this journey to discover what really knowing you can mean, please open my mind and heart to your beauty, your power, and your majesty. By your Holy Spirit, reveal yourself to me in fresh ways, and cause me to hunger for a deep and intimate relationship with you. Amen.*

# 2

# What Keeps Us
# from Knowing God?

We have seen that we don't have to "settle" for merely knowing *about* God; we can *know him* in a real and personal way. So why don't we do it? Why aren't we pounding on the door to the place that holds God's riches? Or maybe we should ask, why do we become so complacent and content with a mediocre walk with Christ?

A. W. Tozer addressed this issue when he wrote the following words: "I have for years carried a burden of sorrow as I have moved among evangelical Christians who somewhere in their past have managed to strike a base compromise with their heart's holier longings and have settled down to a lukewarm, mediocre kind of Christianity utterly unworthy of themselves and of the Lord they claim to serve."[1]

We become stagnant and stunted and strive for the same things the rest of the world does. We've heard the latest Christian speakers and singers. We listen to Christian music in the car and even have little fish symbols—sometimes a whole family of them—on our bumpers. Yet our worship holds no glory, church services provide no challenge, and the Bible offers no enticement to us. We don't have time to worry about those who don't belong to Christ because we have to get home and start dinner before our kids leave for soccer practice. We rear our children to be content with the same casual, convenient, comfortable Christianity that defines God as good only when we get a new car or find a choice parking place at the mall. Our experience with God never goes beyond the superficial.

Bruce Wilkinson wrote about this stale condition of the church in *First Hand Faith*. He compares our walks with God with three chairs extending out from God's throne. As Christians, we choose which of the chairs we will sit in. The first chair, the one closest to God, is the chair of "commitment," where people experience firsthand God's miraculous work. The second chair is the chair of "compromise." People who choose this chair know about God's miraculous work but do not experience it themselves. They become lukewarm and content with knowing about God secondhand through those in the first chair. The third and most distant chair from God is known as "conflict." Those in this chair never get to know Christ, either because they lack opportunity or because they never take the time to discover truth for themselves.

Wilkinson goes on to suggest that whatever chair we choose, our choices rub off on our children and on others closely watching our lives. The further we seat ourselves from God, the less impact we'll have on the lives of others. Eventually our spiritual experiences become like the childhood game of telephone, in which players take turns whispering a message to each other. The third- or fourth- or fifteenth-hand message is so distorted that it bears no resemblance to the original message. For those in the third chair, all the magic, enthusiasm, and passion vanish.[2]

In the Bible we see how Joshua sat in the first chair and found there a vibrant, firsthand, personal walk with God. The elders sat in the second chair, where they leaned on Joshua in a secondhand way and discovered only pseudoenthusiasm for spiritual things. Then in the next book of the Bible we read the sad result of choosing to live a mediocre, compromising, nonintimate Christian life: "Another generation grew up, who knew neither the Lord nor what he had done for Israel" (Judges 2:10, NIV).

A. W. Tozer writes, "If angels can weep, they must weep salty tears upon seeing a proselyte who has never really met the Lord talking to another proselyte who will also never meet the Lord."[3] Yet we all call ourselves Christians. We share the same umbrella under the name of Christianity, third-chair men and women standing alongside those who daily experience a firsthand faith. It has become almost fashionable to call ourselves Christians, but too often we have allowed the word that means "like Christ" to mean "like everyone else."

In contrast, author Calvin Miller describes what spiritual intimacy looks like. On a trip to the Great Barrier Reef in Australia, Miller and his wife observed the reef by snorkeling on the surface of the water while their son chose to see the reef by scuba diving. Miller writes: "What amazes me most is what we reported upon returning from the Great Barrier Reef. Ask me if I've been there, and I will hastily answer yes. So will my son. However, the truth is that the content of our experience was greatly different. . . . Only our son really knew the Reef; only he understood the issue of depth. . . . It seems to me that much of Christianity is a conversation of snorkelers talking to each other of scuba experiences. . . . It is those who read and pray, not those who philosophize and chatter, who arrive at lives of real power."[4]

As a whole, we as a body of Christians have become content with a secondhand relationship with God. We have ceased striving for anything better than the norm and what we've known all along. We have become satisfied with snorkeling on the surface rather than plunging into the depths. This abnormal, distorted way of living the Christian life has begun to appear normal, and for many different reasons, we refuse to seek anything more.

## WHAT KEEPS US FROM KNOWING?

When I was a child, I spent lots of time in the woods behind our home. I loved the bubbling brook where I caught crayfish with earthworms wiggling to be free from the Christmas-tree-ornament hook that held them to the end of my fishing line. I loved the feel of the cool gray clay as I dug it from the ledge in the rocks to create dishes for my playhouse. But most of all, I loved the fence post where I sat and dreamed for hours about all I would grow up to be, the man I would marry, the children I would have, the work I would do. I felt special, unique, set apart, chosen, as I perched high above the world around me. I sat by myself, but I wasn't alone. No one was around to acknowledge the words I didn't even dare to speak out loud, yet joy and peace overtook me there and sustained me until I could return on another day. Discovering such a treasure made me want to tell others about it, but as with the room in my dream, I struggled to find someone with whom to share my special place. Not many would understand that such a location existed. Some were too busy, and most wouldn't care. But when I found those who *did* understand and *did* care, I pulled them to my fence post and let them soak in its solitude and ministry.

This experience made me aware of the presence of someone else, One whom I couldn't see and who loved me in a way I didn't necessarily understand. In the silence of that special place, I found eyes and ears to seek and discover the special places that would come later in my life, yet I continued to find few other people to share my enthusiasm for that experience. Miller describes the frustration of not finding others to go along on our quest for the deeper things of God: "Real spiritual divers are so in love with the depths that they don't spend much of their lives trying to make oceanography real in a world where birdbaths define smaller passions. . . . The inscrutable glories of the deep cannot be described to those hooked on the safety of shallow-ness."[5]

There are several reasons why we can get hooked on spiritual shallowness and become so content with a nonintimate walk with God.

## We Don't Really Know about Spiritual Intimacy

I recently shared a cold drink with a friend on a summer afternoon, and we caught up on what was happening in each other's lives. I told her about something I felt God was teaching me, a new place he was taking me. The glazed look in her eyes told me that my friend wasn't tracking with me.

"Oh, that's nice," she said when I had finished sharing from the depths of my being, and she moved on to the next topic.

God doesn't love me any more than he loves my friend. She also serves him, but she had had no one earlier in her life modeling a first-chair relationship with Christ, nor does she have stories of a special fence post behind her home. We read in Philippians 2:12, "Work out your own salvation with fear and trembling," but working out our salvation happens only in shallow waters if we don't know that deeper waters exist. When my children were young, they were never content splashing in the baby pool once I introduced them to the wonders of the deep. Our spiritual lives can be the same. Once we have begun to know about and experience the deep riches of intimacy with God, we will be unable to remain satisfied with less.

## We Find the Idea New and Strange

Finding a deeper walk with Christ is new and often uncomfortable, and it requires a lot of work. And sticking with the "safe" and the "familiar" comes easier to human nature than mystery and adventure do. Until something happens in our lives to convince us that the adventure of finding spiritual intimacy is worth the risk, we won't approach this new and deeper relationship with Christ.

## We Fear the Loneliness of the Journey

Many resist the idea of being "different" from other people, but the journey to knowing God is a solitary one. No one can make the trip for you, and you can't just inherit your place in the first chair. It may intersect with others' journeys, and they may have a great impact on ours, but the bulk of the journey happens individually. In Dietrich Bonhoeffer's classic book *The Cost of Discipleship,* we read often of the loneliness involved in choosing to follow Christ to the extreme: "Through the call of Jesus, men become individuals. Willy-nilly, they are compelled to decide, and that decision can only be made by themselves. . . . Every man is called separately, and must follow alone. But men are frightened of solitude, and they try to protect themselves from it by merging themselves in the society of their fellow-men and in their material environment."[6]

Don't expect lots of others to share in your enthusiasm for knowing God to the extreme. Those who hear the call into the deeper things of God are always going to be in the minority here on earth, but the more you know him, the less that matters. And the more you get to know him, the less dependent you will be on the acceptance of others. Instead, the mysteries God reveals to you, the secrets he tells you through his Word, and the things he confides in you through the Holy Spirit settle at the roots of your being and manifest themselves not in outward testimonials but through inward manifestations, through changed goals, responses, and commitments.

## We Believe We're Not Suited for Spiritual Intimacy

We often see intimacy, depth, and really knowing Christ as being more for the Martin Luthers and the Amy Carmichaels of the world, not for "ordinary" people like us. Since the Fall in the Garden of Eden, Satan has worked to cloud our understanding about how precious we are to Christ. We can be painfully aware of our weaknesses, yet we still strive to do things our own way and to become the masters of our own fates. When we read the psalmist's words, we find it impossible to grasp that "my frame was not hidden from you [God] when I was made in the secret place" (Psalm 139:15, NIV), and that the secret place he bids us to come back to in Psalm 91:1, "He who dwells in the secret place of the Most High," is the one in Psalm 139:15 where we had our beginnings.

My friend Tonya faced the pain of her husband's unfaithfulness several years ago. Though he came back home, their marriage remained lifeless. I began meeting with another woman and Tonya for a weekly Bible study, and we watched the twinkle return to her eye as she devoured God's Word and sought his will despite what had happened to her marriage. Week by week I watched Tonya take her first-chair seat in the secret place, and one day Tonya expressed her absolute joy in her newfound intimacy with God: "I'm free and loved. I've been in bondage for so long. Now I crave the Word of God."

Knowing God is not *reserved* for great people. Knowing God *creates* great people, set-apart people with an insatiable appetite to know him more and more. Tonya is one of the greatest people I know.

## We Don't Think We Need It

When things are okay just as they are and we have no pressing needs, we don't look to God. Often we don't seek him until we encounter trouble. C. S Lewis wrote, "God whispers to us in our pleasures, speaks in our conscience, but shouts in our pains: it is His megaphone to rouse a deaf world."[7]

Comfort and abundance deafen our ears to the whispers of God. I squelched the beckonings I'd sensed in those early years in my secret place on the fence post—until life grew unmanageable. I came to the end of myself and responded to God's wooing. I turned to him and surrendered my life. On the day Desert Storm began in 1991, as our pastor drew us together in prayer, he said, "Our country has been cursed with blessings; now I have a feeling it will be blessed with cursings."

Without exception, everyone who has encountered hardship and dared to turn everything over to God agrees that knowing God took preeminence over everything else. It was through the harder things in life that they found the deeper things in God.

## We're Too Busy

We will talk about our busyness in depth later in the book, but it bears mentioning briefly here. Our many good activities in service to God don't leave time for anything else. Singing in the church choir, cooking for potlucks, and serving in the nursery can be wonderful endeavors, but often the intensity of our involvement robs us of the time, energy, and motivation to actually seek God. Doing *for* God can never of itself teach us to also *know* him.

## We Tend to Think Small

We put God in a box when we focus on only certain aspects of who he is. We trust him to guide us but don't know if he can heal our sickness or bless us financially. We may presume that his miracles and personal contact with people are something that happened only in the past and aren't for us today. As a result, writes Calvin Miller, "We are stopped short of the deep hunger to know him by our contentment to play in the shallows of our little 'asking.' . . . We have a fear . . . or worse, an apathy toward the depths."[8]

## We're Afraid to Trust

Many of us carry wounds inflicted by people we should have been able to trust. They betrayed us and left us with a nagging suspicion of others, a fear of getting too close to them, and a belief that we don't really need intimacy. We see God as an extension of the untrustworthy people in our lives. I heard an atheist on TV just the other day say, "The only thing worse than finding out there is no God is finding there is one who allows all these bad things to happen."

Although as Christians we hope that we wouldn't go as far as this unbeliever did, without admitting it, we often cling to the same mistrusting mind-set.

## We're Not Ready for It

Many of us see knowing God as something we'll get to later. Ann was like that. During her childhood she developed a deep hunger for God. She pursued him until her late teens, when she said, "God, I want to live like a normal teenager for a while. I'll get more serious with you later on."

Nearly twenty years have passed since Ann made that decision. She pushed aside God's sweet beckonings and his invitation to dance, with him in the lead. She chose to do things herself. I spoke with her some time ago as she talked about her recommitment to God. She wept as she recounted the things that had replaced the blessings God offered, including divorce, abortion, alcoholism, and an immoral lifestyle.

The best time to plant a tree is twenty years ago. The second best time is today. Ann could have set out without distraction to get to really know the Lord twenty years ago, but at least she's doing that today.

## We Aren't Encouraged to Hunger

I spoke with my brother-in-law Larry recently about his mother, Virgie, who raised her fourteen children alone after her husband left. Though Virgie went to be with the Lord many years ago, Larry's description of his memories made her come alive for me once again. She studied the Bible for hours a day and often laid several Bibles out on her bed, open to different passages containing promises applicable to her needs. Neighboring farmers allowed people to pick up corn that remained after the fields had been harvested, and Virgie had her children gather corn and store it in the barn for the pig that God would provide for their food. Larry said, "We often had that corn for a long time before we got the pig, but God always provided."

My own memories of Virgie include people making fun of her and discounting her quest for an intimate relationship with God. I find this true today. Often our church leaders don't encourage us to question, probe, or inquire too deeply into God's character. Hungry hearts and active brains threaten established systems. So the seeds of desire for intimacy with the Almighty often die in the hearts of those expressing it.

## We Allow Sin to Hinder Us

Plain, old-fashioned sin has been tagged with other names today: Addiction. Heredity. Codependency. These are some of the excuses we use to convince ourselves that sinful behaviors are not really our fault. But sin is just as real as God's call on our lives, and we need to deal with it just as completely.

God does not blink at sin. What *was* sin to him is *still* sin to him. And he will not reveal his mysteries, confide his secrets, or show his beauty to those who allow sin to stand in the way.

Satan has much to lose when we find intimacy with Christ, so he crafts each obstacle to fit the person involved. He doesn't want us to realize there's anything more, and he definitely doesn't want us to get to know God personally. But we can start beating Satan at his own game by examining our motives for wanting to really know God.

## HUMANITY'S MOTIVES

Several years ago I embarked on a new professional opportunity in my own life. It was a Christian venture that could easily contribute much to God's kingdom. Early on the morning I was to attend my first meeting with someone who would help me in this new direction, I read an entry in Henry Blackaby's book *Experiencing God* that talked about Psalm 24:3-4: "Who may ascend the hill of the Lord? Who may stand in his holy place? He who has clean hands and a pure heart" (NIV).

Blackaby emphasized how in the Old Testament, a person's hands represented his or her activities. Clean hands symbolized purity. Priests washed their hands before serving in the temple to symbolize that only those who were cleansed could worship God.[9]

The moment we become Christians, we begin a relationship with the Lord. If we persist in sin, that sin will separate us from God and keep us from enjoying fellowship with him and getting to know him intimately. If we follow God's basic commandments but resist every time God gives us specific, personal directives, we will never fully experience the depths of God's Person. If, like the psalmist, however, we begin to understand the holiness of God, we will respond to God's prompting so that we can really know him.

Moving forward with God, getting to really know him, requires clean hands (remaining sinless) and a pure heart (keeping our motives pure). Before we ascend the hill of the Lord, we need to check our hands for sin and our hearts for wrong motives. We can do that by asking ourselves *who, what, when,* and *why* questions about our desire to really know him:

- **Who** should get glory from my journey to know God: God or me?
- **What** is my goal in embarking on this journey to know God?
- **When** will I use this new information and experience?
- **Why** do I want to know God intimately?

Knowing God is not an end in itself. We don't do it just to acquire knowledge, though we'll certainly gain knowledge along the way. We don't do it to put ourselves in a better class of Christians. We don't do it in order to look down on those who don't embark on the quest of knowing him.

Until we can search our motives and honestly answer the who, what, when, and why questions in a way that is pleasing to God, our journey will take us to a dead end. It will come to nothing. It will benefit no one. J. I. Packer writes: "To be preoccupied with getting theological knowledge as an end in itself, to approach Bible study with no higher motive than a desire to know all the answers, is the direct route to a state of self-satisfied self-deception. We need to guard our hearts against such an attitude, and pray to be kept from it. . . . There can be no spiritual health without doctrinal knowledge; but it is equally true that there can be no spiritual health with it, if it is sought for the wrong purpose and valued by the wrong standard. In this way, doctrinal study really can become a danger to spiritual life."[10]

- **Who** should get glory from my journey to know God? God and only God.
- **What** is my goal in embarking on this journey to know God? To learn his truths and conform my life to them.
- **When** will I use this new information and experience? In my motives, character, maturity, and example to others through the words I speak, the deeds I do, and the plans I make.

- **Why** do I want to know God intimately? Not only because one day I will look just like him but also because every day on this journey called life my resemblance to him will be greater. I'll talk and act and respond and think like him better than I did a year ago, with more maturity than before. And in so doing, I will become a vessel God can use for his glory.

Knowing God is a process, the greatest, most comprehensive journey we can ever make in this life. And the earthly part of that journey will end only when we stand before him. Knowing God is the means to an end—an eternal end. We learn God's truths so that our hearts might respond to those truths and our lives might be conformed to them. Some of those truths provide a glimpse into God's motives.

Jesus said, "I have come that they may have life, and that they may have it more abundantly" (John 10:10). But living abundantly is impossible unless we really know God. In 1 Corinthians 15:57-58 the apostle Paul writes, "Thanks be to God! He gives us the victory through our Lord Jesus Christ. Therefore, . . . stand firm. Let nothing move you. Always give yourselves fully to the work of the Lord, because you know that your labor in the Lord is not in vain" (NIV). But living victoriously is not possible without really knowing God either. Again, J. I. Packer writes: "Disregard the study of God, and you sentence yourself to stumble and blunder through life blindfolded, as it were, with no sense of direction and no understanding of what surrounds you. This way you can waste your life and your soul."[11]

It's time to stop stumbling and blundering through life blindfolded. Studying God can give us new direction. Knowing God can give us new life.

LORD, am I stagnant in my spiritual life, stunted in growth? Am I content to sit in the second chair in my relationship with you? Show me by your Spirit what holds me back in knowing you. Is it that I didn't know about it before? that I have never done it before? I've done lots of other things that were new to me. Is the prospect of the journey a lonely one? Knowing you will more than compensate for that. Help me to look deeply and honestly at my life and discover the answers to these questions so that nothing, ever again, will keep me from knowing you. Amen.

# 3

# Grasping God's Love for You and Your Love for Him

Some time ago I sat on a plane beside a man who talked about his work and his reason for making that trip. "I have some unpleasant business to take care of," he said, and went on to say that he was experiencing a nasty divorce.

When the man stopped talking, I leaned my head against the seat and closed my eyes in exhaustion. Suddenly, though, I knew what I had to do. Turning to him, I asked, "Do you know that Jesus loves you? Do you know that he knows everything you've been through and where you're going? He knows your name and the number of hairs on your head. If you were the only person in the whole world, he would still have died for you."

The man cupped his face in his hands and began to weep. I prayed with him and gave him some Scripture references to read in his hotel room and some further contacts to make regarding the issues he faced. I don't even know that man's name, but Jesus knows him completely.

Now let me ask you, do you know that Jesus loves you, too? Our human minds often have difficulty grasping the fact that God knows each of us individually and loves us unconditionally. Many years ago God taught me much about his love. I was in the middle of my divorce and my dad's illness and was raising five-, three-, and one-year-old children alone while working on my doctorate. One night my children's father called to talk to them. Courtney stood in the kitchen beside me saying, "I love you, too, Daddy."

I wanted to grab the phone from her and describe the things he had done to us. But long after Courtney was off playing, God was still setting me straight. He seemed to speak to my heart: *Does Courtney love you any more when you fix a good meal than when you fix a bad one? Does she love you more when you're kind than when you're grumpy? No, she always loves you the same. She loves you just because she loves you. You didn't earn her love, and her love does not depend on anything. That's how she loves her father, too. And that's how I love you.*

God's unconditional love is called *agape*. It is not dependent on anything, and nothing can change it. Agape love just *is*. The apostle Paul had experienced God's agape love, and in his letter to the Ephesian believers, he wrote about his desire for them to realize the truth of it too: "I pray that out of his glorious riches he may strengthen you with power through his Spirit in your inner being, so that Christ may dwell in your hearts through faith. And I pray that you, being rooted and established in love, may have power, together with all the saints, to grasp how wide and long and high and deep is the love of Christ, and to know this love that surpasses knowledge—that you may be filled to the measure of all the fullness of God" (Ephesians 3:16-19, NIV).

Grasping, or comprehending, this love allows us to be filled with God's fullness. This fullness means full measure and completion, and it is the same Greek term used to describe a ship with a full cargo or a town with no vacant houses. If we live our lives without comprehending God's love for us, we never realize this fullness or completion. Paul determined to achieve this fullness in its entirety by understanding God's immense love for him: "I am persuaded that neither death nor life, nor angels nor principalities nor powers, nor things present nor things to come, nor height nor depth, nor any other created thing, shall be able to separate us from the love of God which is in Christ Jesus our Lord" (Romans 8:38-39).

Author Brennan Manning writes: "Do you really accept the message that God is head over heels in love with you? I believe that this question is at the core of our ability to mature and grow spiritually. If in our hearts we really don't believe that God loves us as we are, if we are still tainted by the lie that we can do something to make God love us more, we are rejecting the message of the cross."[1]

Do you know that Jesus loves you? Do you know that he knows everything you've been through and where you're going? He knows your name and the number of hairs on your head (Matthew 10:30). If you were the only person in the whole world, he still would have died for you. Grasping this love is essential to really knowing Christ.

## HIS LOVE FOR YOU

One snapshot of God's individual love for us comes from Genesis 16. Hagar, a servant of Abraham's wife, Sarai, fled from her mistress's mistreatment and found herself in the wilderness. God's love for Hagar was not foremost in her mind, but God's love for Hagar did not diminish just because she couldn't feel it or was unaware of it: "The Angel of the Lord found her by a spring of water in the wilderness. . . . And He said, 'Hagar, Sarai's maid, where have you come from, and where are you going?'" (Genesis 16:7-8).

God called Hagar by name and let her know that he knew her completely. He knew her past, her employment, and the details involved with her pain. He knew her present—where to find her and how to ease her hurts. God also addressed Hagar about her future: "Where are you going?"

The man I met on the plane might have asked, "If God loved me so much, why did he allow me to go through divorce?" Hagar could have stood up to God and said, "If you love me so much, why do I

have to be out in this wilderness in the first place?" A person dealing with sexual abuse, the loss of a loved one, or a terminal disease
might ask similar questions.

But somehow when God's Spirit speaks to us, we cannot deny
God's love. When he indicates he knows us thoroughly or when he
hears and answers the smallest—or largest—of our prayers, we
know we are in full, undeniable, unconditional possession of his
love. By the end of this encounter with God in the wilderness,
Hagar had become convinced of God's love for her: "Have I also
here seen Him who sees me?" (Genesis 16:13).

I have seen evidence of God's love for me, too. Again and again
he has convinced me that he loves me unconditionally. One such
event happened after I had finished my doctoral dissertation in
June of 1990 and had taught at the same university the following
year. During the summer my children and I had flown from Ohio
to Arizona to visit my mother, and I thought I would be teaching at
the same institution in the fall. But I received a phone call while in
Arizona. The department head informed me that because the
university had rules against hiring their own graduates, they would
be unable to renew my contract. I was devastated. How would I
find a job to support my family at this late date? I didn't know how
desperate I really was until I seriously considered a job teaching
statistics for another institution. But when I remembered how
much I hated to balance my checkbook, I decided this job wasn't
for me. So in desperation I continued my search—and my
panic—and one afternoon, I poured out my heart to God.

That night I dreamed that I owned the house that had previously
belonged to my parents. I had revamped the yard except for one
location, so I called in a landscaper, who carefully studied the L-
shaped parcel and then planted three bushes, one at each end and
one in the middle. Then he said, "I've put what *has* to be there, now
what else would you *like* to have there?"

The next day, while taking a walk in my mother's neighborhood, I remembered the dream. "God," I said, "was that you? Are you telling me you've lined up things in my life as you want them and yet you're asking me what I want too? Do my desires matter to you?"

I wasn't sure my dream had come from God, but I know that I filled God's ears about things I desired, and I remember saying, "I want to be home with my children, and I love to write. Help me to write what you want me to write and to get my books published."

Even as I worked on the manuscript for this book, I smiled. The children are mostly grown now, with only our seventeen-year-old son remaining at home. The years brought opportunities for this single mom to be there for her children and even to take them to some exciting places as we celebrated the release of each book.

"Have I also here seen Him who sees me?" Hagar asked.

I had almost missed this important characteristic of an intimate relationship with Christ: he cares about everything we care about. But my discovery depended on one powerful truth. Before I brought my list of desires to God, I had first desired *him*. I wanted him more than anything else. Since my surrender to Christ in September 1985, which I described in the introduction, I sought after him the best way I knew. Sometimes I did well at it; other times I made mistakes. But through it all my greatest desire continued to be to know Christ more.

King David understood this truth long before I did. He wrote in Psalm 37:4, "Delight yourself also in the Lord, and He shall give you the desires of your heart." What David knew and I later discovered was that when we delight in the Lord, our delights become his desires. He causes us to want what he wants.

God loved us so much that he gave us his only Son. That fact is true whether we grasp it or not. And because of his love, we can see him who sees us and love him who loves us.

## YOUR LOVE FOR HIM

Understanding the undeniable and perfect love of God for you is one thing; examining your love for him is quite another. To try to grasp our spiritual love for God, we can take a look at what psychologist Robert Sternberg called a Triangular Theory of Love. In Sternberg's 1986 study he writes about different kinds of love between a man and a woman, and he maintains that love varies from one relationship to another because of its varying mixture of ingredients. He suggests that love has three possible components: intimacy, passion, and commitment.

*Intimacy* (feeling close and bound together by mutual affection) makes up the emotional component of love. *Passion* creates love's motivational component. Passion is the drive that leads to romance, physical attraction, and sexual consummation. *Commitment* comprises the cognitive component of love. Commitment decides to label a certain relationship "love" and to seek to maintain that relationship over time.

Sternberg described what different combinations of intimacy, passion, and commitment—or the lack of them—look like and the kind of relationship each combination creates:

- *Liking* consists of intimacy without passion or commitment.
- *Infatuation,* or love at first sight, is passion alone, in the absence of commitment or intimacy.
- *Empty love* occurs when a person is committed to a relationship that lacks both intimacy and passion.
- *Romantic love* is intimacy and passion combined, without much commitment, although commitment may come later.
- *Companionate love* develops when passion is absent but intimacy and commitment are present. This kind of love sometimes occurs after many years of marriage.
- *Fatuous love* takes place when passion and commitment are

present without intimacy. This type is found in a marriage that follows a whirlwind courtship. The partners have a strong sexual attraction and have decided to share their lives, but they have not yet developed much knowledge of each other or deep feelings of emotional closeness.

- *Consummate love* is the richest of all. It consists of all three components—intimacy, passion, and commitment.[2]

We can use Sternberg's model to help us assess our spiritual relationship with Christ. We may say that we "love" Christ, but what does that really mean? Liking? Infatuation? Empty love? Romantic love? Companionate love? Fatuous love? Or have we found true consummate love?

Psychologists didn't exist in Jesus' day, and obviously the triangular theory of love didn't either. But love did, and Jesus saw all kinds and combinations of it in the people he encountered. By looking at men and women from the Bible, perhaps we can take the first step in discovering what kind of love we have for God.

## Liking: Intimacy without Passion or Commitment

Did you ever feel really close to someone but found you weren't willing to make the commitment necessary to take your relationship to the next level? The rich young ruler in Matthew 19 felt intimacy with Jesus but lacked passion and commitment. He had followed Jesus' teachings and knew him well enough to talk to him directly. His question was an honest one, though he had much to learn: "Teacher, what good thing must I do to get eternal life?" (Matthew 19:16, NIV).

Jesus responded that he needed to keep the commandments. Immediately the young man answered as if to say, "No sweat, Jesus. I've been keeping them since I was a kid. What else do I lack?"

Jesus cut to the young man's true passions and commitments: "If you want to be perfect, go, sell your possessions and give to the poor, and you will have treasure in heaven. Then come, follow me" (Matthew 19:21, NIV).

Intimacy, or close feelings, alone could not sustain this young man. After all, true intimacy comes at a great cost and requires lots of work. It may mean sacrificing the things we cling to the most, something this young man was not willing to do. His passion for and commitment to his riches caused him to turn his back on Christ: "When the young man heard this, he went away sad, because he had great wealth" (Matthew 19:22, NIV). This man's love for Jesus never became all it could be because it lacked passion and commitment.

## Infatuation: Passion without Commitment or Intimacy

When two people are first "courting," they exchange cards, candy, and flowers and spend lots of time together. Neither person can get enough of the special attention. But as time goes on, the passion can wane. That's the way it was with the believers in the church at Ephesus. They felt strong passion for Jesus, but the intensity of this passion by itself kept the Ephesians unaware of the need for building commitment and intimacy, too. In Revelation 2:4, John wrote to the Ephesians, "I have this against you, that you have left your first love."

Passion alone wasn't enough. The Ephesians' lack of commitment and intimacy caused them to slide into a mediocre love for Christ. The passionate flames in their hearts had begun to die down. Their ecstasy had vanished, and John commanded them, "Remember the height from which you have fallen! Repent and do the things you did at first" (Revelation 2:5, NIV).

If that's the case for us, we need to go back to our "first love," back to the time when just speaking about God excited us. When reading the Bible was delicious. When sharing God with others was the highlight of our day. When our devotions were consistent and deep. But while we're at it, we also need to work at building increased intimacy and commitment in our relationship with Christ. This trio—passion plus commitment plus intimacy—will sustain us over the long haul.

**Empty Love: Commitment without Intimacy or Passion**
I once heard a husband say, "I don't know why my wife is so upset. I bought her two new lamps for Christmas!" This man possessed all the commitment in the world, but he lacked the intimacy and passion he needed to really make his marriage work.

The teachers of the law and the Pharisees did too. They prided themselves in making their commitment public by wearing Scriptures on their foreheads and looking sad when they fasted. But Jesus let them know it wasn't enough. He pinned them down on their lack of intimacy and passion: "Woe to you, scribes and Pharisees, hypocrites! For you are like whitewashed tombs which indeed appear beautiful outwardly, but inside are full of dead men's bones and all uncleanness" (Matthew 23:27).

Though their commitment was good, the teachers of the law and the Pharisees—like the husband above—never did find a vibrant, deep relationship with Jesus because they neglected the need for intimacy and passion.

**Romantic Love: Intimacy and Passion without Commitment**
Many people experience romantic love. Their passion and intimacy toward each other grow quickly, and they want to get married, but they have no idea about the commitment involved in building a strong marriage.

Many young Christians do the same. They meet Christ, develop passion and intimacy with him through prayer, Bible reading, and fellowship, but they don't realize the rigors, challenges, and sacrifices that following Christ may involve over time.

The woman in John 4 who met Jesus at the well was a half-breed Samaritan who had been married five times and was now living with a sixth man. Jesus asked her for a drink of water. When she questioned the fact that he was asking her for water, he described the special water he could give her so that she would never thirst again. Jesus immediately captured the woman's heart. Passion and intimacy were no problem for her. She left her watering jar behind (John 4:28) and went to tell others about "a Man who told me all things that I ever did" (John 4:29). We know that Jesus' encounter with this woman brought many others to Christ (John 4:39), but what happened to the woman? In the days and weeks that followed, when Jesus wasn't standing in front of her, did she find what it took to stay committed as well as intimate and passionate in her relationship with Christ? I think she probably did, although her commitment would develop and be tested over time.

## Companionate Love: Intimacy and Commitment without Passion

Many married couples find their relationship in trouble once the passion is gone. They might know each other intimately and be committed to staying married, but an individual is also made for passion.

Jesus found twelve men going about their daily lives and asked them to become his disciples. All of them except one stayed committed to Jesus until the end, and they got to know him deeply by living alongside him every day. But we read often how Jesus' three favorites were Peter, James, and John. They accompanied him to places such as the Mount of Transfiguration, which we'll talk about more in chapter 15, and to the garden of Gethsemane the night he was arrested. I can't help but wonder why these three men stood out to Jesus. The others knew and followed Jesus too, but I think it might have been their passion that singled out Peter, James, and John. It sometimes got them into trouble, but it also brought them close to Jesus.

Most of us fail to demonstrate passion consistently, as Peter, James, and John did. We allow our spiritual journeys to become "routine," and we find ourselves merely going through the motions. Jesus still sets apart time to reveal himself in greater ways to those who seek to fill their hungry, passionate hearts.

## Fatuous Love: Passion and Commitment without Intimacy

Author and relationship expert Gary Chapman wrote a book called *The Five Love Languages.*[3] His premise is that everyone expresses and experiences the reality of the words *I love you* in one of five ways: through gifts, touching, words of affirmation, time spent with someone, or acts of service. The love language of Martha of Bethany, sister of Mary and Lazarus, was acts of service, and she expressed her love this way to everyone she met. She loved them by doing for them and expected others to do the same.

Martha was committed to Jesus, and together with her brother and sister, she was passionate about spending time with him as a family friend. But the *way* she spent her time indicated the quality and depth of their relationship. Martha stayed so busy serving that there was no time left for intimacy with Jesus. She felt strong passion and commitment to him, but she lost out on really getting to know him and developing an emotional closeness.

In contrast, consider the way Mary, Martha's sister, spent time with Jesus.

## Consummate Love: Intimacy with Passion and Commitment

Like the most fulfilled of married couples, Mary of Bethany found the richest kind of love. It consisted of all three components—intimacy, passion, and commitment. Luke 10 describes how Martha prepared food in the kitchen while Mary sat at Jesus' feet, listening to what he was saying. Martha became "distracted by all the prepa-rations that had to be made" (Luke 10:40, NIV), but Mary fell more and more in love with Jesus as she spent time with him. Martha approached Jesus, stood above him, and didn't have time to listen to what he had to say; Mary's heart was hungry to hear Jesus talk and to learn about issues of eternal importance.

What was Jesus response to these two different kinds of love? "Martha, Martha, you are worried and bothered about so many things; but only a few things are necessary, really only one, for Mary has chosen the good part, which shall not be taken away from her" (Luke 10:41-42, NASB). Mary's love for Jesus demonstrated all three elements necessary for a deep, lasting, and meaningful rela-tionship with the Lord she loved.

As we continue our journey together, understand that you, too, are looking for "the good part," which can never be taken away from you. That good part can be found only through really knowing Christ. It is not a destination you visit once, find the treasure, and then leave. Rather, the knowing-Christ life becomes a dwelling place for those willing to make the sacrifices that passion, intimacy, and commitment require. "The good part" is the result.

How would you classify your love for Jesus today? How would you like for that love to be?

Though Jesus died on the cross soon after this visit to Bethany, the good part Mary had experienced remained. She faced some rough times during the remainder of her life, but still she held on to that intimacy with Jesus—along with her passion and commitment. She watched Jesus die, but the knowing relationship she had found with him remained alive. She had chosen the good part, and no one could ever take that away.

*DEAR GOD, I often have trouble grasping your love for me. I still struggle against thoughts that I have to do something to earn it. When it comes to my love for you, I wonder what that looks like in my life. I say, "I love you, Lord," but what has that really meant? Help me to look honestly at my love for you. Show me what is missing. I want to choose "the good part" as Mary did and experience the joy of sitting at your feet. Help me to find true consummate love with you. Show me the way. Amen.*

# 4

# Unmasking Love's Intimacy

The "good part" that Mary of Bethany found in her relationship with Jesus didn't come overnight. It became a reality over time. Her knowledge of him developed and grew little by little. Day by day. Place by place.

When I was a child, my family attended a church thirty-three miles from our home across country roads. Sometimes on the way my dad pulled the car to the side of the road, and he and my mom would pray. As a child I dreaded those times because it meant that our family faced another crisis and we needed help to make it through.

Because our church was very young at the time, the people did not yet know how to wait on God and find his answers for desperate situations. So my parents would ask God to tell us what to do and where to go to find someone to help us pray. We would usually end up at another church some distance away, where we'd receive special intercession and counsel.

We never could have found those answers by the side of the road if my parents had not developed an intimate relationship with God during times alone with him in their secret places. Growing intimacy happens in places, over long periods of time. Joni Eareckson Tada writes: "God meets us in *places*. . . . He strolled with Adam through the Garden in the cool of the day. He wrestled with Jacob through a long night by a stream called Jabbok. He comforted the fugitive David in a dank limestone cave called Adullum. . . . He meets us *anyplace*. But He also meets with us *someplace*."[1]

Joni goes on to tell about her Uncle Vince, who had a prayer room he took her to visit one day. Joni wondered why he had to have a specific place to meet with God when God could meet with him anyplace. But in later years Joni discovered her uncle's wisdom in meeting with Jesus in a particular place. She writes, "That's probably the reason why he could pray on the golf course and when he went hiking with us. Uncle Vince encountered God every place . . . because he had one place."[2]

Because my dad and mom and Joni's Uncle Vince had "one place," they found intimacy with God that they could use anyplace.

## INTIMATE ENCOUNTERS

I, too, have one place where I meet with God regularly. It's a green leather recliner in the corner of my study, where I spend daily time with God. I talk to him, and he talks with me through his Word. We grow more familiar with each encounter, and as I talk to him and read his Word, I discover aspects of God I never knew before. Like a child on an Easter egg hunt, I can run right past the prize egg if I don't spend time on my searching. I have spent more of my life than I care to admit missing out—staying too preoccupied with other things—to uncover the riches of spending time with God: Sometimes I still get too busy or caught up in my schedule to go after him. When that happens, anxiety replaces peace, insecurity replaces love, and I end up going it alone instead of having God's help. On the other hand, the more I share with him, the more I want to share. The more I share with him, the more he shares with me. The more I share with him, the more loved I feel. The more I share with him, the more I miss it when I don't.

Secret places with God, wherever they are, shut out invasive noises of the world so that we can hear the sounds of another place and another voice. It's what the words of C. Austin Miles's old hymn

"In the Garden" describe: "I come to the garden alone, while the dew is still on the roses. . . . And he walks with me, and he talks with me."

Intimacy, the emotional component of love, grows in places. It evolves as a result of a regular, personal, prolonged encounter with someone, which bonds you together with mutual affection. The longer and closer the individual association, contact, or familiarity becomes, the deeper the intimacy grows.

Psychologists define intimacy as "the ability to commit oneself to a close relationship that demands sacrifice and compromise."[3] It involves one's deepest, most private nature. Intimacy requires vulnerability and sharing one's deepest fears without shame. John Eldredge defines spiritual intimacy as romance, as God woos us to himself and awakens in us a yearning for beauty and adventure with him. Eldredge writes: "Romance has most often come to us in the form of two deep desires: the longing for adventure that requires something of us, and the desire for intimacy—to have someone truly know us for ourselves, while at the same time inviting us to *know* them in the naked and discovering way lovers come to know each other on the marriage bed. The emphasis is perhaps more on adventure for men and slightly more on intimacy for women. Yet both desires are strong in us as men and women. In the words of friends, these two desires come together in us all as a longing to be in a relationship of heroic proportions."[4]

Pastor and author Joseph M. Stowell calls intimacy "heart relationships," and he writes about what intimacy with God is *not*:

- It's not about what he will do for us when we get close.
- It's not an informal buddy-relationship with God.
- It's not the same for everyone.
- It's not something we can experience the fullness of in the here and now.
- It's not available to the partially surrendered life.[5]

Stowell goes on to define intimacy with God as he sees it: "Intimacy is what we experience as we grow more deeply conscious of, connected to, and confident in him and him alone as our unfailing resource in life."[6]

Intimacy, romance, heart relationship with God—these are privileges he offers to his people who dare to seek them, and there have always been those who do.

## EARLY INTIMACY WITH GOD

Moses' place of intimacy with God was a portable sanctuary called the tent of meeting. Wherever Moses stopped as he led the Israelites through the wilderness, he set up the tent of meeting and talked to God about challenges they faced and direction they sought: "Now Moses used to take a tent and pitch it outside the camp some distance away, calling it the 'tent of meeting.' Anyone inquiring of the Lord would go to the tent of meeting outside the camp. . . . As Moses went into the tent, the pillar of cloud would come down and stay at the entrance, while the Lord spoke with Moses. . . . The Lord would speak to Moses face to face, as a man speaks with his friend" (Exodus 33:7-11, NIV).

When I read this description, my mind flashes back to my childhood experiences with my family by the side of the road. I can see Moses in my mind and feel the dread of his "kids" looking on: *Oh, no! another crisis,* they must have thought as Moses "pulled over" and began to set up the tent of meeting. Then they prayed. How would they make it through the next challenge? Where would the provision or the strength come from?

But Moses found a spot, over and over again, where he erected the tent and went inside. There, with a cloud hanging above, God spoke to Moses as a man speaks to his friend.

I can't count the times I have called my own caravan to a halt and erected my tent of meeting in my car or my bed or my tub—

anyplace I could be alone with the only One who could help. I have talked to God about things that concerned me, and he has provided another set of directions, fresh strength, and renewed wisdom.

So what made the tent of meeting or the spot where Moses set it up so special? What made the church my parents visited on those Sunday mornings any different from the one we usually attended? What was there in those early encounters that allowed me to hear from God? Why did God use those places to answer his children?

Because we came to him in faith, prepared to hear what he had to say. Those tents of meeting would not have become holy places or memorials of answered prayers had not the individuals who occupied them known the One to whom they prayed. It was not the tents themselves or the eloquence of the prayers that mattered; it was the surrendered hearts of those who dared to seek the Father. Those meeting places would have remained dry spots in the sand had the men and women who walked inside not found those quiet moments with God and looked to him for their sufficiency day after day.

Moses knew where to go during a crisis because he had walked with God in the good times. He had gotten to know him intimately. So when the bad times came and Moses needed help, he pulled over and sought the God he already knew. And that's why my mom and dad could find him when they needed him. Face-to-face. Friend to friend.

## UNMASKING LOVE'S INTIMACY

Every person is created for intimacy with God. Seventeenth-century mathematician and philosopher Blaise Pascal said that there is a God-shaped vacuum in our lives, and only God can fill it.

True intimacy allows us to be privately naked and unashamed.

We saw this type of intimacy demonstrated at the beginning of humankind. In Genesis 1:27 we read that God created man and woman in his own image. Adam and Eve found naked-and-not-ashamed intimacy with God and each other together in the Garden (Genesis 2:25). They spent lots of time together, talking about everything and being vulnerable. But after they ate the forbidden fruit, Scripture tells us, "The eyes of both of them were opened, and they knew that they were naked" (Genesis 3:7).

To cover their nakedness, Adam and Eve made clothes, an evidence of their destroyed intimacy. They forfeited *their* intimate contact with God—and of all humankind's to come, including yours and mine—and we've needed to work hard to regain what was a free gift in the beginning.

Today our society does not encourage intimacy—especially with God. Hank Hanegraaff writes that without intimacy with God, we live "outward" lives. He writes, "The tragedy of contemporary Christianity is that we measure the success of our prayer life by the size and scope of our accomplishments, rather than the strength of our relationships with God. We are fixated on the outwardness, while God is focused on our inwardness."[7]

In *Telling Secrets,* Frederick Buechner writes that "our shimmering self gets buried so deep that most of us end up hardly living out of it at all. . . . Instead we live out all the other selves which we are constantly putting on and taking off like coats and hats against the world's weather."[8]

John Eldredge writes about divine intimacy in his book *The Sacred Romance:* "There is a busyness, a drivenness, the fact that most of us are living merely to survive. Beneath it we feel restless, weary, and vulnerable. . . . What shall we do when we wake one day to find we have lost touch with our heart and with it the very refuge where God's presence resides?"[9]

Divine intimacy, by whatever name we call it, is available to

God's people, but it is also elusive. If we're going to recapture lost intimacy, we first have to discover why it is gone.

## BREAKING THE INHIBITORS

In a physical sense, many of us *want* closeness, but our need to maintain a safe emotional distance inhibits us from achieving intimacy. Psychotherapists study various factors that keep people from finding intimacy. They call these factors intimacy inhibitors. Three common intimacy inhibitors, which often begin during childhood, include issues of control, trust, and priorities. These same factors may also inhibit our intimacy with God:

### Fear of Losing Control

When someone has lorded power over us during vulnerable times in our lives, we often develop an inordinate need to maintain control and protect our rights. As a result, we become assertive, expansive, and self-protective, and we choose arenas in which we can play a dominant, controlling role. The possibility of intimacy makes us too vulnerable and causes us to retreat to situations where we can rebuild the defensive walls. Loving and growing close involve too much risk, so the person who insists on maintaining control never finds true intimacy.

Fear of losing control can also keep us from turning our lives over to God. Women, especially, often like to remain in control. This need becomes even greater when we've been subjected to controlling people who were important parts of our lives. But Jesus taught his disciples about the need to surrender control to him, no matter what they'd been through in other relationships. Contrary to the way we're accustomed to thinking, Jesus explained that it's not until we voluntarily lose our lives that we end up finding them: "If anyone desires to come after Me, let him deny himself, and take up his cross, and follow Me. For whoever desires to save his life will lose it, but whoever loses his life for My sake will find it. For what profit is it to a man if he gains the whole world, and loses his own soul? Or what will a man give in exchange for his soul?" (Matthew 16:24-26).

Loving another person always involves a certain amount of risk, and the same is true when it comes to finding intimacy with God. But until we're willing to take that risk and give up our need to stay in control, we'll never enjoy the bliss of intimacy with the Almighty.

Relinquish control. Those interested in real intimacy are more expressive and disclosing, and they listen to the One with whom they are seeking intimacy. God loves to hear us admit we can't "do life" without him. The surrender of our own strength and control engages the strength and control of God. When we lose our life to him, we gain true life at last.

### Fear of Trusting

Trust is an essential component of intimacy. Many of us have been betrayed by someone we should have been able to count on. When this betrayal has happened at the hands of someone as close as a father, we resist allowing ourselves to trust again. And without trust, intimacy cannot happen.

I believe that at the root of most of our struggles with God is the inability to really trust him. We don't trust that he knows what's best. We don't trust that he won't withhold good things from our lives. We don't trust him with choosing our spouses or jobs or ministries. We don't trust him to protect us from the devil, disease, or disaster. We just don't trust him.

My second husband, Dave, and I once planned a ski trip to Crested Butte, Colorado, with our children. Part of that plan involved sending our children, ages thirteen to thirty, Bible verses about trust. When we arrived at the condominium where we would stay, we spent time talking about trusting God. One child ques-tioned God about whether she should marry. Another about what college she would attend. Another about her faith as a whole. We read Psalm 37:3: "Trust in the Lord, and do good; dwell in the land, and feed on His faithfulness."

For someone like me, who had experienced a first marriage marked by every imaginable example of deception, discovering that I could trust God and he would not fail me was music to my ears. I've learned to look at even bad stuff when it happens and still see God as faithful, because trust is not dependent only on what you can see. Trust is built on experiences of past faithfulness, so as you move forward through the hills as well as the valleys, you can continue to remember and trust God's faithfulness.

## Fear of Making Intimacy a Priority

Some of us have never known anyone who knew how to be intimate in relationships, so we have no model to follow. As a result, intimacy does not become a priority for us. We hold our relationships at arm's length and justify ourselves by feeling that it's good that we have any relationship at all. This nonintimate mentality flows over into our time with God, too. We say we're Christians, but intimacy is just not something we strive for. We may know in our heads that intimacy is important for a meaningful relationship, but because we've never seen what intimacy in a relationship looks like, we have no desire to enter that secret place with God. We don't know what we'll find there.

The solution to this difficulty is found in Matthew 6:33: "Seek first the kingdom of God and His righteousness, and all these things shall be added to you." *Seek first the kingdom of God.* Even if you've never experienced intimacy in a relationship with someone, value intimacy with God as your most prized possession. Pursue it with all your might. God's secrets are the ultimate prize in life. We can have money, fame, even wonderful relationships, but these things pale in comparison when we begin to see God's

words in Isaiah 45:3 fulfilled in our lives: "I will give you the treasures of darkness, riches stored in secret places, so that you may
know that I am the Lord, the God of Israel, who summons you by
name" (NIV).

Love him. Spend time with him. Talk to him every day. Read his
love letters to you. In exchange, you'll find intimacy with the
Almighty.

In *Dancing in the Arms of God,* author Connie Neal describes spiritual intimacy in terms of dancing with God, as "a relationship
between you and God that is based on love and mutual respect.
The two of you communicate in a close, intimate setting. He holds
you, but his embrace is the embrace of a lover, not the restraint of
an oppressor. As partners in this dance, God leads, and you let
him, moving with the flow of his leading. You are not enveloped
in God, losing your identity as a unique person; you are who
you are, retaining your freedom and individuality at every
turn."[10]

We will never know complete intimacy with God until we get
to heaven and stand face-to-face with Jesus. Until then, like
Moses, we can meet with him daily. Find your tent of meeting.
Put your fear of losing control, fear of trust, and fear of making
intimacy a priority behind you and begin to learn to snuggle close
with God.

As a robin is a harbinger of springtime, so intimacy with God
provides a taste of what's to come. "Until then," Joseph Stowell
writes, "the healthiest and most fulfilled pursuit of life is to turn our
eyes toward the day and focus our lives on getting as good a look as
possible now—to connect with him as intimately as possible."[11]

Now's the time. Today's the day. Connect with him. Dance with him. Dare to become intimate with him.

---

*LORD, I have struggled with intimacy in many areas of my life, and that struggle has spilled over into my relationship with you. I want to experience the joy and freedom of knowing you intimately. Help me to break away from the things that have inhibited me and kept me from knowing you as you desire. I'm learning that intimacy happens in places and over time. Help me, show me, teach me how to be intimate with you. And then show me how to bring that intimacy into my relationships with other people. Amen.*

# 5

# Igniting Love's Passion

Barb fell into temptation with an Internet romance. When her husband found out, turmoil erupted, and for five years the scorching lava of pain and unforgiveness on the part of Barb's husband flowed down to engulf their lives. It didn't matter that their two little boys were waiting to get on with the business of living.

I lived nearby. The fact that Barb, who had been a Christian for a long time and attended church regularly, had succumbed to such an obvious trap of Satan, shocked her into changing some things in her life. She asked for forgiveness, first from God and then from her husband. She also sought out Christian counseling and committed herself to Bible study and prayer. Making her marriage work became Barb's burning passion. But as we all know, when a marriage is in trouble, it takes two to *want* to make it work. I talked and prayed with the couple many times, and often thought there was no hope. Finally, however, Barb's husband decided that he really did not want his family to break apart. He also developed a desire to rediscover the woman he had fallen in love with and then, with her, to find depths of intimacy they'd never known before. Eventually the couple moved out of state, but they recently visited, and Barb updated me on their marriage: "It's like we've been on a three-year honeymoon," she said. Passion had returned to their marriage.

## WHAT IS PASSION?

One dictionary defines passion as "an intense . . . or overmastering feeling or conviction; a strong liking or desire for" something.[1] In chapter 3 we looked at passion as love's motivational component and the drive that leads to romance. We experience passion when we want something more than anything else in the whole world. It often becomes ungovernable in its intensity. It means we choose, covet, crave, enjoy, fancy, want, wish, hanker, and hunger for the object of our passion. Passion causes us to pine, pant, yearn, thirst, aim, and long for. It leads to romance, attraction, and ultimately consummation. It has been the subject of popular songs for centuries.

Bill and Kathy Peel draw attention to the subject of passion in *Discover Your Destiny:* "Passion is the God-given ability to feel so deeply about something that it causes you to move toward the object of desire. This passion stems from an urge *given by God,* a burden, an emotional response to a need or opportunity He wants us to move toward. . . . Passion is the birthplace of a dream, the trailhead of a new path God wants us to follow. Passions give us direction . . . help us know where we want to go. They provide us with a kind of nozzle to focus our energy. Passion keeps our purpose clear before us."[2]

Calvin Miller calls passion *appetite.* He writes, "Martyrs are not necessarily those who are hungry to die. They are mere souls with an excessive appetite to please Christ."[3]

In *The Awakened Heart,* author Gerald May calls passion *heart:* "There is a desire within each of us, in the deep center of ourselves that we call our heart. We were born with it, it is never completely satisfied, and it never dies. We are often unaware of it, but it is always awake. . . . Our true identity, our reason for being, is to be found in this desire."[4]

The psalmist wrote, "My soul longs, yes, even faints for the courts of the Lord; my heart and my flesh cry out for the living God" (Psalm 84:2). His heart beat with a passion for God.

## LIFE WITHOUT PASSION

The prophet Jeremiah called his passion for God's Word "a fire shut up in my bones" (Jeremiah 20:9, NIV).

I, too, see passion as a fire, a flame that has been burning inside me since I was about fourteen years old. I had learned an old hymn written by Audrey Meier. I would sit at the upright piano my father had purchased from a university dormitory in our hometown, and I would sing the words of the song with tears in my eyes:

> *I've a yearning in my heart that cannot be denied.*
> *It's a longing that has never yet been satisfied.*
> *I want the world to know the One who loves them so,*
> *Like a flame it's burning deep inside.*
> *To be used of God,*
> *To sing, to speak, to pray;*
> *To be used of God to show someone the way.*
> *I long so much to feel the touch of His consuming fire.*
> *To be used of God is my desire.*

Though the flame is unquenchable, it has not always burned brightly in my life. During my most healthy and productive times, this yearning has remained my focus and has kept me striving toward it. At other times, however, I have misplaced that yearning and allowed the flame to flicker. It was my own doing, and it began with small areas of compromise. A little give here and a little take there ultimately sapped the passion. I lost my way. I no longer had a dream or a goal to keep my eyes on and my feet plodding toward. Desperation and resignation invariably resulted and caused me to make wrong choices and pursue wrong things. Life's passion was gone.

Even for us as Christians, without passion, our lives become ho-hum. Like a car stuck in the snow, we can't move forward. Instead, we go through the motions of living and only spin our wheels. We go to work, we come home. We go to church, we come home. Life offers no desires, so it offers no excitement. It creates no guidelines and so provides no direction.

John Eldredge sees passion as desire, and he writes about the passionless condition in *The Journey of Desire*:

> Desire, both the whispers and the shouts, is the map we have been given to find the only life worth living. . . . Bringing our heart along in our life's journey is the most important mission of our lives—and the hardest. It all turns on what we do with desire. If you will look around, you will see that most people have abandoned the journey. They have lost heart. They are camped in places of resignation or indulgence, or trapped in prisons of despair. I understand. I have frequented all those places before and return to them even still. Life provides any number of reasons and occasions to abandon desire. Certainly, one of the primary reasons is that it creates for us our deepest dilemmas. To desire something and not to have it—is this the source of nearly all our pain and sorrow?[5]

Poet Langston Hughes calls passion *dreams*, and in his poem "Dreams," he describes the barrenness of a life without passion or dreams:

> *Hold fast to dreams [desires, passions]*
> *For if dreams die*
> *Life is a broken-winged bird*
> *That cannot fly.*

*Hold fast to dreams*
*For when dreams go*
*Life is a barren field*
*Frozen with snow.*[6]

## THREATS TO SPIRITUAL PASSION

It seems clear that a life without passion lacks depth or "color" or "desire." This is particularly true of spiritual passion. If we know that we don't want to live a passionless life, then what kinds of things threaten our passion for knowing God? In *Renewing Your Spiritual Passion,* author Gordon MacDonald lists seven conditions that threaten our spiritual passion:

- *The drained condition* comes when our gas tank hits empty. It is the result of depleted or exhausted energy or resources.
- *The dried-out condition* results when we fail to take anything into the inner chambers of life to fill our spiritual tank. It results in unchecked emotions such as irritability, impatience, and deceit.
- *The distorted condition* takes place when we allow the world's lies, alternatives, and messages to obscure or distort our view of the way things really are.
- *The devastated condition* manifests itself as fatigue and weariness. It originates when people and events vigorously oppose what we stand for.
- *The disillusioned condition* results from the deflation of a great dream.
- *The defeated condition* is the product of a personal defeat and is the most common kind of weariness.
- *The disheartened condition* sets in when we feel intimidated and see people, events, or institutions as more powerful than God.[7]

Whatever you call passion—appetites, hungers, desires, "fire in your bones," or yearnings in your heart—you can lose it or never discover it at all if you are not aware of the option of passionate living. Whether you've smothered the flame or never ignited it in the first place, a heart and flesh crying out for the living God, as the psalmist's did, will turn you toward spiritual passion.

In the classic movie *Braveheart,* William Wallace, played by Mel Gibson, said, "Every man dies, but not every man really lives."[8] With passion we have the opportunity to really live. It points us in the direction of God's purpose for our lives. And just like a fire, passion demands that we do two things: first, ignite it; second, sustain it.

## IGNITING YOUR PASSION

We saw that lack of intimacy with God often creates the absence of intimacy with other people, too. The same is true for passion. If you have never experienced a passionate relationship with Christ, take a look at these things that will help you to ignite it:

### Determine Right Passions

Greeks in Bible times saw passions in terms of both good and bad desires. The Greek word *epithumeo* means "to set one's heart upon, eagerly long for, covet, greatly desire, lust after." The emphasis was on the intensity of the desire, not the object of the desire. It referred to an affection of the mind.

We realize that we need passion to grow spiritually, but since passions can take us in both positive and negative directions, we must be sure that we develop passion for the right things. If we allow our passions to center on evil things, they can quickly lead to lust. If our passions for Christ are motivated only by what he can do for us, they will take us in selfish directions and never bring us to a "knowing" relationship with him. As Calvin Miller writes, "To desire only what Christ gives and not to desire Christ Himself is to be bought off by little trinkets, never to own the greater treasures of His indwelling presence."[9]

If the urge to get ahead or to establish ourselves powerfully and securely becomes our motivation for what we give our passions to, we will find ourselves getting out of line. This motivation becomes most dangerous when it settles into the cracks of the heart and tempts us to weigh every situation in terms of the possibility of advancing into a position where we find fame or reward. Ambition is tiring and overcomes spiritual passion. It leaves us weary from constantly playing the mental game that starts with "what if?" and moves on to "if only." Fatigue results from dissatisfaction with where one is and what one is doing.

Wrong passions will result in sin. If they have gotten you into trouble in the past, pray for redirection. Ask God to show you how to conquer your ungodly desires. Jesus understands your situation. He was tempted the same way we are, but each time, he overcame the temptation. That's why Paul says we can boast about our weaknesses, including our passions, because when we are weak, the Lord is strong (2 Corinthians 12:9).

If passion comes naturally to you, your task is to channel it in the right direction. Be sure the things you desire square with God's Word. If you're not by nature a passionate person, start loving God. Tell him aloud how much you love him. Keep up that habit, and you'll find you've ignited your passion.

**Pinpoint Your Passions**

What do you weep about? What issues and problems motivate you? What needs would you like to meet in the world? What idea would you love to see come to fruition? What things deeply concern you? What gets you excited?

If you list the things that bring about strong emotion in you, you will be on the right trail in discovering your passions. And as your love for God grows, so will your passions. He will masterfully weave together your passions for him and the gifts and abilities he has given you. Then he will provide opportunities for you to plug them in to the right places.

**Pursue Your Passions**

Once you've discovered which passions are good ones and what your own particular passions are, it's time to pursue them. Your passions are a gift from God, and he desires that you use the abilities he has given you to go after those passions.

Pursue your passions with your whole heart. A. W. Tozer writes, "Thirsty hearts are those whose longings have been wakened by the touch of God within them."[10] Thirsty hearts stay alert to things that will feed and satisfy the appetites within us. Surrender your quest for passion with God. Make a paraphrase of Colossians 3:23 a regular part of your prayers: "Lord, whatever I do, help me to do it with my whole heart, as if I'm working for you and not for other people." This will help you keep the goal before you and still retain God in his rightful place.

**Watch for God's Leading**

I've had a passion for radio since I was a young girl. The church my dad pastored launched a radio broadcast when I was twelve years old. It lasted until I was nearly thirty, and my siblings and I took part in various aspects of the program. As I grew to love and know God more and more, he started weaving together my passion for him and my passion for writing and radio. Every week now when I talk to my listeners, I have the opportunity to convey my passion for Jesus through my passion for radio. Only God knew me that well. Only God loved me that much.

Once we surrender our passions to God, he uses them for our

good and for his glory. His leading will attract your passions like a magnet. Pray for opportunities and for eyes to recognize them, and prayerfully respond to them.

## Hang In There

I know many people who have determined, pinpointed, and pursued their passions, but they haven't yet seen them come to fruition. As a result, they have become frustrated, and some have even let the fire of their passion die.

Don't do it. God builds passion within each of us, and he does all he can throughout our lives to get us to pursue desires we feel. Sometimes we have to wait for the fulfillment of those things that we are passionate about. God's Word not only acknowledges our godly desires but also promises that God will fulfill them: "The vision [desire, passion] is yet for an appointed time; but at the end it will speak, and it will not lie. Though it tarries, wait for it; because it will surely come" (Habakkuk 2:3). If you have felt a yearning in your heart for a long time but haven't seen it come to fruition, keep surrendering it to God and stoking the fire of passion within you. If you keep it alive, he'll show you a place to use it.

## SUSTAINING YOUR PASSION

Igniting the fire of God-given passion is important, and sustaining it is essential. Unless you tend it carefully and fuel it constructively, your passion will fizzle and eventually extinguish altogether. Instead of letting it smolder and smother, you want to make your passion ignite and then explode. You can do that by feeding your passion with the right things:

### Associate with Other Passionate People

Individuals around you can either feed or squelch your own spiritual passion. The faith hall of fame in Hebrews 11 mentions

Abraham, who believed, and "it was credited to him as righteousness" (Romans 4:22, NIV). Did Abraham retain his belief in God by surrounding himself with people who didn't believe? No way. He hung around with people of like passions: "By faith Abraham obeyed when he was called to go out to the place which he would receive as an inheritance. And he went out, not knowing where he was going. By faith he dwelt in the land of promise as in a foreign country, dwelling in tents with Isaac and Jacob, the heirs with him of the same promise" (Hebrews 11:8-9).

How do the people we associate with affect our spiritual passion? Gordon MacDonald writes:

- Resourceful people ignite our passion.
- Important people share our passion.
- Trainable people catch our passion.
- Nice people enjoy our passion.
- Draining people sap our passion.[11]

The kinds of people you choose to hang around with have a great bearing on whether or not you are able to sustain your passions over the long haul. They need passions of their own, and your passions must not be threatening to them. They should have a healthy view of how to nurture their own passions and time for helping you nurture yours. Find your Isaacs and Jacobs, heirs with you of the same promise and passions, and become an Isaac or Jacob who can help others sustain their own passions.

**Take Care of Your Body**
Passion will die in a tired body, and misdirected passions can *create* a tired body. Sometimes we can work so hard on our own passions that we wear ourselves out.

Be sure to get adequate rest, exercise regularly, and eat right. God ordained your passions; look to him for outlets for them too. Even in your pursuit of a passionate relationship with God, don't pursue passion for its own sake. Instead, love God with all your might, and when you do, passion will result. Participate in things that feed your passion. We should guard the passions God has given us by taking care of our bodies, and we should give them back to God to do with as he pleases. Once we have done that, we can rest as he puts the pieces in place.

## Make Small Strides

You have probably heard the saying, Rome wasn't built in a day. Don't expect to accomplish all we've been saying about spiritual passion in a day either. Instead, as you see opportunities to direct your passion, begin in ways that are doable. Add them gradually to the mainstream of your life. If you don't, you'll overload and burn out and put out the fire of passion that brought you to that point.

## Evaluate Your Strides

Put other godly, passionate people in your life to observe you and hold you accountable. Let them watch to see how you're playing out your passions. Allow them to help you set goals and give you feedback about how you're doing.

By focusing on a target and evaluating the direction in which we are going, we can have some idea of our progress. But sometimes the target seems to move, or the path seems to be taking another direction. I've encountered a lot of disappointments in my attempts to pursue my passion. But is passion still there? Sure it is. Passion keeps going when external rewards drop out of sight. True spiritual passion isn't fickle. It's intrinsic. It can withstand pain and delayed gratification along the way: "Do you not know? Have you not heard? The Lord is the everlasting God, the Creator of the ends of the earth. He will not grow tired or weary, and his understanding no one can fathom. He gives strength to the weary and increases the power of the weak" (Isaiah 40:28-29, NIV). Passion is a renewable resource that keeps us steadfast when obstacles appear.

**Unleash Your Emotions**

When we love someone—whether a spouse, a child, a family member, or a close friend—with only part of our hearts, souls, minds, and strength, we live a pretty passionless relationship. But allow those expressions to come alive, and *wow!* Just imagine where passion can take us. Permit yourself to go wild in expressing your passion for Jesus, too. There's no limit to where that passion will take you.

"As the deer pants for streams of water, so my soul pants for you, O God" (Psalm 42:1, NIV). Passion requires stoking if its flame is to continue burning. Our daily challenge is to both ignite and sustain our passion. Calvin Miller says, "Spiritual growth occurs by ever starting, starting, starting every day some creative new thing that will sponsor a creative, never-boring walk with Christ."[12]

Passion, love's motivational component, is the drive that leads to genuine romance with God. Passion for God allows us to really live and puts excitement into our knowledge of him.

---

*LORD, you are a God of passions. It is your passionate love that seeks those who don't know you. And it is your longing for your creatures that drove Christ to the cross. Appetite, longing, hunger, a yearning for you. I want these in my life. I want to understand your passion for me, and I want to feel passionate about you. I want a desire that keeps me running to spend time with you. The drive that gets me up in the morning, excited about spending time with you. Show me how to ignite it and then how to sustain it. Give me renewed passion for you. Amen.*

# 6

# Making Love's Commitment

Daniel Harmon attended the church my dad pastored in rural Indiana. Though I was only in junior high, I remember Daniel well. In his late twenties, Daniel battled alcoholism and came to church only sporadically with his wife and three young children. But then Daniel had a heart attack, and when he got out of the hospital, we saw him often at church—for a while.

One night he stood to share his testimony of how God had spared his life. The light reflected off his black hair, smoothed back from his face. Tears rolled from his chin and onto his chest as, with arms crossed over his potbelly, Daniel said, "I'm ready to die for Jesus."

I asked my dad about Daniel's words as we made our way home later that night. My dad said, "I think that Daniel is ready to die for Christ, but I'm not sure he's ready to *live* for Christ."

Daniel's attendance dropped off soon after that emotional night, and I heard that he had gone back to the comfort of the bottle. A few weeks later, while Daniel and his wife drove to town to do some shopping, Daniel slumped over in the driver's seat. His wife knew he'd suffered another heart attack. She ran to the driver's side of the car, moved him over, and drove quickly to the hospital. I later heard her say that she felt he'd stay alive as long as she could keep him propped up and leaning against her. But such was not the case. That October afternoon, at only twenty-eight, Daniel was pronounced dead.

## THE MEANING OF COMMITMENT

Webster defines *commitment* as "an agreement or pledge" or "the state of being obligated or emotionally impelled."[1] Commitment is the cognitive component of love, the part that involves awareness or judgment; that is, making a conscious, deliberate choice. It's the part of love that decides to hang in there over the long haul. The Bible uses the word *commit* in terms of turning something over to another. Synonyms include *decide, pledge, vow,* and *swear.*

I think of commitment as meaning that something is a settled issue or there is no turning back. Aerospace experts might define commitment as a point of no return. Airplanes reach a place where they have only enough fuel to keep flying toward their destinations. To turn back to their place of origin would require more reserves than they have.

Marriages require commitment. We've all seen what happens to marriages when at least one of the partners is not committed. True commitment doesn't require only onetime lip service as we say our marriage vows: "to have and to hold from this day forward, for better for worse, for richer for poorer, in sickness and in health, to love and to cherish, till death us do part." Instead, marriage requires daily commitment. When worse replaces better and we get poor instead of rich or sick instead of well, commitment must commit all over again if the marriage is to endure.

My husband, Dave, learned the hard way what commitment meant. He and his first wife, Dianne, were married for thirty-two years, and Dianne was sick from day one. Many different afflictions kept their life together from becoming what both of them had imagined it to be. When things got really hard, only Dave's commitment kept him strong.

The same is true in our Christian walks. The Bible doesn't tell us to be committed to Christ only when things are going well. Shadrach, Meshach, and Abed-Nego renewed their commitment to God and stood up to King Nebuchadnezzar when he threatened to throw them into the fiery furnace if they didn't bow to him. They affirmed their belief that God could deliver them, but even if he didn't, their commitment would remain strong (Daniel 3).

One morning while I soaked in the bathtub, I poured out my heart in prayer for one of my children. I said, "Lord, you don't owe me this, and I'll still serve and be committed to you, even if you never show yourself mighty to me again. But please, Lord, hear and answer this prayer for my child."

Commitment to God had become a settled issue in my life. Like the situations with Dave in his first marriage and with the three Hebrews before Nebuchadnezzar, commitment did not depend on circumstances or on receiving new revelations from God. Commitment happened first, and then God honored that nonnegotiable commitment by changing circumstances.

The Bible doesn't beat around the bush when it comes to the subject of real commitment. At the end of Joshua's life he stood before the Israelites and said: "Choose for yourselves this day whom you will serve, whether the gods which your fathers served that were on the other side of the River, or the gods of the Amorites, in whose land you dwell. But as for me and my house, we will serve the Lord" (Joshua 24:15).

Elijah also made a strong commitment. When he confronted the Israelites on Mount Carmel about their idolatry, he said: "How long will you waver between two opinions? If the Lord is God, follow him; but if Baal is God, follow him" (1 Kings 18:21, NIV). Elijah knew there could be no compromise, no middle ground.

Jesus spoke firmly to the church in Laodicea about their noncommitment. He said, "I know your deeds, that you are neither cold nor hot. I wish you were either one or the other! So, because you are lukewarm—neither hot nor cold—I am about to spit you out of my mouth" (Revelation 3:15-16, NIV).

The Bible is clear that commitment is not optional for God's people. He will not share our affections with anyone or anything else. He insists on being number one in our lives:

- "I, the Lord your God, am a jealous God." (Exodus 20:5)
- "You shall worship no other god, for the Lord, whose name is Jealous, is a jealous God." (Exodus 34:14)
- "The Lord your God is a consuming fire, a jealous God." (Deuteronomy 4:24)

God is a jealous God, who does not want us to straddle the fence. He desires that we settle the issue of "forsaking all others as long as we both shall live." A. W. Tozer reminds us that God wants all of us; giving him only a part will not do. Yet commitment remains a struggle for many Christians.

## NONCOMMITTAL COMMITMENT

Many of us see commitment as a form of bondage. We try to keep our options open and protect our freedom. We thrive on lives of noncommitment in our marriages, our churches, and our political parties. Like Daniel in my dad's church, we're ready to die for God, but we're not committed to fully living for him. We find ourselves thinking like the Hollywood couples I once read about. The article described the "like" rings Hollywood couples were giving to their significant others. Without demanding any kind of permanent commitment, the givers of such rings conveyed to the other person, "I'm 'in like' with you." This noncommittal approach also provides an easy way out if desired.

The Bible says, "Where your treasure is, there your heart will be also" (Matthew 6:21). Rooted in self-centeredness, we treasure our jobs, cars, homes, and families, and as we do, our hearts—and our commitments—follow. Jerry White, author of *The Power of Commitment,* writes, "The accoutrements of wealth, position, power, and success take their silent, demanding toll on the Christian who begins to value them."[2]

Noncommitment often comes masked in busyness. Activity, attendance, and right answers replace determination to hang in there even when things get hard. We often fail to commit to a first-hand relationship with Christ because of our busyness *for* Christ. Sanctified hassle leaves no room for significant commitment to God. Again Jerry White says, "It is easy to be a Christian in our society today. It is wholly acceptable, even commendable. It takes so little in the way of commitment to be totally accepted in the world and in the church. The demands are small. Compare this to the level of commitment required in a society where Christians are despised or persecuted."[3]

Generally speaking, our struggles with commitment come in four areas: possessions, positions, plans, and people. Let's take a look at each of these.

## Our Possessions

Jesus told his disciples: "It is hard for a rich man to enter the kingdom of heaven. And again I say to you, it is easier for a camel to go through the eye of a needle than for a rich man to enter the kingdom of God" (Matthew 19:23-24). Jesus doesn't hate people who have money; he just hates money having people. He knows that owning things has a tendency to take over one's life and affections.

I once heard Chuck Swindoll relate a story in which God told a man to give him all his possessions. "Okay," the man said, "here's everything. Here's my life savings, my home, my car, and my boat."

"There's more," God said. "What about your wife and children?"

So the man gave his family to God. When he did, God said to him, "I'm going to give these things back to you to use for a while, but just remember from whose hands you received them."

James 1:17 says it like this: "Every good and perfect gift is from above, coming down from the Father of the heavenly lights, who does not change like shifting shadows" (NIV).

We clutch our material possessions to us and refuse to surrender them to God when they belong to him in the first place. They are gifts he has given us to use for a while, but we often become more committed to the gifts than to the Giver. The trick to releasing our possessions to God is opening our hands. Holocaust survivor Corrie ten Boom once said that we should hold everything loosely because it hurts when God has to pry our fingers away.

We need to work on this ourselves, and the sooner we start teaching it to our children, the sooner they'll begin to make it a habit too. You can overcome the messages that entice them to make commitments to the wrong things as you share and model the truth of God's Word.

### Our Positions

Joni Eareckson Tada writes, "There are no little people in God's kingdom, because there are no big people."[4] When the disciples asked Jesus who was the greatest and who had the highest position, Jesus said, "Whoever humbles himself as [a] little child is the greatest in the kingdom of heaven" (Matthew 18:4).

We sometimes make gods out of the positions we hold. Even in our churches we may place benefits, perks, and titles above God. Once, after I finished my doctorate and sought direction for what I should do with my life, God directed me to these verses: "Do not speak with a stiff neck. For exaltation comes neither from the east nor from the west nor from the south. But God is the Judge: he puts down one, and exalts another" (Psalm 75:5-7). I understood that any position or title I ever received would be from God and, so, belong to him. Keeping that in mind keeps the credit where it belongs. And keeping the credit where it belongs keeps me from being committed to the wrong things.

## Our Plans

In chapter 5 we talked about our passions. Passions are good, and God wants us to have them. But in an effort to follow our passions we can make our own plans and go our own way when, once again, the job of planning belongs to God: "'I know the plans I have for you,' declares the Lord, 'plans to prosper you and not to harm you, plans to give you hope and a future'" (Jeremiah 29:11, NIV).

God makes the plans; we fulfill them. We don't hold tenaciously to our plans and then ask him to work around them. Instead, we pray the prayer that Jesus taught his disciples: "Our Father in heaven, hallowed be your name, your kingdom come, *your will be done on earth as it is in heaven*" (Matthew 6:9-10, NIV, emphasis added).

Keeping a balance between praying for God's will and at the same time seeking to fulfill our passions and approaching God's throne with confidence (Hebrews 4:16) will help us make commitments to the right things. Don't commit to *your* plans for your life; commit to God's plans for your life: "'My thoughts are not your thoughts, nor are your ways My ways,' says the Lord. 'For as the heavens are higher than the earth, so are My ways higher than your ways, and My thoughts [higher] than your thoughts'" (Isaiah 55:8-9).

## Our People

Not long ago I drove to Boulder, Colorado, to spend the afternoon with my daughter who attends college there. On the way I prayed for every member of my immediate family. I named them one by one and pictured lifting each of them to God. I knew this was part of my role as a godly mom, and I knew I should continue to be there for each of them. But once again the need to find a delicate balance came into play. I had to check my own heart. Was my commitment more to God or to the family members that I love? Did I love Dave or any of our six children more than I loved God?

It's often not the bad things we commit to that challenge our unfettered commitment to Christ. It's the good things and the good people. Children, parents, friends, spouses—they're the ones who tend to mean too much to us and threaten the unchallenged place Christ should have in our lives.

As with our possessions, our positions, and our plans, we need to hold our loved ones loosely. Present each one to God, and then let them go. Be first committed to God, and then let him show you how to have a proper commitment to the people in your life.

## COMMITMENT WITHIN REACH

If living a life of complete commitment to God remains a challenge for you, look to the Scriptures to show you how. God's Word tells us that commitment

- *happens day by day, decision by decision:* "Commit to the Lord whatever you do, and your plans will succeed." (Proverbs 16:3, NIV)
- *sustains us through trials:* "Those who suffer according to God's will should commit themselves to their faithful Creator and continue to do good." (1 Peter 4:19, NIV)
- *passes the truth on to others:* "The things that thou hast heard of me among many witnesses, the same commit thou to faithful men, who shall be able to teach others also." (2 Timothy 2:2, KJV)
- *requires trust:* "Commit your way to the Lord, trust also in Him, and He shall bring it to pass." (Psalm 37:5)

- *demands surrender:* "Into your hands I commit my spirit." (Psalm 31:5, NIV)

Commitment is not a onetime thing. If we are to endure, it will require continued commitment in every aspect of our lives. But take heart. This commitment is not out of reach because when we commit our lives to Christ, he promises that "[we] can do everything through him who gives [us] strength" (Philippians 4:13, NIV).

Take some time to examine your commitment to God. What about your possessions, your positions, your plans, your people? Do any of these stand between you and God? The psalmist wrote, "Search me, O God, and know my heart" (Psalm 139:23). Ask God to do the same for you. Tell him you want to be committed to him. Then be quiet and let him show you how.

Commitment is hard work, but life is easier when you commit, and commitment is essential to really knowing God. A. W. Tozer writes:

> There is no limit to what God could do in our world if we would dare to surrender before him with a commitment like this: "Oh, God, I hereby give myself to You. I give my family. I give my business. I give all I possess. Take all of it, Lord—and take me! I give myself in such measure that if it is necessary that I lose everything for Your sake, let me lose it. I will not ask what the price is. I will ask only that I may be all that I ought to be as a follower and disciple of Jesus Christ, my Lord."
>
> If even three hundred of God's people became serious, our world would never hear the last of it. They would influence

the news. Their message would go everywhere like birds on a wing. They would set off a great revival of New Testament faith and witness. God wants to deliver us from the easygoing Christianity so fashionable today.[5]

True commitment comes at a cost, but that cost is not as high as the cost of noncommitment: "If the ax is dull, and one does not sharpen the edge, then he must use more strength; but wisdom brings success" (Ecclesiastes 10:10). When you don't stand for something, you'll fall for anything. When you don't commit to God, you'll never know him as he really is. Sharpen your ax. Sharpen your commitment to God.

---

*DEAR GOD, commitment is a challenge in every way. You are a jealous God, and you alone are worthy of first place in my life. Long ago I said I committed my life to you, but I think I've taken too lightly what that really means. Today I want to recommit my life to you. I want to restate my vows. Help me commit my possessions to you by not holding on to material things. Help me commit to you my aspirations for position and the need to make a name for myself. Help me commit my plans to you and want only what you desire for me. And help me commit the people I love to you. I want to do it, but I need your strength and guidance. By your Spirit let me begin today a life of true commitment to you. Amen.*

# 7

# Taking the Knowing Step

All of us reach places in our lives when we stand between where we are and where we know we can be. The time for examining benefits and weighing costs lies behind us, and only the journey and the decision to go forward lie ahead.

In the classic allegorical book *Hinds' Feet on High Places,* author Hannah Hurnard describes the character Much-Afraid standing at such a place. Would Much-Afraid stay where she was or make the trip into the High Places? The Shepherd has shown her the benefit and the cost of making the trip, and in the process, Much-Afraid comes to know these words well: "The Lord God is my strength, and he will make my feet like hinds' feet, and he will make me to walk upon . . . high places" (Habakkuk 3:19, KJV).

Much-Afraid weighs her options: She could return to the way things used to be, like most other people she knew, or she could do what it took to make the journey to the High Places, where a whole new life awaited her. What would she do?

Then the Shepherd speaks: "If you will climb to the heights this once . . . even though it may seem a very long and in some places a very difficult journey, I promise you that you will develop hinds' feet. . . . Never for a moment shall I be beyond your reach or call for help, even when you cannot see Me. It is just as though I shall be present with you all the time, even though invisible. And you have My faithful promise that this journey which you are now to make will be the means of developing your hinds' feet."[1]

What Hurnard calls developing hinds' feet I call getting to really know God, but both represent a journey and a decision, which each of us Much-Afraids must make individually. No matter where you found yourself spiritually when you opened this book, I hope the chapters so far have helped you realize that there's more. A deeper, richer, more knowing life with Christ awaits all those who choose to find it. I hope you now realize that being a Christian doesn't have to consist only of a marriage of convenience but that it can become an intimate, passionate, committed union with the King of kings. I hope you're now aware that you can have a vibrant, knowing relationship with God. And the time has come for you, as it did for Much-Afraid, to decide whether you want to do what it takes to really know him. Will you pursue high places with God? He's holding out his hand to you, beckoning you, calling you by name, inviting you to join him for a richer, fuller, newer relationship.

When the Israelite tribe of Dan was looking for a place to settle, they sent spies to check out the territory. When the spies returned with their report, their response was, "Come on . . . ! We have seen that the land is very good. Aren't you going to do something? Don't hesitate to go there. . . . When you get there, you will find . . . a spacious land that God has put into your hands, a land that lacks nothing whatever" (Judges 18:9-10, NIV). The tribe of Dan had only to choose to go, and the land would be theirs.

God invites you to enter the rich territory of really knowing him. This is your opportunity to do that.

## MAKING THE KNOWING DECISION

Before we take a trip, we first decide whether we want to go. My husband, Dave's, business required a trip to Hawaii some months back. He really *needed* to go, but neither of us *wanted* to go. We had so many other responsibilities and commitments, and we'd already seen the islands. Though the downside of making the trip seemed to outweigh the benefits, we did go, but we went more out of obligation than out of desire. And because we didn't really want to be there, we missed out on so much Hawaii has to offer.

The journey to really knowing God also begins with a decision to go. All of us may agree that we *should* go, but do we really *want* to? Do we really want to do what it takes to get there? Is it worth the price and inconvenience? Do we want to go there more than we want anything else?

No one can answer these questions for someone else. I can't answer the question for you. Parents can't speak for their children; wives can't respond for their husbands. We can bring back souvenirs for our loved ones from our adventure to really knowing God, mementos that come through our changed lives and the ways we respond to others. But we can only entice them to make the journey for themselves.

We can, however, make the decision for ourselves. If you decide, "No, I don't want to really know God," then you could choose to close this book at this point because the remainder of these pages is dedicated to assisting the Much-Afraids who decide to make the journey.

Once you have made the choice to really know God, the task before you resembles a long-distance run.

## THROWING OFF OUR HINDRANCES

My son Clint participates in cross-country and track. Why anyone would deliberately run seventy to eighty conditioning miles a week and compete in one- and two-mile races is beyond me. But he does, and I'm in on his routine. You see, he knows that all kinds of things can affect his race either for the good or the bad.

So I fix pasta for him the night before and oatmeal the morning of each race. I know he needs no sugar and lots of rest before the actual event. I know that stretching well before he runs can keep him from injury. I know that lots of diligent practice will help him to run his best.

Clint is running to win, and he's getting rid of everything that can keep him from that goal. The Bible gives us similar instructions for running the spiritual race: "Let us throw off everything that hinders and the sin that so easily entangles, and let us run with perseverance the race marked out for us. Let us fix our eyes on Jesus, the author and perfecter of our faith, who for the joy set before him endured the cross, scorning its shame, and sat down at the right hand of the throne of God" (Hebrews 12:1-2, NIV).

The things that could hinder and entangle Clint as he runs to win include eating wrong foods and getting too little sleep. For Mindy, a competitive swimmer I knew, it was the hairs on her legs. Mindy realized that even the tiniest things could keep her from achieving her best swim time. Mindy would let the hair on her legs grow until the day of her meet, when she would shave for the cleanest and smoothest finish. Even the additional drag from leg hairs could hinder her ability to cut through the water cleanly. "Let us throw off everything that hinders. . . ."

Augustine calls the things that hinder and entangle us and keep us from being all we can be in Christ "The Toy Box." He writes: "The very toys of toys, and vanities of vanities, my ancient mistresses, still held me; they plucked my fleshy garment, and whispered softly, 'Dost thou cast us off? and from that moment shall we no more be with thee for ever? and from that moment shall not this or that be lawful for thee for ever?' . . . Yet they did retard me, so that I hesitated to burst and shake myself free from them, and to spring over whither I was called."[2]

C. S. Lewis also writes about hindrances in *The Great Divorce,* where he describes a ghost who approaches heaven toting a lizard on its lapel. The keeper at heaven's gate tells the ghost that heaven allows no lizards on its premises. The lizard begs the ghost not to part with him. The ghost wants to keep his lizard, but he decides he wants entry into heaven more. So he gives an angel permission to kill it. The angel grabs the screaming lizard, throws it to the ground, and stomps it dead. Then, as the ghost watches, the lizard turns into a horse, and the ghost becomes a man and rides the horse into heaven.[3] The ghost in the story knew what he wanted most and literally threw off the thing that was keeping him from it.

Making the knowing decision—the decision to really know God—requires that we lay aside the things that hinder us from making today's journey. I fix Clint the right foods before every race. Mindy shaved her legs before every meet. Our journey to knowing God doesn't require that we have all the answers from now until Jesus comes. It doesn't mean that we have to live a perfect life. It requires, instead, that we do what's necessary one day at a time: lay aside the things that hinder and entangle us now. By doing that every day, we make a fresh commitment to show up, put in the hours, rid ourselves of present encumbrances.

Getting rid of our encumbrances begins with repentance. None of us has really measured up to all we could have been with Christ. Whatever has kept you from really loving Jesus, it's time to ask God's forgiveness for allowing those things to keep you from being all you can be in Christ. When we ask God to forgive us, he is glad to do it. But we're doomed to repeat the same mistakes and get entangled in the same things unless we take steps to avoid that problem. This is where repentance comes in, and repentance is not reserved only for the person coming to Christ for the first time. It is a requirement for every Christian. To repent means to stop going in your present direction, turn around, and go the opposite way.

Henry Blackaby writes: "Repentance indicates a decisive change, not merely a wishful resolution. We have not repented if we continue in our sin. Repentance involves a radical change of heart and mind in which we agree with God's evaluation of our sin and then take specific action to align ourselves with His will. A desire to change is not repentance. Repentance is always an active response to God's word. The evidence of repentance is not words of resolve, but a changed life."[4]

The *desire* to run is not running—*running* is running. The desire to get to really know God will not bring about that knowledge unless action accompanies that desire. Intimacy with God demands that we repent—turn completely away from anything or anyone that we have allowed to keep us from knowing God as we should. Passion requires that we repent of our failure to take the time and effort necessary to ignite our passion for Jesus. Commitment involves identifying those things that stand between us and the decision to go all the way to true intimacy with God.

## FIXING OUR EYES

Once we've repented concerning what lies behind us, we focus on what remains ahead: "Let us fix our eyes on Jesus, the author and perfecter of our faith, who for the joy set before him endured the cross, scorning its shame, and sat down at the right hand of the throne of God" (Hebrews 12:2, NIV).

Abraham fixed his eyes on the goal of following where God was leading and looked away from everything that distracted him. He, along with the other men and women of faith mentioned in Hebrews 11, died before Jesus was ever born, yet somehow they kept their eyes on him: "These all died in faith, not having received the promises, but having seen them afar off were assured of them, embraced them and confessed that they were strangers and pilgrims on the earth" (Hebrews 11:13).

The words translated "were assured of them" actually mean to salute or greet as sailors wave a greeting to a country far off on the horizon. Some translations use the word *welcome*. This long-range view formed Abraham's thinking and provided guidelines for his decisions, including the one he made in the land of Mount Moriah.

God had called Abraham to run a special race. Three visitors, whom the Bible refers to as the Lord, came to Abraham's tent and told him he would have a son (Genesis 18). This seemed odd news to ninety-plus-year-old Abraham and his wife, Sarah, who was not much younger. Their biological clocks had continued to tick, and still there was no child. Yet Abraham kept running the race with faith. He kept believing God and fixing his eyes on the promises while he did whatever came next in obedience to God.

Then it happened. Some time after Abraham's one hundredth birthday, Sarah became pregnant. Here she was, way past hot flashes, and now she had morning sickness! Can you imagine the light in Abraham's eyes when Isaac, his long-awaited son, was finally born? No nighttime disturbances of diaper changings and feedings kept that old man from rejoicing over the birth of his son, the tangible, holdable fulfillment of God's promise to him and Sarah. From the time Abraham first cradled Isaac in his arms, his son was the delight of Abraham's heart.

As the boy grew, so did Abraham's affection for him. God kept a close eye on Abraham's love relationship. It might have taken Abraham's eyes off the goal—which we know to be *the* Son—and onto his own son. So God tested Abraham: "Take now your son, your only son Isaac, whom you love, and go to the land of Moriah, and offer him there as a burnt offering on one of the mountains of which I shall tell you" (Genesis 22:2).

How could God promise Abraham a son, make him wait years for that son, allow him to love that son into his teens, and then ask Abraham to sacrifice him? This definitely tested Abraham's vision of the goal. But Abraham's assignment for many years had been to trust God's promises, and they had never failed, so somehow, some way, he knew God would still come through.

Abraham took Isaac on a three-day journey to Mount Moriah, along with the wood, fire, and a knife for the sacrifice. Isaac, whose whole life had been bathed in his father's love, asked, "The fire and wood are here . . . but where is the lamb for the burnt offering?" (Genesis 22:7, NIV).

At that moment Abraham sealed his decision. Once and for all he lifted his eyes off the boy he loved and onto the God he loved more. Even if God didn't come through for him, he would still obey: "God himself will provide the lamb for the burnt offering, my son" (Genesis 22:8, NIV).

With his distractions behind him, Abraham came to the place God told him, built an altar, arranged the wood, bound Isaac, and laid him on the altar. How Abraham must have wiped the sweat and closed his eyes to keep them focused on obedience. As he raised the knife to slay his son, the Angel of the Lord called to Abraham to stop. "Because you . . . have not withheld your son, your only son, I will surely bless you and make your descendants as numerous as the stars in the sky and as the sand on the seashore. Your descendants will take possession of the cities of their enemies, and through your offspring all nations on earth will be blessed, because you have obeyed me" (Genesis 22:16-18, NIV).

Author A. W. Tozer writes about the significance of Abraham's moment: "Everything [Abraham] had owned before was still his to enjoy: sheep, camels, herds, and goods of every sort. He had also his wife and his friends, and the best of all, he had his son Isaac safe by his side. He had everything, but he possessed nothing. . . . After that bitter and blessed experience, I think the words *my* and *mine* never again had the same meaning for Abraham."[5]

The joy that Abraham fixed his eyes on loomed bigger than the inconveniences and sorrows it cost.

## FOLLOWING JESUS' EXAMPLE

Though Abraham didn't know Jesus' name as yet, he served him nonetheless. Though Jesus hadn't yet been born, crucified, and raised from the dead, Abraham still followed his example.

You and I live "after the fact." Jesus has come. We have the Scriptures to tell us about his life, and we're getting to really know him. And although we differ from Abraham in what we know about Jesus, yet like Abraham, we are to look to Christ's example as we run our race: "For the joy set before him [he] endured the cross, scorning its shame, and sat down at the right hand of the throne of God" (Hebrews 12:2, NIV). What does following Christ's example look like?

### Jesus Endured the Cross

We'll have to endure the cross too. Suffering will be a for-sure part of our journey to really knowing God. Like Abraham, we might be asked to give up our children—or spouses or homes or work or comfort or companionship. Many have. The Bible talks about those who endured torture, mocking, whipping, chains, imprisonment, stoning, and even being sawn in two. These "destitute, persecuted, and mistreated" believers exchanged deliverance in this life for eternal resurrection, and of these unnamed saints the Bible says that "the world was not worthy of them" (Hebrews 11:37-38, NIV).

The types, degrees, and duration of our suffering will vary, but suffering will happen. Getting to really know God comes at a price: "Any of you who does not give up everything he has cannot be my disciple" said Jesus (Luke 14:33, NIV).

## Jesus Scorned the Shame

Abraham must have suffered tons of ridicule. We know that Sarah laughed when she heard that she would have a child (Genesis 18:12). Imagine how others must have snickered and whispered behind Abraham's back as they watched him believe the impossible day after day and serve the Lord with everything he had. Abraham scorned the shame. He saw a city out there whose builder and maker was God (Hebrews 11:10), and that kept him living out of his suitcase here on earth.

Jesus was "despised and rejected by men, a man of sorrows, and familiar with suffering" (Isaiah 53:3, NIV). The Jews rejected him, and even among his followers Jesus sometimes suffered scorn. But he did not love anything more than he loved doing his Father's will, and he commands that *we* do not love our fathers or mothers or houses or possessions more than we love him (Matthew 10:37). Jesus knew what it was to live out of a suitcase: "Foxes have holes and birds of the air have nests, but the Son of Man has nowhere to lay His head" (Matthew 8:20). Earth wasn't his home.

We'll be called on to suffer scorn too. Family members and sometimes fellow believers who haven't made the choice to really know God won't hear the same drummer we do. But for the joy that is set before us, we'll need to endure.

## Jesus Sat Down at God's Right Hand

Abraham got to really know God through the hard places, and his faithfulness was credited to him as righteousness (Romans 4:22). Jesus learned obedience from what he suffered, and in the end he was able to sit in the place of honor at the right hand of the throne of God.

An intimate, passionate, committed walk with God is available to us here on earth. But it's just an appetizer for what is to come when we can finally sit in our Father's presence. That's the joy of all joys that is set before us. That's the reason we throw off everything that hinders us and the sins that can so easily entangle us. That's the reason we run with perseverance the race marked out for us. That's the reason we fix our eyes on Jesus, the author and perfecter of our faith.

The joy that is set before us is to be the reason for everything we do. The crosses and shame we face pale when compared with that joy. Let go of what holds you back, and fix your eyes on the goal of really knowing God. Author Frances Roberts writes it this way:

> When I am become to thee more precious than all beside; when I am become to thee more real than all else; and when thou lovest Me more than thou lovest any other, then shalt thou know complete satisfaction. . . . For I purpose not to strip thee of earthly ties and joys, but I long to have thee give to Me the center of thy life that My blessing may flow out to the circumference. For My Spirit moveth not from the circumference to the center, but from the center to the circumference.
>
> So yield to Me thy very inmost consciousness. Offer Me not some random portion of thine affections, but give to Me that deepest portion of thy heart, yea that which seemeth to be thy very life itself. For in very truth it is so. For thou yieldest Me thy life only as thou profferest thy love. For this reason have I said, love is the fulfillment of the law. So give Me wholly thy heart's affections and I will meet thine every need.[6]

Every journey begins with the first step, and it is yours to take. But when you do, Jesus will come alongside you and walk with you every step from then on: "'I am here,' said Much-Afraid, still kneeling at His feet, 'and I will go with You anywhere.' Then the Shepherd took her by the hand and they started for the mountains."[7]

---

*DEAR GOD, it's time to make the decision to "go with you anywhere." I repent of the sins I have committed instead of following you in every way. I also repent of the things I didn't do that I should have done to really know you. I surrender everything. And I want everything—everything you have to teach me. I want to know you, regardless of the cost. Amen.*

# PART TWO

# A VIEW FROM THE INSIDE

That I may *know* Him.*

*Philippians 3:10*

*emphasis added

# 8

# Submitting to Discipline

I like the word *epiphany,* which means "a usually sudden manifestation or perception of the essential nature or meaning of something."[1] Epiphanies are simple or striking events that provide an intuitive grasp of a truth, almost as if a lightbulb were going on in our brains. We might describe life-changing events in our lives as epiphanies. Moses' epiphanies no doubt included his burning-bush experience. Joshua encountered an unexpected epiphany one day during battle when the sun stood still, allowing Joshua's army to be victorious. God used a talking donkey as an epiphany for Balaam. Epiphanies come at different times and different places for different people, but all epiphanies leave the recipient changed and able to see some aspect of life in a whole new way.

I call epiphanies "aha! moments," and I can identify at least three of these events in the most recent decades of my Christian journey. I discussed one of them in the introduction of this book: the September 1985 surrender of my life to Christ and the invitation to have him do with me whatever he pleased. During the months following that event, God walked with me through the early years of raising my children alone and as I earned my doctorate in education. After I completed the degree in 1990, I felt God telling me to start writing, and so I did. I wrote about everything around me, even children's books for my son, Clint, using the words he practiced in speech therapy. Only Clint saw those children's books, but

God brought some of the other things I wrote during that time to other people's attention and used them to provide future aha! moments.

The second epiphany came on my birthday on February 14, 1994, as I drove home from teaching a class at the university. I had begun to feel my "ship" turning in a different direction, and as a result, I had a sense of finality about the home and church we loved. That night after we had shared the birthday cake my children had made for me, they went to bed, and I prayed, *God, if you're talking to me, speak louder. I can't hear what you're saying.*

The next morning I awoke at four o'clock. Turning on the light, I pulled my Bible from the side of the bed and asked God to speak to me through his Word. Then I read two portions from Isaiah: "Enlarge the place of your tent, and let them stretch out the curtains of your dwellings; do not spare; lengthen your cords, and strengthen your stakes. For you shall expand to the right and to the left, and your descendants will inherit the nations, and make the desolate cities inhabited" (Isaiah 54:2-3), and "I am the Lord your God, who teaches you to profit, who leads you by the way you should go" (Isaiah 48:17).

Three days later I received a letter from Dean Merrill, head of periodicals at Focus on the Family. They had become aware of my writing and were inviting me to contribute to a new magazine they were starting. More than a week later, after I returned from a conference, I called Dean, who asked some questions about my background. Suddenly he said, "Would you consider a staff position with us here in Colorado as the editor of the magazine?"

During spring break at the university I flew to Colorado for an interview for the editor's job. They offered me the position, and somehow I knew this was the place God had chosen to enlarge my tent, so I accepted. I finished out the remaining part of the semester, began the magazine from a distance, sold our house in Ohio, bought a house in Colorado, fulfilled some speaking commitments, and headed across country in a brown Chevy Astro van with three children and three animals. We smelled like Noah's ark by the time we arrived.

I loved every day of my work with Focus on the Family, and I represented that ministry proudly as I traveled throughout the world, writing and speaking by radio on their behalf. Then after six years I felt my ship turning again. One more time I prayed that God would "speak louder."

In March 1999 another magazine editor from Focus introduced me to Dave Bjorklund, a widower. After more than fourteen years as a single mom, I further enlarged the place of my tent and married Dave, my Prince Charming. Several months later the direction of the magazine changed. With some new writing projects before me, I believed that this was yet another place God was leading. So in July 2000 I said good-bye to Focus and hello to the new ways God would teach me to profit and lead me by the way I should go.

## ORDINARY BUT LIFE CHANGING

My third epiphany arrived in a much more subtle, less heralded way, yet it holds the most importance thus far in my quest to really know God. I had grown up with a *passion* for knowing God in a deep way. With my surrender to God in 1985 I sealed my *commitment.* The years that followed began the *intimate* adventure I sought. But I needed more.

Once I began working from the quietness of my home, I saw my spiritual life with clearer vision. For far too long I had been what I call "Miracle-Gro'd" to death. On the surface, observers could see all kinds of pretty blossoms and foliage through the ministry I did and the people I spoke and wrote to, but underneath, my root system remained shallow. With all my family and work responsibilities, I had found little time to take care of myself and little time to spend with God. Countless mornings I was up and well about my day before my cell phone had finished its nightly recharging. Too many mornings I forged ahead doing so much *for* God that I didn't spend time *with* God. As a result, not only did I wear down physically but my testimony wore down spiritually. I no longer delivered a life-giving message because the Life Giver did not have regular access to my life.

Gordon MacDonald begins his book *The Life God Blesses* with a parable about a man who built a boat. His goal was to create the grandest, most talked-about boat that ever sailed, so he spared no expense. Eventually his boat boasted colorful sails, complex riggings, and comfortable surroundings. The man's anticipation of the admiration and applause he would receive from onlookers made him work even harder on the visible things, and soon these appointments began to gleam with excellence.

The man gained the anticipated praise and good wishes from his admirers, and on the day of his maiden voyage, the people of the club joined him at dockside as he set sail in his masterpiece. The boatman swelled with pride as he recounted the numerous things he had accomplished and the things he had under his control—the future, the acclaim, and even the ocean itself.

But everything changed when he encountered a storm at sea. The boat began to shudder, and water swept over the sides. The man's poise began to waver. Perhaps he wasn't as much in control as he had thought. It wasn't long before the ship's sails, riggings, and decks were reduced to shreds. The boat capsized and was unable to right itself because of the lack of weight, resilience, and stability *below* the waterline—where storms are withstood. As a result, the boat and its proud owner were lost at sea.

You and I have lived long enough to name several prominent people in ministry whose stories parallel that of the ship and its owner. Caught up with building the things that are visible, they left the most important, unseen, below-the-waterline parts unfinished, and consequently, these people no longer remain in ministry today. MacDonald writes, "A man who builds only above the waterline does not realize that he has built less than half a boat. . . . Once a foolish man built a house. . . . Once a foolish man built a career. . . . Once a foolish man built a marriage. . . . Once a foolish man built a life."[2]

I read this parable for the first time while preparing to speak at a conference, and in addition to thinking about some of the well-known fallen Christian heroes, I was also challenged to look at myself. Difficulties with one of my daughters during our first six years in Colorado forced me to reexamine my life. While the top of my boat looked pretty good, the part underneath the waterline was woefully lacking and had no ability to right itself. I needed to draw back and focus on some long-overdue rebuilding. I needed to really know Christ in the quiet places of my life before I could ever entice others to know him too.

Since then everything I have done reflects whatever strides I have made in my own quest to really know Christ. My growth has been deeper rather than broader. My interest in the things of the Lord today doesn't necessarily show outward manifestations tomorrow. I have learned that deepness in God and growth in him can happen only in the hidden, unapplauded secret places. The mature Christian life doesn't consist only of epiphanies, where knowing Christ is measurable in a spectacular way. Major Ian Thomas, founder of Torchbearers Ministry, has said that the Christian life is not spectacular, just miraculous. Living the miraculous Christian life mostly means walking in and out of the daily doldrums, having faith that God will guide, protect, and see us through: "Those who hope in the Lord will renew their strength. They will soar on wings like eagles; they will run and not grow weary, they will walk and not be faint" (Isaiah 40:31, NIV).

Paul realized the need to walk and not faint when he wrote the words of Philippians 3:10: "That I may know Him." Paul certainly had his share of epiphanies, such as his sudden conversion on the road to Damascus (Acts 9) and his experience singing with his cell mate, Silas, as God opened their prison door (Acts 16). But most of Paul's postconversion life consisted of the ordinary—not spectacular, just miraculous. And Paul realized that growth in Christ required sacrifice and submission to discipline. That's why he wrote "that I may know Him and the power of His resurrection, and the fellowship of His sufferings" (Philippians 3:10). Knowing requires suffering, which requires submission to discipline.

Our responsibility as children of God is to submit to his discipline, or training—to wait on the Lord. God's job is to enable us to keep running through life's really hard places and not grow weary and to continue to walk through ordinary assignments without fainting. Waiting. It's where we access God's sufficiency, and it happens only as we develop spiritual discipline.

## PRESENT UNPLEASANTRIES

Your decision to read this book indicates your desire to know God in a greater way. You've examined what knowing God really means and your motives for pursuing it. Your continued journey to really knowing means evaluating and troubleshooting your love for God by examining your intimacy, passion, and commitment. Now it's time for discipline.

Our daughter Courtney started playing basketball when she was in the third grade. By age thirteen, when she approached six feet tall, coaches began to notice, urged her to get serious about the game, and taught her more advanced skills. We watched with pride through Courtney's high school years as her team lost only a couple of games. Her senior year brought an undefeated season and a state championship, and Courtney was named Miss Colorado Basketball 3A.

A good two years before Courtney graduated and developed into the best basketball player she could be, she started receiving correspondence from colleges who invited her to play for their team. These letters collected in a corner of Courtney's room. But when the fall of her senior year brought a deluge of notes and phone calls, she started thinking seriously about the direction she would go. She responded to some of the inquiries, colleges started coming to see her play, and she went on recruiting visits. For a while Courtney found the number of choices flattering, but a point came when she had to commit. She prayed and made her choice.

Courtney's commitment signaled the end of one era but the beginning of another. When she arrived on campus in August, her feet hit the ground running in her basketball shoes. Four-hour-a-day practices quickly sealed her commitment, and now it was time to perfect her game. The commitment lay behind Courtney; the discipline of moving toward perfection lay in front of her. And the more potential the coach saw in Courtney, the harder she pushed her.

You and I have come to a similar place in our walks with God. We've committed to the game, but now it's time to perfect it, to work toward completeness. Perfection involves discipline, and lots of it. Discipline corrects, molds, and perfects our mental faculties and moral character. Obedience or order that results helps us to gain control.

The purpose of discipline is not bondage but freedom—freedom to become all that God designed us to be. Our aim is the freedom, not discipline itself. The disciplines are not valuable by themselves. They're important only as a means of setting us before God so that he can give us the freedom we seek. Knowing God is the end, but discipline is the means to the end. Discipline is not the answer, it just leads us to the One who is the Answer.

Discipline is never automatic, quick, natural, or easy, and it takes a lifetime to fully develop. But the more our heavenly Coach sees our potential, the more he disciplines us. The more he loves us, the more he disciplines us. And the one unchanging truth about discipline is that it is never pleasant: "No discipline seems pleasant at the time, but painful. Later on, however, it produces a harvest of righteousness and peace for those who have been trained by it" (Hebrews 12:11, NIV).

## THE PERFECTION PROCESS

Courtney just finished her freshmen year. She still complains about the long and arduous workouts, and she cries from the pain of sore muscles. She has had to undo and then redo her shot form. But when I'm with her she shows me her strong leg and arm muscles and talks about her improved shooting ability. No discipline is pleasant for the present, but in the end, it brings good stuff.

God's goal in disciplining us is to perfect us, to make us mature and complete. As a child, I often heard my dad say, "When God's people are striving for perfection, in his eyes, they're already perfect."

For many years my understanding of the word *perfect* came from the dictionary meaning "to bring to a final form," inferring a finished product. Because perfection means the absence of faults and defects, I found perfection to be illusive—much sought after but never achieved. I tried to be a "perfect" wife and mother. I worked at cooking "perfect" dinners and keeping my house in "perfect" order. I really worked hard at saying "perfect" words and making "perfect" decisions. In all these attempts, however, I fell short.

One night several months ago I awoke, clearly hearing two Bible verses spoken to my heart, Psalm 138:8 and 1 Peter 5:10. We'll discuss the second verse in chapter 19, but here we'll take a look at

Psalm 138:8: "The Lord will perfect that which concerns me." After I read this verse, I examined the Jewish definition of the word *perfect.* It means "to complete, to come to an end, to perform, to finish." The word "concerns" in this passage refers to prepositions, such as *about, at, by, upon, within, beside, among, behind.* This verse could be translated, "The Lord will complete everything that is *in* me, *around* me, *beside* me, *behind* me, *before* me."

The King James Version of the Old Testament describes three men as perfect: (1) Noah: "Noah was a just man and perfect in his generations, and Noah walked with God" (Genesis 6:9); (2) Abram: "When Abram was ninety years old and nine, the Lord appeared to Abram, and said unto him, I am the Almighty God; walk before me, and be thou perfect" (Genesis 17:1); and (3) Job: "There was a man in the land of Uz, whose name was Job; and that man was perfect and upright, and one who feared God, and eschewed evil" (Job 1:1; see also verse 8 and 2:3).

But each of these three "perfect" men exhibited imperfect qualities. Noah struggled with drunkenness, Abram lied about Sarah's being his wife, and Job doubted God's goodness during his trials.

It is through the life of Amaziah, the eighth king of Judah, that we can discover the key to God's idea of perfection: "Amaziah was twenty and five years old when he began to reign, and he reigned twenty and nine years in Jerusalem. . . . He did that which was right in the sight of the Lord, but not with a perfect heart" (2 Chronicles 25:1-2, KJV).

Then I realized that for the child of God, perfection is not a destination but a process. Perfection is not the measure of a perfect life but the surrender of a perfect heart to God's discipline. It is possible, like Amaziah, to do the right things, quote the right verses, and sing the right hymns and not do so with a perfect heart. God would rather have us be like Noah, Abram, and Job and offer perfect hearts to him, even when we make imperfect decisions. Since the heart is the seat of our mind, will, and emotions, submitting to the perfection process involves surrendering our hearts to God's work in us every day. This happens in several areas:

- Prayer (talking to God)
- Study (learning about God)
- Fasting (fasting with God)
- Stillness (listening to God)
- Adoration (worshiping God)
- Hearing (understanding God's will)

If the prophet Daniel could talk to us today, he would probably describe in detail some of the epiphanies of his life. He would talk about the way his body grew stronger than others' when he refused to eat the delicacies of the king (Daniel 1) and about his accurate interpretations of King Nebuchadnezzar's dreams (Daniel 2). No doubt one of Daniel's top three aha! moments was his visit to the lions' den, where the lions lay down like puppies instead of making Daniel their dinner (Daniel 6).

But in between these well-known events, four Babylonian kings came and went, and eighty years passed in Daniel's life. The Scriptures don't say a lot about other mentionable occurrences during that time, but we can be sure that a lot was going on. For Daniel, it was a time of discipline, during which he was spending time in the quiet places where he chose to pray, study, and obey God's commands. In the process he got to really know his Lord. This quiet discipline developed the underside of Daniel's boat so that he could withstand the challenges that were to come.

## GOD DISCIPLINES THOSE HE LOVES

If I were to ask you to describe the epiphanies of your walk with God, what would they include? What events triggered your taking a different path with the Almighty? I hope you allowed your epiphanies to cause you to commit to a disciplined walk with Christ.

In the devotional book *Streams in the Desert,* author Mrs. Charles E. Cowman tells the story of a dream a friend had about the Master, who encountered three women in prayer. He bent over the first woman in tenderness, with radiant smiles full of love, and spoke to her in accents of pure, sweet music. The Master only placed his hand on the bowed head of the second woman and gave her a look of loving approval. When he came to the third woman, he passed her without a word or a glance. The one dreaming thought, *The Master must love the first two more than the third, for he gave her no word at all, not even a passing look.*

Then the Master explained: "The first kneeling woman needs all the weight of My tenderness and care to keep her feet in my narrow way. . . . The second has stronger faith and deeper love, and I can trust her to trust Me, however things go or whatever others do. The third, whom I seemed not to notice, has faith and love of the finest quality. And her I am training by quick and drastic processes for the highest and holiest service."[3]

God gives us epiphanies through his tangible touches and messages, but the depth of our relationships, the extent of our growth, and the degree of our knowledge of God depend on the discipline we subject ourselves to in our everyday walks. As we grow, we no longer need the "spectacular," just the miraculous fact that God loves and knows us individually and desires that we experience that love and knowledge from him in a greater way.

If you will commit to the disciplines of praying, studying, fasting, listening, worshiping, and hearing, you, too, will find yourselves being trained by quick and drastic processes for the highest and holiest service.

And while for the present this discipline may cause you to complain about the long and arduous workouts and cry over the pain of sore muscles, hang in there. Keep submitting to the Coach's perfection process. When you do, the end will bring really good stuff in and from your life. Remember, when you're striving for perfection, in God's eyes you're already perfect.

---

*LORD, we're in for a journey together as I subject my life to your disciplines. I lay my life down for whatever you want to make of me. Through the disciplines you put me through and I submit to, I want to find the freedom to be who you want me to be. I'm ready, Lord, so let's go for the perfection! Amen.*

# 9

# Talking to Him

I called my mother one night and asked her to help me pray about a challenge I was facing. She said something I'll never forget: "I already prayed for that—just the other night—and I remember the spot on the wall I looked at when I gave it to our Father."

The absolute faith and trust my mother conveyed in these simple words were forged through more than fifty years of praying to the One she had come to love. She knew that God cherished every word she brought before him, and she cherished memorials of the places and times of their talks together.

The prayers of God's people are so special to God that he gathers them like trophies in bowls in heaven (Revelation 5:8), receives them personally from an angel's hand (Revelation 8:4), and delights in them (Proverbs 15:8). Allow those words to sink in: The trophies in which God delights are the prayers of his children.

Many great writers talk about prayer. French mystic François Fénelon said that our conversation with God "resembles that with a friend; at first, there are a thousand things to be told, and as many to be asked; but after a time, these diminish, while the pleasure of being together does not."[1]

A. B. Simpson, founder of what became the Christian Missionary Alliance, saw prayer as "the link that connects us with God. It is the bridge that spans every gulf and bears us over every abyss of danger or of need."[2]

The Bible describes prayer in several different ways:

- bowing one's knees (Ephesians 3:14)
- looking up (Psalm 5:3)
- lifting up one's soul (Psalm 25:1)
- lifting up one's heart and hands (Lamentations 3:41)
- pouring out one's heart (Psalm 62:8)
- pouring out one's soul (1 Samuel 1:15)
- calling or crying out to God (Psalms 27:7; 34:6)
- crying out to heaven (2 Chronicles 32:20)
- drawing near to God (Psalm 73:28; Hebrews 10:22)
- pleading or seeking favor with the Lord (Exodus 32:11)
- seeking God's face (Job 8:5; Psalm 27:8)
- making supplication or petition (Job 8:5; Jeremiah 36:7)

Before God's people were known as Hebrews or Christians, they were known as the people who call on the name of the Lord. Prayer is the center of our relationship with God. It is the most fundamental discipline of the Christian faith, and without prayer we'll never know God as he is.

Even Jesus maintained intimacy with his Father through regular prayer. When the disciples needed Jesus, they knew to go to his place of prayer. Prayer guided Jesus' ministry (Luke 6:12). Prayer preceded miracles (Matthew 14:22-27). Prayer was a source of encouragement for Jesus (Luke 9:28-31). Prayer enabled him to go to the cross (Luke 22:41-43). When Jesus withdrew to lonely places and prayed, he found the secret of his power. Author Hank Hanegraaff writes: "[Jesus] performed in public what He'd practiced in private. . . . Public performance is defined by private practice. . . . The secret to prayer is secret prayer."[3]

## JUST DO IT!

Jesus found his strength in prayer. He found his direction in prayer. He maintained intimacy with his Father in prayer. Our strength, direction, and intimate knowledge of God happen only in prayer too. Yet praying is hard work. Samuel Chadwick wrote, "The one concern of the Devil is to keep Christians from praying. He fears nothing from prayerless studies, prayerless work, and prayerless religion. He laughs at our toil, mocks our wisdom, but trembles when we pray."[4] Henry Blackaby writes, "Prayer is not difficult to understand. Prayer is difficult to do."[5]

Joshua learned how important it was to go to God in prayer. Throughout the early part of the book of Joshua, we see evidence that he consulted God. But Joshua learned the hard way what it meant to neglect his time with God. God had clearly instructed Moses and Joshua to destroy all the original inhabitants as they conquered the Promised Land. But when the Gibeonites came to the Israelites and pretended to be from a distant foreign land, Joshua and his men fell for their ploy because "they did not ask counsel of the Lord" (Joshua 9:14). This neglect of prayer resulted in a prohibited covenant with the Gibeonites, a covenant that conflicted with God's instructions for the Israelites and caused years of struggles in the generations to come.

In some aspects of my life I have done well about consulting God, but in others I have regretted the times I haven't prayed. I have moved forward with some decisions that seemed to be no-brainers and have stepped out of God's will as Joshua did. Some-times I have failed to recognize my true position in Christ, or I have questioned the value of prayer in a difficult situation. Other times I simply didn't go to God about something, or I abandoned prayer as an option when the answer to that prayer seemed too mysterious or distant. When I have allowed my emotions to dictate my prayer life, I have tended not to pray when things were going well. Some mornings I have been downright lazy or have prayed in shallow ways on the run. Still other times, legalism, wrong motives, idols, unforgiveness, or just plain lack of desire have kept me from getting through to God.

Whether the things that have hindered your prayer life sound like mine or are altogether different, we all have regrets about times when we didn't pray. And no doubt, we all, like Samuel Chadwick, should have prayed more. I have a basement full of exercise equipment, but just owning the bike, weights, and tread-mill doesn't get me in shape. I have to use them. Similarly, know-ing about the importance of prayer will not make us into effective pray-ers. No books or seminars on prayer will transform us into effective intercessors. We need to adopt the popular Nike slogan and "Just do it!"

## TEN BE-ATTITUDES OF PRAYER

When it comes to prayer, there are no shortcuts. We simply have to do it. Several things help me. I call them Be-Attitudes of Prayer. They have encouraged me as I have pursued "just doing it," and they have helped me to grow in having an effective prayer time.

### 1. Be Pure

In John 9:31 the Bible gives us some profound instruction about prayer and the soul condition of the person praying: "God does not hear sinners; but if anyone is a worshiper of God and does His will, He hears him." This verse tells us that God is not obligated to answer prayers of people who do not know him; that is, those who are not true worshipers. It also implies that for Christians, contin-ued sin by not doing God's will is a hindrance to God's hearing our prayers. The prophet Isaiah agreed: "Your sins have hidden His face from you, so that He will not hear" (Isaiah 59:2).

Because the channel to heaven must always be free from

unconfessed sin, confession—or personal cleansing—should
be a part of every prayer time. Examine your heart. Do you
have unconfessed sins in your life? Are you holding on to bitterness or anger or some other reaction that is unlike God? Confession clears the way for God to hear your petition in heaven.

Norman Vincent Peale tells of an incident from his childhood
when he secretly smoked a cigar he had found. When Norman's
father approached him, the boy hid the cigar behind him and asked
his dad if he could go to the circus. His wise father said, "Never
make a petition while at the same time trying to hide a smoldering
disobedience behind your back."[6]

## 2. Be Honest and Bold

One night twenty years ago I was so angry about what I was going
through that I couldn't talk to God. So I called my mother, who
remained the buffer between my anger and my ability to pray.
After my 4:00 A.M. conversation with Mom, during which she
encouraged me to pray about what was bothering me, I was able
to sort things through and come honestly before God's throne in
prayer. Some time ago my daughter Courtney called me, hurt,
aggravated, and angry about some things she was facing. My
response to her was the same as my mother's had been to me all
those years ago: Go to God in prayer. I advised my college-
student daughter to grab something to drink, drive to a beautiful
location, and talk to God about her concerns. Her call later that
night brought back memories of my own follow-up calls to my
mom. God knows us completely, and he wants us to be honest
with him about the things that concern us: "The Lord is near to
all who call upon Him, to all who call upon Him in truth"
(Psalm 145:18).

When our children want something from us, they don't beat
around the bush. They come boldly and specifically: "I need twenty

dollars." "I need to borrow the car." Jesus wants us to do the same: "Ask, and it will be given to you; seek, and you will find; knock, and it will be opened to you. For everyone who asks receives, and he who seeks finds, and to him who knocks it will be opened" (Matthew 7:7-8).

In this verse, "ask" means to request or petition. The word denotes insistent asking without qualms, not commanding God but solidly presenting a requisition for items he longs to provide. The word usually describes a suppliant making a request of someone in a higher position.

When we "come boldly to the throne of grace," we obtain mercy from God (Hebrews 4:16). Just as my children make their requests clearly known to me and then go about their day, I've learned to come to my heavenly Father, make bold and specific requests, and then go about my day. I ask him to use me and teach me while he is giving, finding, and opening the door to the things I have asked him for.

## 3. Be Persistent

Jesus told two parables about the importance of persistence in prayer. After a man kept repeating his request for bread to a friend, Jesus said, "Because of his persistence he [the man's friend] will rise and give him as many [loaves of bread] as he needs" (Luke 11:8). In the second parable a widow kept coming to a judge and asking for justice, and the judge finally gave in to her request: "Because this widow keeps bothering me, I will see that she gets justice, so that she won't eventually wear me out with her coming!" (Luke 18:5, NIV).

Because of the first man's persistence and because the woman kept bothering the judge, they both received what they requested. Prayer is one place we can afford to be a nuisance. God wants us to keep coming to him day after day without becoming discouraged.

American evangelist R. A. Torrey wrote, "Great revivals always begin in the hearts of a few men and women whom God arouses by His Spirit to believe in Him as a living God. . . . Upon their hearts He lays a burden from which no rest can be found except in [persistent] crying unto God."[7]

I have a friend named Debra who suffers with chronic back pain. I pray for her almost every day, and when I do, I try to pray as if it were my first time praying for her. I resist becoming discouraged and work to exercise a childlike faith that God both hears and will answer my prayers. Though he has collected a lot of my prayers and those of others for Debra, he hears them just as much and is just as capable of answering: "The effective, fervent prayer of a righteous man avails much" (James 5:16).

*Fervent* means "marked by great intensity of feeling."[8] If we feel intensely about something, we are not likely to give up easily. I once heard someone compare long-term prayer to dynamiting through a mountain. It may take two blasts or twenty or two hundred. When you're in the middle of the blasting, it still looks just as dark as when you began. But imagine giving up the hard work when you're almost there. Keep blasting. You don't know which blast of prayer will break through to the other side. God honors the faith we show through persistent prayer.

### 4. Be Consistent

Jesus said, "I stand at the door and knock. If anyone hears my voice and opens the door, I will come in and eat with him, and he with me" (Revelation 3:20, NIV). One day I read this verse in a new way: Jesus stands knocking at my door early in the morning and invites me to do breakfast with him. The choice is mine. I can roll over for a few more minutes of sleep, or I can meet with the King of kings to tell him what's on my heart and hear what's on his. Oswald Chambers wrote, "Prayer does not fit us for the greater works; prayer *is* the greater work. . . . Whichever way God engineers circumstances, the duty is to pray. . . . Wherever God has dumped you down in circumstances, pray."[9]

Until we reserve a specific time and an undistracted place to meet with God every day, our prayer lives will never grow. Only when we make this our top priority will we faithfully keep the appointment. Just as we must visit our closets to get dressed for our day, we must go into our prayer closets to get spiritually dressed for the day. My early morning appointment with God is not penciled in my planner, but it remains the most important part of my schedule. In addition to spending the first part of my day in prayer, I have found several other habits helpful in growing my prayer life:

- Using a prayer list helps me to pray comprehensively.
- Continuing to pray throughout the day enables me to shoot "bullet prayers" to God concerning people and situations I encounter.
- Recognizing ongoing opportunities for prayer provides me with wonderful conversations with God while I'm driving the car or soaking in the bathtub or taking afternoon walks.
- Staying in prayer long enough to both talk and listen to God teaches me much about answered prayer.
- Loving prayer time and recognizing its benefits brings uneasiness when I miss my time with God.
- Praying out loud keeps me focused and assists with my intensity and sincerity.
- Praying when things are going well forges my relationship with God for when hard times come to me and to those I love. My dad often said, "If God's people stayed close to him on the mountaintops, they'd find him already near in the valley."

If we have children, we need to model consistency for them too. I've had my own kids say to me when I was grumpy or imbalanced, "Mom, shouldn't you go spend time with the Lord?"

When my children were young, I heard Pastor Charles Stanley say that before our feet hit the floor, we should arm ourselves for the day from Ephesians 6:14-18. Since then, I have prayed that prayer almost every day with my family. Even now, with only one child left at home, I stand at the door with my six-foot-three son before he leaves for school each morning and pray, "Lord, be with Clint today. Place your helmet of salvation and your breastplate of righteousness on him. Gird him with truth, give him feet that are fitted with the preparation of the gospel of peace, and show him how to use the sword of the Spirit, which is the Word of God."

Has this prayer I've prayed for nearly twenty years made a difference? I may not know in this life, but eternity will tell.

## 5. Be Comprehensive

For much of my dad's career he worked as a rural-route driver for the U.S. Postal Service. He parked his work car outside the garage, and in order to keep off the snow and ice from Ohio winters, he placed a piece of cardboard on the windshield at night. Every morning before he left for work, Dad started the engine and then got back out of the car, removed the cardboard from the windshield, and put it in the trunk. It's obvious that if he had kept the cardboard there, he couldn't have seen through it, around it, or under it. He had to put it completely aside before he could move on.

The same is true of our prayers. We know that we should take every need boldly to God on a consistent basis. But in between we should remove that need from the windshield of our minds, and store it until we pray about it again. If I'm praying about physical healing for myself, I bring my need to God every time I come to him. But in addition to asking him to heal me, I also need to praise him, thank him, pray for others, and listen to what he wants to communicate to my heart and mind.

Using the simple acronym ACTS helps us to structure our prayers and make them more comprehensive. The four elements of this acronym, Adoration (Psalm 66:17), Confession (Nehemiah 1:4, 6-7), Thanksgiving (Philippians 4:6; Colossians 4:2), and Supplication (asking for things; Job 8:5; Jeremiah 36:7), remind us to be comprehensive when we pray. We can be creative about how we do this. One man prayed for years that God would give him a son; it was the greatest desire of his life. But then he would put this ongoing prayer aside and talk to God about other things. He taped his prayer list to the middle of his steering wheel so that while he drove, he could pray for everyone he knew who was in need. He also offered praises to God by singing and playing his harmonica.

God wants our prayer to be comprehensive. Meat is good, but so are vegetables, fruit, pasta, and bread. The best diet consists of a healthy balance of all of these. Similarly, the best prayers consist of taking your needs—or supplications—boldly to God and also adding thanksgiving, adoration, and confession to your daily prayer diet.

## 6. Be Willing to Tarry

The word *tarry* isn't used all that much anymore, but it means "to linger in expectation."[10] This is an aspect of prayer I took for granted when I was a child, and it is the one I miss the most as an adult. The church my dad pastored when I was a child was located in an Appalachian area of southern Indiana. The colorful people who attended the church would never have been invited to join a country club or to attend a society function, but they knew how to "tarry." God was all those people had, and they went wholeheartedly to him with every need. When someone had a physical need, for example, that person would stand or sit in the front of the church, and we would "tarry" in prayer until we felt we had received God's answer. As children, that was irritating to us when we were hungry and wanted to call it quits, but the adults in our lives stayed with what was most important. We saw prayers answered again and again, and because we did, even as children we knew where to go when we needed answers ourselves. In fact, when my brother Phill's cat died, he said, "Let's take it to church and have them pray for it."

We may smile at that now, but that kind of faith was forged in a circle of saints willing to exchange convenience for lingering in prayer as long as it took to see God's answer. Henri Nouwen wrote, "The rest which comes from unceasing prayer needs to be sought at all cost, even when the flesh is itchy, the world alluring, and the demons noisy."[11]

Many churches today may not often do that, but how are we replicating that practice in our personal prayer lives? Are we regularly putting the needs of others ahead of our own when we pray? Are we willing to wait and wait and wait on God if necessary? Are our ears focused on hearing what God has to say to others? The psalmist says, "I waited patiently for the Lord; he turned to me and heard my cry" (Psalm 40:1, NIV).

God answers prayer when we are willing to tarry—for ourselves and for others.

### 7. Be Creative

Be-Attitude 4 emphasized the importance of consistency in prayer. But our prayer life doesn't have to be boring or stale or always done at the same time or in the same place. First Timothy 2:8 encourages us to "pray everywhere, lifting up holy hands."

Daring to alter your prayer techniques helps to keep regular prayer times exciting. One of my favorite ways to pray for others is to insert their names into specific Scripture verses I find. Praying out loud helps me to see God as more tangible in the seat beside me, especially in the case of really desperate prayers.

Once Clint, then eleven, and I drove to a park near our home, where we ran around the lake and through the pine trees. When we finished, we sat down on a log. With my arm around my son, I said, "Let's shoot thank-you prayers to God."

Typical of my eleven-year-old son, Clint said, "Thank you for my tennis shoes." Then he laughed. I followed with thanks for health and the ability to run and for the beautiful place we live. Clint and I continued to send up prayers of gratitude, and our time ended with some tears, a hug, and a race back to the car.

It's important to have a set time and place for prayer. But having a spontaneous and fun side to your praying is important too. Praying everywhere can be so enjoyable!

## 8. Be Growing

Gary Smalley writes about the growth and development of mature relationships with the people we love: "Every fully realized relationship is a trip from surface emotions down into the depths, descending through five distinct levels of intimate communication that move from shallow levels to the fifth and deepest level. At this fifth level, a couple feels absolutely safe and accepted for what they feel they need as unique individuals."[12] According to Smalley, growth in relationships begins and develops like this:

- Speaking in clichés: consists of surface talk
- Sharing facts: requires deep breaths, thinking, and feeling
- Sharing opinions: discusses individual opinions, concerns, expectations, goals, dreams, and desires

- Sharing feelings: helps each other feel safe sharing deep emotions; can also create conflict
- Sharing needs: becomes the most intimate part of loving communication, when people feel safe revealing unique needs to one another[13]

According to this author it takes about six years for couples to learn to share feelings and needs. Our prayer lives can grow, too, but it doesn't have to take six years. We may begin with surface talk, but as our relationships with God develop, we learn to share our most intimate concerns.

Sometimes I look up and wrinkle my nose at God when I see him answer a prayer. He understands. After all, he knows me, and I'm coming to know him in greater ways as I grow.

## 9. Be Willing to Be Changed

Prayer does not change God; it changes us. As we find purity, honesty, boldness, persistence, consistence, comprehensiveness, creativity, and growth in maturity in our prayer lives, we see ourselves changing.

My two daughters once befriended some non-Christian girls who started leading them down the wrong path. Like a mother bear, I fought back to protect my cubs. I wanted those girls out of our lives, regardless of their own spiritual needs. One Sunday morning as we were preparing to partake of the Lord's Supper, our pastor told us to check our hearts for things that needed God's forgiveness. As I did, I clearly felt God saying to my heart, "I love those three girls as much as I love your three children." I realized that I didn't love those girls and I wasn't praying for them, but things began to change that day. I put them on my prayer list along with the names of more than sixty other teens I knew, and I prayed for them as well as for my children. Through prayer, God had changed me.

God used the time he spent with Moses to change the way Moses thought. Moses climbed Mount Sinai and spent forty days communing with God. During that time God revealed the wickedness of Israel, which Moses had not realized before that point. Following that encounter, Moses offered to have his own name removed from the Book of Life if God would spare the people.

God uses our prayer time to soften our hearts and change our focus. As we pray for others, the Holy Spirit gives us God's compassion for them. God changes other people by changing us. He changes situations by changing us. And God works those changes in us as we spend time in prayer with him.

## 10. Be Faith-Filled

One Wednesday night when my children were about ten, eight, and six, I had such a headache that I didn't think I could make it to the midweek youth services we regularly attended. But it was part of our routine, the kids loved it, and a neighbor girl usually went along, so I felt I had to go. I parked the car in front of the church and walked them inside; then I got back in the car and pulled it to a corner of the parking lot where I could wait. As I leaned back against the headrest, I prayed, "Lord, I need help. Please touch me."

I had scarcely gotten these words out when *pop!* my headache and nausea were gone. Later that night I asked God why he answered as he did. In response, God used two verses to help me understand: "You do not have because you do not ask" (James 4:2) and "Whatever you did for one of the least of these brothers of mine, you did for me" (Matthew 25:40, NIV). I felt that God was telling me through his Word that he was pleased that I had put the children's spiritual needs before my physical ones. He also let me know that he wasn't pleased with my not asking earlier and therefore not really demonstrating faith that he would do as I asked.

Doubt is a hurdle I am determined to conquer. The Bible tells us over and over not to doubt God, and though I have a long track record of answered prayer, I still doubt at times. But while doubt-free prayers still elude me, I keep praying. By looking back on the victories, I'm seeking to build my faith and trust. As long as I still have relapses, I'll keep praying.

Recently our pastor posed this question to the congregation: "If God's power in our church depended on your prayers, where would we be?"

What if we ask that question about our own prayer lives: Are we praying enough for our churches? our spouses? our children? our country? our leaders? our enemies? Hank Hanegraff writes, "Prayer does not simply maintain the Christian life, it *is* the Christian life reduced to its barest essence. Can there be any [greater] joy—in this world or the next—than to commune in the secret place with the living God?"[14]

I began this chapter with a story about my mother's prayer life. I hope I've continued her tradition of going regularly to God in prayer and of passing it on to my children too.

One Sunday night after Dave and I had been married only a month, I propped him up on pillows in bed as he dealt with the symptoms of bronchitis, and I made my way to the kitchen. I asked Clint, then thirteen, to pray for Dave with me. Back in the bedroom, Clint sat on the edge of the bed, picked up Dave's hand, and started to pray. "Lord, it's us again," he began with friendlike familiarity. Clint continued, asking God to heal Dave's body.

Before I left to pick up our daughter from a friend's house, I peeked into Clint's room to say good night. He was reading his Bible in bed. When I returned home, Dave told me the rest of the story. Clint had gone back to Dave and said, "I want to pray for you again, but first I want to share some Bible verses that have come to mean a lot to me."

Dave never got bronchitis—not that week or any week since—despite having suffered recurring bouts of it for forty years. The God of the universe heard and answered the prayers of a thirteen-year-old boy who had come to believe in his faithfulness. Clint's prayers, lifted to God in angels' hands, had landed in God's trophy bowl and become God's delight.

---

*LORD, I've heard that I need to pray. I've read that I need to pray. Have I seen personally how much I need to pray? Help me to "just do it"! Give me a heart to pray all the time about everything. Show me a special spot for meeting with you, and help me to keep that daily appointment. Help me to be faithful. And through my prayers, help me to know you more than I ever have before. Amen.*

# 10

# Learning
# about Him

I sat at a table in the back of the room, taking feverish notes. I still couldn't believe I had the opportunity to take some classes at Fuller Theological Seminary. As we studied the Gospels, the professor talked about academic things, Greek word origins, and meanings I had never known before.

Then the professor took us to Luke 10:42, where Jesus told Mary of Bethany that she had "the good part" because of her choice to really know him, as we discussed in chapter 3. As this "expert" talked about the story, I found my mind flashing back to 1986 and an Indiana driveway where I was washing my van. I had been raising my children alone for several months by this point, and during that time, I had pored over God's Word, watched Christian programming on TV, and listened to Chuck Swindoll and Dr. James Dobson on the car radio. I wanted to learn everything I could about the Lord I had gotten to know.

With a sudsy sponge in my hand and three children playing in the puddles, I prayed, "Lord, I don't thank you for what I'm going through, but I do thank you that I now have time to spend with you—to read and pray more than I ever did before." Suddenly I heard these words spoken to my heart: *You've chosen the good part.*

I was still immature in my faith, in my familiarity with Scripture, and in my knowledge of God. I didn't recognize the source of those words. That night after the kids had gone to bed, I read my Bible.

As I reached to turn off the light, my heart heard those words again: *You've chosen the good part.*

I switched the light back on and prayed, "God, show me where these words come from." Suddenly I knew; it was Mary and Martha. I searched the concordance until I discovered the passage in Luke 10, and I found myself in Mary's sandals. After my world had crashed around me through divorce and my father's impending death, I had planted myself at the feet of Jesus every day, crying, praying, laughing, and beginning my first real journey of knowing him.

## SWEET KNOWLEDGE

Academic knowledge of God's Word is wonderful, but the heart part of God's Word is spectacular. Job said, "I have treasured the words of His mouth more than my necessary food" (Job 23:12). The prophet Jeremiah wrote, "When your words came, I ate them; they were my joy and my heart's delight" (Jeremiah 15:16, NIV).

To Job and Jeremiah and me—and I hope to you—the Scriptures are more than just words on a page. They have places and times and promises, and many of them are wet with tears—from the earliest times of God's people.

The study of Scripture has always been important to the Jews. The main purpose of education in Bible times was to train the whole person for a life of obedient service in knowing God. Jewish education emphasized holiness, a set-apartness so that a person could belong to God. While the Greeks embraced a secular education, for the privileged only, and saw education as a development of talents, abilities, and the acquisition of intellectual and technical knowledge, the Hebrews valued education for all people and for the whole person. Study and learning were based on relationship. The headmasters of the Jewish schools were called school fathers; pupils were called school sons; and teacher/student relationships became like those of father and son. Fathers were seen as living conveyors of divine truth to sons, and their job was to convince the learners to obey and submit to divine authority.

The Greeks learned in order to comprehend; the Hebrews learned in order to revere. In Luke 10:27, Jesus, in response to a question about what was required in order to inherit eternal life, answered by directing the questioner to read what the Scriptures said: "You shall love the Lord your God with all your heart, with all your soul, with all your strength." One can't help but wonder whether Jesus answered as he did because this passage, from Deuteronomy 6:5, was the first portion of the Scriptures Jewish children learned.

The Hebrews became known as "people of the book," people who valued study because they knew their religion and their culture could perish if they failed to pass that learning on to their children. A common Jewish saying of the day summed up this value of study and learning: "If you have knowledge you have everything." The Jewish people knew they could lose everything—except knowledge. So learning for them was not a matter of status, as it was for the Greeks. Rather, it became the key to their survival.

In chapter 1 we talked about how the definition of the word *know* goes beyond mere intellectual activities. It also means to act. The Hebrew word for wisdom, *hokhmah*, means to have good sense, aptitude, or technical skill. It includes common activities or personal know-how applied to various realms and experiences of life. The Hebrews impressed this idea on each child from birth. Midwives rubbed the palates of newborns with honey and date juice so that the children would develop a taste for sweet things. As they grew older and received their educations in their homes, learning continued to be a positive and active achievement. Chalkboardlike teaching tools with vowels, consonants, and portions of the Scriptures written on them were coated with honey. The child who successfully recited the information earned the privilege of licking the honey from the board. This Hebrew affinity for gaining wisdom, connecting learning and doing, and connecting the natural life with the spiritual life, brings new meaning to the words "Eat honey, my son, for it is good; honey from the comb is sweet to your taste. Know also that wisdom is sweet to your soul; if you find it, there is a future hope for you, and your hope will not be cut off" (Proverbs 24:13-14, NIV) and "How sweet are Your words to my taste, sweeter than honey to my mouth!" (Psalm 119:103).

Once I embarked on my journey to really know God, study became an integral part of that journey. I began with the book of Romans and even asked two women to join me for Bible study, but I didn't understand what I read, and the study didn't last long. I kept at it, however, and joined another Bible study where we covered the book of Matthew. That's when I started using Bible commentaries, which helped clarify the biblical text. That's when the Scriptures really started becoming mine.

Almost daily study in the years since has turned into an adventure I scarcely have words to describe. I have identified with Bible characters who dealt with something then that is totally relevant to me now. Countless times when I have faced discouragement or needed direction, I have found a verse that brought me peace, a new perspective, and a way to pray about what I was facing. And while I have found the Scriptures comforting, I have also found them challenging. They haven't always told me what I wanted to hear, but they have always told me what I *needed* to know to keep growing in my knowledge of God. One day I complained to God about something one of my sisters was doing that I thought was wrong. After I prayed about my sister, I read my Bible and found an admonition—not for her but for me: "First remove the plank from your own eye, and then you will see clearly to remove the speck from your brother's eye" (Matthew 7:5).

I allowed that verse to seep into my spirit, not with a feeling of condemnation but with the deep knowledge that God knew and loved me. I was worth the trouble he took to show me how to be more like him in yet another way. Several months later I spoke with my sister by phone, and out of the blue she began telling me what God was doing in her life. And that issue I thought was so wrong? God had taken it away—even without my help!

> *If you accept my words*
> *and store up my commands within you,*
> *turning your ear to wisdom*
> *and applying your heart to understanding,*
> *and if you call out for insight*
> *and cry aloud for understanding,*
> *and if you look for it as for silver*
> *and search for it as for hidden treasure,*
> *then you will understand the fear of the Lord*
> *and find the knowledge of God.* (Proverbs 2:1-5, NIV)

Wisdom has become sweet to my soul, and God's words are sweeter than honey to my mouth.

## HEART STUDY

If you get the chance to attend seminary or Bible study classes, by all means go for it. But whether or not you get to study the academic side of Scripture, be sure to discover the heart aspect of it. You need both the big picture of what Scripture means and the small picture of how it plays out in your life: "What I am commanding you today is not too difficult for you or beyond your reach. It is not up in heaven, so that you have to ask, 'Who will ascend into heaven to get it and proclaim it to us so we may obey it?' Nor is it beyond the sea, so that you have to ask, 'Who will cross the sea to get it and proclaim it to us so we may obey it?' No, the word is very near you; it is in your mouth and in your heart so you may obey it" (Deuteronomy 30:11-14, NIV).

What an adventure it is to realize that although these verses were written for God's people in the Bible, they were also written for each one of us to read as God's personal love letters and instructions for our individual lives. If your study time is not sweet, doing the following things can help make it so:

## Make It a Regular Habit

Once again, just do it! Reading my Bible as well as various writings of other people in the morning sets the tone for my day. When I visited my daughter recently at college and saw her Bible in the backseat of her car, she explained how she liked to read it between classes.

The specific time and place where you read Scripture is not important. What *is* important is that you make it a daily habit. You may not describe your time in God's Word as I do mine, but I guarantee that you're in for an exciting adventure. The experiences God provides while you're reading are as individualized as the words themselves and how they apply to you.

## Vary Your Diet

I like to read at least one daily devotional book. I find having one or more of these going for the day is like talking to someone about a lesson God is teaching them. Some are more valuable than others, but I get a lot of nuggets from their content. I also like rereading a couple of these devotionals every year and glancing at comments I have written in each. It helps me to measure how much I've grown.

## Read the Bible in Doable Ways

For two years in a row I read a Bible designed to be read in one year. It was set up so that each day's reading covered a couple of chapters from the Old Testament, one from the New Testament, and a section from Psalms. By the end of the year, a reader has covered the whole Bible. I gained a view of the big picture as well as the opportunity to highlight particularly meaningful verses.

I also study passages of Scripture in one of three basic ways: subject, character, and book:

*Subject studies* involve using a concordance to look up all the verses containing a certain word or concept and then studying those throughout the whole Bible. I also take time to look up Hebrew and Greek meanings of specific words.

*Character studies* have allowed me to become personally acquainted with lots of real people in Scripture. Jehoshaphat faced a battle like every one of us does, and his life is an example for us to follow in fighting our own battles. Many Bible women, such as Phoebe, Dorcas, and Ruth, have taught me different aspects of being a godly woman.

*Book studies* provide the big picture of lives and events when we read a book from the Bible in its entirety. I have studied the life of Joshua in depth, and someday I want to have a talk with him and tell him how many of his strategies worked in my life too.

## Get Involved in a Group Bible Study

Bible study is a personal thing, but sharing it with others can greatly enhance your study program. Dave and I started a neighborhood Bible study for nonbelievers, and we watched a whole family come to faith. The dad, mom, and three teenage girls gather at our home on Sunday nights for Bible study and popcorn. "Where do I start?" they all asked when we told them they needed to study the Bible on their own. The dad began with Genesis and is working his way through systematically; the mom moves around. We had to skip several weeks during the Christmas holidays, and when I saw the dad on the street, he said, "I miss our Bible-study time together." The mom said, "I can't believe I just open the Bible and read something that shows me what to do today, as though it is written just for me!"

It would be hard to overemphasize the value of gathering together with other people interested in learning the truths of God's Word. Youth groups, Sunday school classes, lunchtime Bible studies with coworkers—these can do much to augment your own personal study of God's Word.

## Take Time to Memorize

One Friday night we had a scare concerning my husband's health. As I quickly decided to drive him to the emergency room, Bible verses I knew by heart echoed back to me: "Whenever I am afraid, I will trust in You" (Psalm 56:3). "God is our refuge and strength, a very present help in trouble" (Psalm 46:1). As with the theme of my radio show, "bringing God's Word alive in women's lives," God's Word came alive at a time when I needed it most.

Sometimes memorized verses help me make decisions or choose the right way to respond. Whether it's through straight memorization of Scripture or times when I put it to music, God's Word continues to come alive to me as I allow more and more opportunity for it to affect my life. One of my memory verses is Hebrews 4:12, which reminds me of that aliveness: "The word of God is living and powerful, and sharper than any two-edged sword, piercing even to the division of soul and spirit, and of joints and marrow, and is a discerner of the thoughts and intents of the heart."

## Seek Guidance from God

I have a friend I'll call Gail. She has become discontented with her marriage, and she's looking for any way out. I sat with her as she talked about her unmet needs and decisions she would need to make in the months to come about ending her marriage. Though the marriage has suffered a lot of neglect, Gail's husband is a Christian and has been faithful to their vows. So I asked Gail for justification from the Bible for her leaving the marriage. Of course, she could not give me that, but she went on to describe the deep neglect, regardless of biblical instruction.

Paul wrote to Christians who either didn't or couldn't learn and apply God's Word to their lives: "Though by this time you ought to be teachers, you need someone to teach you the elementary truths of God's word all over again. You need milk, not solid food! Anyone who lives on milk, being still an infant, is not acquainted with the teaching about righteousness. But solid food is for the mature, who by constant use have trained themselves to distinguish good from evil" (Hebrews 5:12-14, NIV).

Never neglect covering your daily study time with prayer. Ask God to reveal his Word to you. Ask him to guide you into its mysteries and truths. Ask him to open your mind to receive what he has to give. Ask him to help you apply the truths of Scripture to your life in new ways.

The steps of a righteous man or woman are ordered by God (Psalm 37:23), but we have to learn the steps and do what it takes to walk in them.

## Keep a Journal

There are many good books that show you how to keep a journal of the things God is teaching you. You may find a technique in one of them that works especially well for you. But I have found that the simpler I make it, the easier it is to stick with it. Journaling doesn't have to be any more elaborate than writing in a spiral notebook the things you learn, and if you're not discovering anything new on a particular day, lay your writing aside.

You can be spontaneous about this too. During a movie or a sermon, Dave is no longer surprised when I pull out a deposit slip and write down a quote. I usually journal the things I'm learning on my laptop and then fold them into my writing where appropriate. But several files in my office are filled with quotes or information written on napkins or scraps of paper. Your goal is to keep your eyes open to the lessons God teaches you and then to capture them in a way you can remember. Journaling can help you do that.

## Collect Good Resources

I've heard people say that if their house was on fire, they would be sure their families were safe and then they would grab their family photos. So would I, but next, I think, I would go for some of my Bible-study materials. The covers on more than one Bible have literally fallen off. Some of my reference books are so dog-eared that I'm ashamed for others to see them.

One night I flew back from Chicago, where I had done some TV and radio appearances, and I was trying to get home before my children went to bed. I thought I could wait until morning to put gas in my car, but about two miles from home I learned differently. While I walked along the interstate to the gas station to get more fuel, someone broke into my car and stole my luggage. They got one of my favorite blouses and skirts, but that didn't matter nearly as much as the Bible they stole, which had chronicled my study with God up to that point. After I had bemoaned my loss for a while, I set out on a new adventure with a new Bible and began to discover the fresh things God had to teach me.

Much good reference material exists for studying Scripture, but in my opinion, no serious student of the Bible should be without the following resources:

- *Multiple Bibles* in readable versions with good notes or commentary, cross-references, concordances, and word definitions. Using several versions together can expand your information base. Don't hesitate to write and underline and even scribble dates in your Bibles. Each entry will allow you to

capture what God teaches you at that moment and will help
you build one lesson onto another.

- *An exhaustive concordance.* This allows you to find Scripture
verses by searching under key words and also gives Old Testament Hebrew and New Testament Greek meanings. Using a
concordance adds a dimension to your study of Scripture you
can't find anywhere else.

- *Bible dictionaries and atlases.* Especially in these days, with
Israel and various Arab nations in the news, I find it interest-
ing, for example, to learn that in Bible times, Iraq was Babylon
and Iran was Persia. Looking up people and places quickly to
find what others have already learned about them enriches
your own study.

- *Bible commentaries.* These contain a wealth of information
about key concepts. They also help you understand wider
meanings of the text with regard to the times and culture in
which the words were written.

- *Good books.* I like to read reputable and readable authors about
certain topics of interest to me. God reveals different aspects of
issues to different people. Sometimes I find others' material of
little or no value to my own study, sometimes of great value,
and still other times it sparks a whole new component to the
study that I hadn't considered before. Just be sure that you
don't allow the results of others' study to take the place of your
own study of the Bible.

For those of you who are computer savvy, there are lots of good
computer programs that contain the resources listed above,
although they can be costly. The resources above are also often
available from stores that sell used books.

"Do your best [or "study"] to present yourself to God as one
approved, a workman who does not need to be ashamed and who

correctly handles the word of truth," says 2 Timothy 2:15 (NIV). Whatever it takes, however long it takes, whichever direction it takes—study to show yourself approved. As you study, you'll find that you are wanting to eat God's Word, like Jeremiah and Job. In the process you'll find new ways of knowing God that you never realized existed.

When I was a child, my dad taught us a poem about prayer and Bible reading. This poem is branded forever in my heart, and I know exactly what the author was writing about:

*I met God in the morning*
*When the day was at its best,*
*And His presence came like sunrise*
*Like a glory in my breast.*

*All day long the presence lingered,*
*All day long He stayed with me;*
*And we sailed in perfect calmness*
*O'er a very troubled sea.*

*Other ships were blown and battered,*
*Other ships were sore distressed;*
*But the winds that seemed to drive them*
*Brought to us a peace and rest.*

*Then I thought of other mornings,*
*With a keen remorse of mind,*
*When I, too, had loosed the moorings,*
*With His presence left behind.*

*So I think I know the secret*
*Learned from many a troubled way;*
*You must seek God in the morning*
*If you want Him through the day.* [1]

Seek him early or late; just seek him. Find the nuggets of truth and direction he has for you every day for everything you'll face. When you do, you, too, will find God's words sweeter than honey to your mouth—and we don't even have to feel guilty about eating those sweets!

---

*LORD, I am learning to cherish your Word more than my necessary food. The Bible holds your love letters to me. Help me to read them consistently and to understand their meaning in fresh ways, both with my head and in my heart. You have told us that when we draw near to you, you will draw near to us. Please draw near to me through your Word in my life. Amen.*

# 11

# Fasting with Him

I was about ten years old when my family went on a monthlong vacation from Ohio to Arizona. I don't remember what all we saw or who we visited that summer, but I do remember something my dad did. He fasted for forty days for the salvation of his older brother, Conley. Dad drank only water and juice for those weeks, and his weight dropped drastically, but he had decided to add the discipline of fasting to his everyday prayer for his brother's salvation. I must admit that for me as a child, Dad's fast didn't hold any appeal, especially when Aunt Alma made her tasty tacos. I also got pretty tired of hearing Dad pray out loud for Conley, and only as an adult did I wonder how many more of his faithful prayers were spoken privately.

Dad's long fast ended without Conley's coming to faith. Dad's prayers seemed to have gone unheeded when my father died in 1988 with Conley still rejecting the gospel. It was not until 1998 that I realized what Dad's discipline and faithfulness had really produced.

I had booked an April speaking engagement back in Ohio, so I took Courtney and Clint with me to visit family. When we arrived, I called my oldest sister, Sue, to tell her we would get to her house soon, and together with our other sister's twin daughters, we arrived to spend the day. Sue said, "Let's visit Uncle Conley before we get going."

The mere mention of Conley's name reminded me of Dad's prayers for him. I agreed, and soon we were knocking on his door.

We walked into his house, and the four children sat on one of the couches. Sue and I took our places on another couch in front of the window, and Uncle Conley perched on the coffee table in front of me as he leaned on his cane.

"Cain't walk so fer as I used to," he said. "My heart is plumb give out. When I look at them two cows out thar, I see five of 'em. And this here," he said, as he pointed a shaky finger to a spot on his lip, "is cancer, and I'm skeert it's gonna spread to the rest of my body."

"Uncle Conley," I said, "are you able to talk to the Lord about these things?"

"Oh, no," he said. "Me and the Lord ain't friends. I done too much." And Conley continued to talk about his health concerns.

"What would you like the Lord to do for you?" I said.

"Well," he said, "I'd like him to fergive my sins ifn' he could."

"Then look up and tell him that," I said.

In a moment the six of us will never forget, Uncle Conley's eyes traveled to the ceiling, and with a tear on his cheek, my uncle said, "God, do you think you could fergive my sins?"

I finished by leading my uncle in the sinner's prayer. As we pulled away from Conley's home, I rejoiced at God's faithfulness. Not only had he honored my dad's prayer and fasting for his brother's salvation, but God did it after Dad's death with his two oldest children and four grandchildren looking on.

Conley died the following December at age ninety-one. I can only imagine what my dad said to him when he arrived in heaven: "Con, do you know how many prayers and meals your ticket here cost me?"

## FASTING'S ROLE IN BIBLE HISTORY

The Hebrew meaning of the word *fast* means "to cover the mouth, to abstain." It was thought in early days that the gods were jealous of the pleasures of men and that abstinence would regain their favor. As a result, they found fasting to be a religious duty. Later, the expression used in Hebrew law meant "to humble your souls," implying the sacrifice of one's personal will. We find several examples of this in Scripture:

- "So it was, when I heard these words, that I sat down and wept, and mourned for many days; I was fasting and praying before the God of heaven." (Nehemiah 1:4)
- "Then I set my face toward the Lord God to make request by prayer and supplications, with fasting, sackcloth, and ashes." (Daniel 9:3)
- "After they had fasted and prayed, they placed their hands on them and sent them off." (Acts 13:3, NIV)

Eventually, however, fasting was abused. The Pharisees used fasts as a frequent and ordinary pious exercise, and they carried about a downcast demeanor so that onlookers would know that they were fasting and would admire them for their great spirituality. Jesus rebuked the Pharisees for their hypocrisy (Matthew 6:16-18), but he did, however, draw attention to the importance of combining fasting with prayer as a way of growing in our faith.

The story is told in Mark 9. Jesus, Peter, James, and John were just returning from the Mount of Transfiguration. They arrived to hear the scribes disputing with a crowd of people. Jesus questioned the scribes, "What are you discussing with them?" (v. 16).

A man from the crowd answered, explaining how he had brought his son, who was possessed by a demonic spirit that deprived him of speech. He had asked the disciples to pray for the boy's healing, but the disciples had failed to get the job done.

I wonder whether Jesus' emotions on hearing those words might have been similar to what I felt one day. Dave and I were traveling, and we called seventeen-year-old Clint to tell him about our exciting day. Clint apparently not having heard a word we said, responded, "Mom, I'm hungry. What can I eat?"

I said good-bye to my son thinking, *Do I have to do it all? Can't you do anything without me there?*

Jesus' words reflected a similar response: "O faithless generation, how long shall I be with you? How long shall I bear with you? Bring him to Me" (v. 19).

To make a long story short, Jesus commanded the spirit to leave the boy, and the boy was delivered.

But that wasn't the end of the subject. The disciples listened and wondered why Jesus' words to the deaf and dumb spirit hadn't worked for them, too. After all, Jesus had given them power over evil spirits (Mark 6:7). Why hadn't their prayers worked? Once they had gone indoors, they asked Jesus to explain, and he answered without hesitation, "This kind [of spirit] can come out by nothing but prayer and fasting" (Mark 9:29).

Those words created the reason that we still fast today. Some things require more-powerful praying, and our prayers become more powerful when we combine them with fasting. The use of prayer and fasting together allows us to focus our attention more fully on God for a specific purpose over a specific period of time. Dad empowered his prayers with fasting, and that may have made the difference in Uncle Conley's coming to faith.

How many serious situations have we prayed about during this past week? How many of those things could use the extra measure of power that fasting would give?

## THE DISCIPLINE OF FASTING

I have to pause here and admit that I did not naturally inherit my dad's devotion to the discipline of fasting. I remember once as a child trying to fast for a day. I made it through breakfast. I trudged through lunch only by distancing myself from the rest of my family while they ate. Later that afternoon I met my downfall as I walked through the kitchen on my way outside. The lunch table had not yet been cleared. I looked around, and while no one was watching, I grabbed a spoon and stuffed a giant bite of potato salad into my mouth. So much for those early attempts!

Fasting still does not come easily to me. Although I love God with all my heart and want to know and please him, I had never fasted for fasting's sake. It was not a discipline I regularly used. But I turned the corner when I took the time to find out more about fasting and why it lends so much power to our prayers. This is what I learned about why, when, and how we fast.

## Why Do We Fast?

There are a number of reasons for fasting. And keeping each of these benefits in mind can increase our motivation to continue when we're trying to fast and feel like grabbing that big bite of potato salad.

*We fast to put the body in its proper place.*

The apostle Paul wrote, "I fight: not as one who beats the air. But I discipline my body and bring it into subjection, lest, when I have preached to others, I myself should become disqualified" (1 Corinthians 9:26-27). The words "discipline my body" refer, as you might guess from what comes before them, to going into a boxing ring and fighting a fight. To fast is to put up a fight, not just with Satan but with myself and my own desires.

In early Bible days, God told Israel to set aside the Day of Atonement for the purpose of afflicting their souls (Leviticus 16:29) or denying themselves (NIV). This allowed the "spirit" to take precedence over the body as the people denied themselves food. Fasting became a way for believers to inform their bodies that the spirit was in charge.

I try to fast one day a week for one, two, or all three meals.

During the breakfast, lunch, and dinner times when I would ordinarily be eating, I pray for people and situations on my prayer list. When I feel hunger pangs from fasting, I try to use them as a reminder to pray. When we add fasting to our arsenal of disciplines, we free our minds from earthly matters and distractions and devote ourselves to contemplating divine things. Is your spirit in charge of your body, or do your body and its appetites still reign supreme?

*We fast to gain compassion for others.*

The theme verse for this part of the book is "That I may *know* Him" (Philippians 3:10, emphasis added). That's not the complete verse, however. In the New International Version the entire verse reads: "I want to know Christ and the power of his resurrection and the fellowship of sharing in his sufferings, becoming like him in his death."

Really knowing God does not come without pain. And for us to know him most, we need to agonize over the people he loves. "Nice" people all around us—people in the post office, at the grocery store, and next door—are going to face an eternity in hell if something doesn't happen to change their hearts.

Dave and I decided that when we walk the dog together, we would pray for the families in the houses we pass. Recent missionary estimates say that more than sixty thousand people around the world come to Christ every day. That's no doubt happening through someone's prayer and fasting. Prayer and fasting will give you greater compassion for those who don't know Christ.

*We fast to help us make right decisions.*

Many times when I faced a major decision involving one of my children or perhaps a job choice, I fasted in addition to praying. While I fasted, I focused on talking to God about the decision and the answers he would give me. The discipline of fasting makes our minds and hearts more receptive to what God's Spirit has to teach us. Even Jesus, who was God himself, fasted and prayed before he chose his disciples. As we face major life decisions and need God's wisdom, what better way could there be than to seek it with a heart and mind made receptive by the discipline of fasting and prayer?

*We fast to defeat Satan.*

Many years ago I faced a family crisis that came as a direct attack from Satan. I cried and prayed a lot about it. Then I fasted for two days and headed to the mountains. I sat on the couch in a cabin I had borrowed from a friend, and I set a chair in front of me. I needed to see something tangible as I directed my prayers and intercession to God concerning this matter.

The next day, I went skiing. Through prayer and fasting I had put everything I had into fighting Satan in this matter. Now, as God honored my faith in him, I enjoyed spending the day doing something I loved.

We've already seen that Jesus' deliverance of the demon-possessed boy with the words "I command you, come out of him and enter him no more" (Mark 9:25) could truly have occurred only by prayer and fasting. Spiritual battles require spiritual weapons.

Professor Ole Hallesby compares the use of fasting to the transmission of electrical power: "The greater the volume of power to be transmitted, the stronger the connection with the power house must be; that is, the larger the cable must be. Fasting helps to give us that inner sense of spiritual penetration by means of which we can discern clearly that for which the Spirit of prayer would have us pray in exceptionally different circumstances."[1] Are you facing a spiritual battle with Satan? Strengthen yourself through prayer and fasting.

*We fast to overcome temptation.*

Immediately after Jesus' forty-day fast, Satan tempted him three times: "If You are the Son of God, command that these stones become bread." "If You are the Son of God, throw Yourself down [from this pinnacle]." "All these [kingdoms of the world] I will give You if You will fall down and worship me." (See Matthew 4:1-10.)

If Jesus could not escape the temptations of Satan, we can't either. No matter how mature we are or how much we really know God, we will still face temptations as long as we live on earth. But Jesus stood up to Satan and claimed his rightful success over the enemy. Surely the power he had gained through forty days of prayer and fasting enabled him to stand strong. What was the result? "Then the devil left him, and angels came and attended him" (Matthew 4:11, NIV).

If you have encountered temptation, it might be something that you can defeat only through prayer and fasting. Although it is diffi-cult to explain, fasting releases spiritual power that we need to win our battles with Satan and with ourselves and our desires.

*We fast to prepare ourselves for new challenges.*

Whether we need leadership abilities or wisdom or something else, we know that God is the One who can give us what we need when we face new challenges. Prayer and fasting can become the pathway through which God gives us what we need. Don't neglect going to God for these things. Never assume that you already have everything it takes. Tap into God's sufficiency through prayer and fasting.

**When Do We Fast?**

To find out when it is appropriate to fast, we can take a look at when the Hebrews fasted in the Old Testament:

*They fasted in the midst of difficult circumstances (2 Chronicles 20:3).*

Jehoshaphat, king of Judah, encountered a war against the Moabites and Ammonites. There was no way Judah could win the battle by themselves. So what did Jehoshaphat do? He "feared, and set himself to seek the Lord, and proclaimed a fast throughout all

Judah" (2 Chronicles 20:3). Not only did he know that fasting would help him find victory, but he taught this same truth to the people he led. Judah went on to win an overwhelming victory against insurmountable odds, and fasting helped that happen.

Our prayer list grows long with people facing nearly impossible situations physically, emotionally, spiritually. Fasting can help to give your prayers power in these desperate situations. I have often taken part in partner fasting, in which several people fast around the clock for someone's need.

### They fasted during times of misfortune (1 Samuel 31:11-13).

In 1 Samuel 31 we read about the death of King Saul and his sons. Although Saul had been a less than honorable and godly ruler, he had been the Lord's anointed to lead God's people. Therefore, those who buried his bones spent seven days fasting. Whether it be the loss of a loved one, joblessness, or divorce, some crises are so grave that they require more strength and power than we have to work through them. That power can come through much prayer and fasting.

### They fasted in times of impending judgment by God (1 Kings 21:27-29).

It's easy to watch the news and shake our heads at the way America has turned its back on God. But how often do we pray and fast for our country? Fasting will help you set your focus and seek God's mercy on our nation: "If My people who are called by My name will humble themselves, and pray and seek My face, and turn from their wicked ways, then I will hear from heaven, and will forgive their sin and heal their land" (2 Chronicles 7:14).

### They fasted in times of sin (Ezra 10:6).

When we fail, one sure way to help us get back into fellowship with God is to fast and pray. God will give us forgiveness, healing, and the strength to overcome our own desires when we get serious enough to come before him with both prayer and fasting.

*They fasted before impending calamity (Esther 4:1, 3, 16).*

Nothing gets us on our knees and causes us to push back our plates more than a sense that disaster is imminent. On the Wednesday night that our nation declared war on Iraq, I went to church, where our pastor called us to pray throughout the entire service, and he challenged us to fast. Until we as humans see that things are bigger than we are and are beyond our control, we will want to stay in charge. A sense that calamity is approaching shakes us from that godlike way of thinking and makes us serious about our need to pray to the One who is in control.

*They fasted during times of national disaster (Judges 20:24-26; 2 Chronicles 20:3).*

The days following 9/11 did much to enforce our need to pray and fast. Who knows what lies ahead? Who knows what comes next? Only God knows the future. It is enough for us to realize that if disaster occurs again, prayer and fasting now will help us to be prepared and to shine the light of God's truth to others.

### How Do We Fast?

The ancient Hebrews had different kinds of fasting. When a fast lasted only a single day, they usually abstained from food of any kind from one evening until the next. Private fasts of a more prolonged nature meant refusing to eat ordinary foods. To manifest a still more profound humbling of the soul before God, those fasting would often repent, tear their clothes, put on sackcloth, and throw ashes over their heads.

Our fasts can vary too. We can go without all food or some food. A fast may or may not include water and/or juice. A fast can be long or short. Always consult a doctor about any health concerns related to your choice to fast, and then become informed about proper ways to fast. The late Bill Bright, founder and president of Campus Crusade for Christ, published a helpful pamphlet titled "Seven Basic Steps to Successful Fasting and Prayer." Briefly, these seven steps are as follows:

*1. Set your objective.*

Ask the Holy Spirit to clarify his leading and objectives for your prayer fast.

*2. Make your commitment.*

Making a commitment ahead of time will help you sustain your fast. When doing this, think about what kind of fast it will be, how long it will last, what physical or social activities you will restrict, and how much time you'll spend in prayer and study.

*3. Prepare yourself spiritually.*

Unconfessed sin will hinder your prayers. Confess your sin and accept God's forgiveness (1 John 1:9). Seek forgiveness from those you have hurt. Make restitution. Ask God's Holy Spirit to give you confidence in the promise of 1 John 5:14-15 (NIV): "This is the confidence we have in approaching God: that if we ask anything according to his will, he hears us. And if we know that he hears us—whatever we ask—we know that we have what we asked of him." Meditate on the attributes of God: his love, sovereignty, power, wisdom. Reading verses from the Bible, such as Psalms 48:9-10 and 103:1-8, 11-13 can help with this. Begin your fast with an expectant heart (Hebrews 11:6), but don't underestimate the possibility of spiritual opposition to what you are doing.

*4. Prepare yourself physically.*

Consult a physician. Don't be in a rush to begin your fast. Prepare your body by eating smaller meals before you begin your fast. Avoid high-fat and sugary foods. Instead, eat raw fruits and vegetables for two days beforehand.

### 5. *Put yourself on a schedule.*

Schedule time to be alone with God. Listen for his leading. The more time you spend with God, the more meaningful your fast will be.

### 6. *End your fast gradually.*

Break an extended water fast, during which you've drunk only water, with fruit such as watermelon. As you begin eating again, add fruit or vegetable juices, raw salad, baked potato without butter or seasoning, and steamed vegetables. Gradually return to eating a regular diet by eating several small snacks during the first few days after a fast.

### 7. *Expect results.*

If you sincerely humble yourself before the Lord; repent, pray, and seek his face; and consistently meditate on his Word, you will experience a heightened awareness of his presence (John 14:21). Just as we need fresh portions of the Holy Spirit, we also need new times of fasting before God. Many Christians have found a twenty-four-hour fast once a week greatly rewarding.[2]

I don't know who else prayed and fasted for Uncle Conley besides my dad, but I do know Dad did. He realized that although not everything on his prayer list would come about only through much prayer and fasting, his brother's salvation most likely would. When you think of fasting, you, too, might feel the urge to grab a bite of potato salad. But one thing is certain, your prayers will never be as powerful as they can be without the discipline of fasting.

DEAR LORD, this one is hard for me. The busy life I lead requires nourishment for my body, but I need quality time with you even more. Thank you for the discipline of fasting, which can accomplish what no other discipline can. Help me to add regular fasting to my arsenal of spiritual weapons so that my spiritual life will be one of power. Amen.

# 12

# Being Still and Listening to Him

The clock in my car said 9:15 one Friday night, and I was just getting home after a day of work, errands, and kids' sports events. Exhausted, I turned right at the stop sign and headed the last two miles toward our house. Immediately I saw the red lights of a state police car flashing in my rearview mirror. I pulled over and watched the officer climb out of his car.

"I stopped you," he said, "because you didn't come to a dead stop back at the sign. I'm going to give you a warning this time, but if you don't start coming to a complete stop, you'll have to pay the price at some point."

The next morning I was up by four. I got ready for work, put dinner in the Crock-Pot, left written instructions for the children, pulled together my notes, and headed to Denver to speak at a conference for the day. As I drove on the interstate, I leaned against the headrest. Suddenly I remembered the police officer's words: "If you don't start coming to a complete stop, you'll have to pay the price at some point."

That man's words suddenly meant more to me than just obeying traffic rules. As a single, working mom I had huge responsibilities. I talked to God regularly—usually on the run—but I didn't give him the chance to talk to me. Though I was busy doing good things, the hectic level I had allowed my life to reach had impeded my ability to hear from God.

## COMPETITORS OF QUIETNESS

The prophet Elijah's life was filled with good things too. He stood for God in Israel at a time when godly voices were few. In 1 Kings 19 he found himself on the run from Queen Jezebel and King Ahab, who had vowed to kill him because of his convicting message.

Elijah fled for his life into the wilderness and sat down under a broom tree, where he even prayed for God to take his life (v. 4). God knew that part of Elijah's discouragement came from exhaustion, so he had Elijah sleep. After he had eaten food brought by an angel, he rested again. When the angel returned a second time, he told Elijah to get up and eat again, "for the journey is too much for you" (v. 7, NIV). So Elijah ate a second time and was then able to travel for forty days and nights until he came to a cave, where he spent the night. At that point God had Elijah tap into the source that would give him the power he needed for the difficult journey ahead. God had Elijah be still. Stop his striving. Cease his talking. Close his mouth and open his ears and eyes. God told Elijah, "'Go out, and stand on the mountain before the Lord.' And behold, the Lord passed by, and a great and strong wind tore into the mountains and broke the rocks in pieces before the Lord, but the Lord was not in the wind; and after the wind an earthquake, but the Lord was not in the earthquake; and after the earthquake a fire, but the Lord was not in the fire" (vv. 11-12).

Today our winds could be the uncertainties of life, which blow us about at will. Disasters, like earthquakes, shake us to the core. Fires ignite and consume everything we thought we had achieved and earned. Our tendency, like Elijah's, is to tremble, run, complain, grow fearful, and sometimes even pray to die. But God communicated profound truth through what was the most simple. He made himself known through quietness: "After the fire came a gentle whisper" (v. 12, NIV).

God has things to communicate to us. He wants to express his love for us, encourage us, and give us direction. But he isn't inclined to scream at us above the clamor of life's distractions. If you're having trouble hearing what God has to say, you might be distracted by other things that compete for your attention. At least three of these—materialism, busyness, and noise—will most surely mute his voice.

## Materialism

Materialism places an inordinate value on acquiring things. Our society promotes materialism with the popular notion that the person who has the most toys wins. We may call it covetousness, ambition, hoarding, or prudence. Our full houses—and garages and even storage units we rent to store the overflow of things we have—seem to indicate that we've bought into the thinking that having more and more things takes priority over almost everything else and that our personal worth is somehow related to our material worth.

I grew up in a family with eight children, so we didn't have much. My dad's postman's salary was never more than sixteen thousand dollars. His paycheck came every two weeks, and my mother received fifty dollars to buy enough groceries to last us for fourteen days. Mom clipped coupons and planned meals according to what was on sale and then made rounds to three different grocery stores. Because of our shortage of possessions, I liked to sit with one of my sisters with a Sears catalog spread across our laps. Together we pretended that I got everything displayed on my side of the book and my sister got what was on her side. I pictured myself wearing the beautiful dresses and sparkling jewelry. Once the game was over and we had closed the catalog, it was back to real life—and invariably a sense of disappointment.

Materialism squelches contentment and breeds greed. Unless we keep these tendencies in check, the more we get, the more we want. And the less emphasis we place on knowing God, the more time and energy we tend to devote to acquiring things. A lack of divine center causes a deep insecurity and an inordinate attachment to things, and this dries up our longing for spiritual things:

- "Whoever trusts in his riches will fall." (Proverbs 11:28, NIV)
- "Though your riches increase, do not set your heart on them." (Psalm 62:10, NIV)

Growing materialism is directly proportional to plummeting spirituality. Author Calvin Miller writes, "When we trade our spiritual treasures for mere trifles, the grand dream we had for serving God seeps away through the glitzy pores of our greed."[1]

To keep materialism from becoming a problem for you, regularly check how you're doing in these areas:

*Growing spiritually.*

When we get hungry for something sweet, if we feed that craving with something nutritious, our body benefits. The same is true of materialism. If instead of catalogs we spend time with the Bible across our laps, God will satisfy our deeper hungers, our deeper thirsts, with things that really satisfy. Again Calvin Miller writes: "Striving for, clinging to, and hoping in all that is within our grasp displaces God from His rightful place in our lives. We were built for God. Only He can satisfy the vacancy in our souls. His nature, provisions, power, and wisdom are the only realities that will unfailingly buttress our lives with that which truly sustains and secures."[2]

God does not and will not compete or share his space with anyone or anything. As we fix our hope on him alone and focus everything we do on getting to really know him, we become convinced that the only real, lasting, valuable assets in our lives come from above.

*Buying wisely.*

I've always liked to dress well, and I love to find bargains on quality clothing.

One day I ran across quite a sale. I purchased three items, and when I brought them home and went to hang them in my closet, I saw three other garments just like them already there. My taste was the same whether the clothes were old or new. Now I try to buy things for their usefulness rather than for their trendiness or the status of a particular label. And when I pay with cash only and not credit, I can keep my spending in line.

*Watching addictions.*

Don't eat, drink, watch, or read anything you can do without. For me that includes everything from TV to caffeine. If you're unsure, ask God to show you the things you think you need but can really do without.

*Giving things away.*

If you haven't worn it or used it during the last year, give it away. Call Goodwill Industries or the Salvation Army or some other charity. Often they will even come to your house and pick up your donation. You may also know people in your church or other needy people who would be grateful for those things you no longer need or want. Just be sure that if you give things away to people you know, you are careful not to embarrass the recipients or take away their dignity.

*Recognizing propaganda.*

I played a game with my children once, having them help me recognize various examples of advertising pressure or propaganda: "Everybody has it." "Get on the bandwagon." "Don't be the last person on your street to have. . . ." Not only do you need to recognize and resist propaganda, you need to teach your kids to do it too.

*Appreciating simple things.*

If you have children, allow them to help you develop an appreciation for simple things. As a young child, my daughter Ashley loved to take a family outing to pull rocks out of a creek or to climb a mountain. "This is living," she said once when we hiked while visiting my mother in southeastern Arizona.

One time I said to my young children, "Let's do something fun today. What would you like to do?" In unison, they all asked to stay home. Take a walk with your child or your pet. Listen, smell, look at the sky. You'll have lots of fun and scratch your materialism itch at the same time.

*Enjoying things without owning them.*

There's nothing wrong with having things as long as those things don't have you. One missionary came to our church and talked about how he had sensed that God was telling him to give one thousand dollars toward a building project going on at his new place of assignment. All he had of value were three chess sets from the three countries where he had served. Hesitantly he considered his only real possessions, and again he felt that God was telling him to give one thousand dollars. The missionary sold the three sets for exactly one thousand dollars, and he gave the money to the church. Someone else found out what he had done, and as weeks went by, different members of the congregation purchased the chess sets back and returned them to the missionary as gifts. As he spoke at our church, he set one piece from each of the three sets on the podium for us to see. "God really needed my chess sets for the kingdom, right?" he said. "No, God really needed me, all of me, and giving up my most prized possessions gave him access to the rest of me."

## Busyness

Busyness is the bedfellow of materialism, especially within the church. Our I'd-rather-burn-out-than-rust-out mentality causes us to serve on too many church committees, and we rationalize all the hassle by telling ourselves that we're running for the Lord. We don't understand the truth in the Greek motto "You'll break the bow if it's always bent." Fast living and fast spending keep company. Calvin Miller writes that "hurried Christians beget hurried disciples beget a hurried church."[3]

Once, after speaking at a Life on the Edge conference, I made my way to the book table. When I arrived, I was excited to see the long line of people waiting to receive their signed copy of my book. My enthusiasm was quickly dashed, however, when I realized that they had seated me next to Frank Peretti. I took my seat at the table beside Frank and his wife, signed the dozen or so books people handed to me, and then chatted with the Perettis as I watched Frank sign his hundreds. I asked about their plans for the summer, imagining the exotic place they would travel for Frank to pen his next best-seller. Their answer both surprised me and reminded me of the reason Frank could write his next book: "We're going to stay home and trim our bushes."

The Perettis could have afforded an exotic trip, but they had discovered that God's wisdom comes through simplicity. Simplicity is the antidote to busyness. We don't need to go to extremes in our simplicity. But simplicity does free us from the bondage of pretense. It replaces anxiety and fear with joy and calmness. Simplicity is the result of inward habits that result in outward life-styles. But trying to simplify outwardly without inwardly focusing on God turns into a whole different kind of bondage called legalism. To avoid falling into that trap, follow these suggestions:

- Simplify your schedule, and meet with God at the same time every day. In your car, at lunchtime, or in bed, study, pray, and take time to listen to what God wants to teach you.
- Eliminate the need to serve the urgent. Clocks can make us

good stewards of time, but if every moment of our day is governed by planners or PDAs, we can become slaves of the very things that we thought would simplify our lives.

- Say "no" more often, and cancel the things that you can so that you aren't overcommitted.
- Organize and eliminate the clutter in your closet, desk, car, purse, etc.
- Get out of debt.
- Plan ahead, and think through your schedule.
- Take time for leisure and rest.
- Take care that the high-tech luxuries you have don't complicate your life.

## Noise

Noise, noise, everywhere. As soon as we take notice of silence, we reach for the TV remote and switch on Fox News. Because I do talk radio, I usually find myself turning on the radio in the car instead of enjoying the quietness. Many people don't have good memories of being by themselves, so they resist getting silent before God and never experience the benefits it brings.

But we can't hear God speaking to our hearts unless we find pockets of silence and solitude with him. Jesus modeled the need for solitude as he withdrew on a boat (Matthew 14:13), and he showed the disciples how to build in their own times of solitude too: "He took them and went aside privately into a deserted place" (Luke 9:10).

Writer Richard Foster distinguishes between loneliness and solitude:

> Jesus calls us from loneliness to solitude. . . . Our fear of being alone drives us to noise and crowds. . . . But loneliness or clatter are not our only alternatives. We can cultivate an inner solitude and silence that sets us free from loneliness and fear.

Loneliness is inner emptiness. Solitude is inner fulfillment. Solitude is not first a place but a state of mind and heart. . . . It is in solitude that we come to experience the "silence of God" and so receive the inner silence that is the craving of our heart. . . . The fruit of solitude is increased sensitivity and compassion for others. There comes a new freedom to be with people. There is new attentiveness to their needs, new responsiveness to their hurts.[4]

When God met Elisha at the cave, he was not in the wind, the earthquake, or the fire. He was in the gentle blowing of the "still small voice" (1 Kings 19:12). Cultivating silence and solitude may be a brand-new concept for you. If so, here are some suggestions from Richard Foster:

- Determine your silent place with God, and visit it daily.
- Instead of always praying aloud, reserve some time for silence.
- Find little moments of solitude every day, without radio, earphones, telephones, or TVs.
- Find silent places outside your home, such as a church, park, even a storage closet.
- Discipline yourself so your words are full and few. Have something to say when you speak.
- Set aside times during the year to go off by yourself for three or four hours to be still and reorient your life goals.
- Take study retreats, and make silence/solitude a major part of them.
- Listen.[5]

## HEARING THE GENTLE WHISPER

Once we learn to exchange materialism for contentment, busyness for simplicity, and noise for silence or solitude, we're in the right place to hear God's voice. However, contentment, simplicity, and silence will not of themselves allow us to hear him speak. We need to also cultivate the discipline of listening, and for women who like to talk and to be in charge, that's not always easy to do. Many times we spend too much time talking in prayer and not enough time listening. Instead of saying, "Speak, Lord, I'm listening," we say, "Listen, Lord, I'm speaking."

Author Dick Eastman writes these truths about listening:

- Listening is a quieting of the soul.
- Listening is a time of release from other worlds.
- Listening is heart communication.
- Listening is the better half of conversation.
- Listening is the key to creative prayer.[6]

On the morning I worked on this chapter, I had risen early, while the rest of my world continued to sleep. I sat in my green chair with God. I sat in silence, even before I talked to him about my heart, heavy over news I'd heard the night before about wrong choices someone I dearly loved was making. I had awakened throughout the night, wondering if she would ever turn her life over to God. After a while I opened my Bible and silently read Psalm 119. As I continued to read, I scribbled verses that jumped off the page: "Forever, O Lord, Your word is settled in heaven. Your faithfulness endures to all generations; You established the earth, and it abides. . . . The entrance of Your words gives light; it gives understanding to the simple. . . . My heart stands in awe of Your word. I rejoice at Your word as one who finds great treasure. . . . Great peace have those who love Your law, and nothing causes them to stumble" (Psalm 119:89-90, 130, 161-162, 165).

When my time with God ended, the winds still blew. The earth still shook. The fires still burned. But I had been learning to listen. I had heard the still, small voice whispering, *I am here.*

Before I leave the topic of silence, I must address those times when God is silent. When there is no still, small voice. When we go in silence to find him and we find only silence as the wind, earthquakes, and fires continue to rage around us.

When Courtney was about two years old, I was faced with divorce, the birth of my third child, and my dad's battle with pancreatic cancer. Added to those challenges, Courtney had started waking several times through the night and crying for me. After many nights of interrupted sleep, I cried out to God one morning. I waited, but I heard nothing. No relief came. No voice spoke to my heart. No calm overtook me. I cried out to God, "Don't you hear me? Don't you understand? Don't you care?"

Soon, my newborn son had joined his sisters, hungry for breakfast and to get going with his day. I did mom stuff all day, and before I knew it, it was nighttime again. Once I had tucked the children in for the night, I planned my strategy for getting Courtney to sleep through the night: I would just ignore her cries until she realized I would not come, and then she'd sleep.

It wasn't long before my opportunity came. My much-needed sleep was interrupted by the wails of the two-year-old down the hall. I slipped out of bed and tiptoed to a hidden spot beside her door where she could not see me. I wanted to be sure she was okay, but I also wanted to teach her an important lesson. She cried, and I watched. Finally she gave in and fell asleep. Victory was mine, and I went back to bed.

Unfortunately, my success was short lived. Courtney awakened and cried out again. Again I took my place at the hidden spot and watched her. She shook the sides of her crib, trying to get a response, and after much too long a time, she again gave in to slumber.

Not long after I had finally drifted off again, Courtney's third disruption sounded. Exhaustion and anger overwhelmed me as I stood outside her door once again. Tears dropped off her cheeks as she seemed to say, "Don't you hear me? Don't you understand? Don't you care?"

Where had I heard these same questions before? Then I remembered my prayers just hours before. I slid down the wall and listened to the silent explanations from God. Just as I remained silent when Courtney cried out to me, God needed to teach me to trust him. Just as I had watched over her completely when it seemed to her that I didn't care, God was doing the same with me. Just as I didn't bat an eye or move from my place of protection until she was fast asleep, neither did God. Just as I had my hidden spot near Courtney's place of misery, God remained in a hidden spot not far from me.

It has been nearly eighteen years since I discovered that late-night treasure. In the days and nights, joys and sorrows since, I continue to discover that silence grows from my being still. I find out more about who God is. How it happens I can't explain, but it does. I let go and be still, and God reveals himself to me. When I hold on and refuse to be still, I miss out on what God wants to reveal to me. If you and I do not "come to a complete stop" and find time for silence, we'll just have to wonder who God really is.

Be still, and know that I am God.

*Psalm 46:10*

---

*DEAR LORD, even as I begin this prayer, I'm tempted to fill it with lots of words. Teach me stillness without distraction. Show me how to hear your silent words. Amen.*

# 13
# Worshiping Him

Imagine what you would do if you were outside walking and suddenly the rocks on the ground started to sing. What if the mountains broke forth in worship to God? We may not know how we would respond, but the Bible tells us why they would be doing it. The rocks would cry out in praise because God's people were remaining quiet.

It was the apostle Luke who recorded this graphic description. As Jesus entered Jerusalem before his crucifixion, onlookers honored him by spreading their clothes on the road. The disciples joined in the worshipful moment and began to loudly rejoice and praise God for all the mighty works they had seen. Then the Pharisees called to Jesus from the crowd and asked him to rebuke his disciples. Jesus responded with a clear emphasis on the importance of worship: "I tell you that if these [people] should keep silent, the stones would immediately cry out" (Luke 19:40).

Worship does not need an occasion or a reason. It is spontaneous and happens as the overflow of a loving and grateful heart. Joni Eareckson Tada has spent more than thirty years as a quadriplegic as the result of a diving accident. I once heard her say, "The only thing worse than not having arms to raise and praise the Lord is having arms and not doing it."

John Calvin wrote, "The ceremony of lifting up our hands in prayer is designed to remind us that we are far removed from God, unless our thoughts rise upward; as it is said in the psalm, 'Unto thee, O Lord, do I lift up my soul.'"[1]

Virginia Whitman, author of *Mustard: The Excitement of Prayer Answered*, wrote: "It is a good practice to begin every prayer with thanksgiving and praise. (The former rejoices in the gift, the latter in the Giver.)"[2] Her words echo the pattern of Psalm 100:4 (NIV): "Enter his gates with thanksgiving and his courts with praise; give thanks to him and praise his name." The Hebrew translation of that verse can add clarity to its truth: "You can get a quick audience with God by thanking Him, and praise will take you with Him into his enclosed yard."

Within the body of Christ, some people are called to preach, others to serve as missionaries, teachers, or evangelists. But all believers—every one of us—are called to worship God, and that happens through the discipline of thanksgiving and praise.

## THANKSGIVING

Thanksgiving is the expression of gratitude. It means thanking God for what he has done. Specifically, thanksgiving involves listing blessings and benefits from God and saying thank-you to him for his kindness.

Joshua talked to God regularly. Chapter 12 of the book of Joshua lists thirty-one victories God had already given Joshua and the people—thirty-one battles they'd already won.

Think about that. Joshua stopped and listed everything so the people could remember what God had done. What if you do the same right now. Stop reading, and number from one to thirty-one on a blank piece of paper. Now, brainstorm every good thing that God has done for you—physically, emotionally, spiritually, or financially. Include thanks for things God has done for others you know and love.

If you're like me, you don't have to work too hard to come up with thirty-one things you're grateful for. Taking time to express thanks to God is not something you should reserve for that special holiday in November. He wants us to come into his gates every day with thanksgiving. Doing so does two things: First, as you *give* thanks for thirty-one things God has already done for you, you develop a heart that is both grateful and trusting. You begin to realize that since God has been so good to you already, he'll continue to be good to you when you face battles number thirty-two and thirty-three. Second, when God *receives* your thanks, he knows that he can entrust you with more mature things, and he goes to work on the new challenges you face. Dare to enter his courts with thanksgiving. It's a habit worth developing. God will love it, and you'll like what it does to you.

## PRAISE

Thankfulness naturally leads to praise. E. M. Bounds writes, "Gratitude arises from the contemplation of the goodness of God. . . . Praise is so distinctly and definitely wedded to prayer, so inseparably joined, that they cannot be divorced."[3]

While *thanksgiving* means showing gratitude to God for what he has done, *praise* means adoring God for who he is. Praise allows us to verbalize our love for God just because he is God. Miller writes, "Praise is the language of spiritual lovers. It is the joy of such togetherness, the clock disappears."[4]

Thanksgiving gets us into God's presence, but praise takes us to special places of intimacy with him. Intercession could be thought of as the highest form of prayer, but praise is the highest form of worship. Praise should be the major goal of our prayers and the purpose for our living. We should live to give God praise.

Jehoshaphat, King of Judah, is the man I remember when I think of praise. In 2 Chronicles 20 we see how he faced a huge battle against the Ammonites and the Moabites. He prayed and fasted, then "he appointed those who should sing to the Lord, and who should praise the beauty of holiness, as they went out before the army and were saying: 'Praise the Lord, for His mercy endures forever'" (2 Chronicles 20:21).

God did the rest. When God's people began to sing and praise the Lord, the Lord sent ambushes and defeated the enemy.

Do you ever think of praise as a weapon against your enemies? Put this book down again, and think about one huge challenge you're facing. What Ammonites or Moabites are you up against? Look up to God and sing a praise song. Open your Bible to a psalm and read it aloud to the Father. Tell him how glorious he is.

Paul and Silas sang praises in jail, and the prison door swung open (Acts 16:25-26). While bringing the ark of the covenant into Jerusalem, King David praised God with all of his strength (2 Samuel 6:12-15). When Jesus was about to go to Gethsemane and to the cross, he and his disciples sang a hymn (Matthew 26:30). Their praise helped them to focus on the One who gives ultimate victory.

Your praise does too.

## MAKING WORSHIP A WAY OF LIFE

Once we develop the habit of daily worshiping God, we can't wait to talk to him about everything. Lovers discuss even the most incidental events of their day; so it is with the ministry of thanksgiving and praise. To make the most of your worship times, try these suggestions:

### Allow Your Worship to Be Both Spontaneous and Structured

Make a habit of building thanksgiving and praise into every one of your prayers, but also offer thanksgiving and praise spontaneously. I like to sing praise songs when I drive. I thank God every time my plane lands safely, and I praise him for who he is. A great example of spontaneous praise is Mary's song in Luke 1:46-47: "My soul magnifies the Lord, and my spirit has rejoiced in God my Savior." Mary was overwhelmed by the Lord's goodness to her, and she sang one of the most profound songs of praise found in Scripture. You can no more stop praise from a thankful heart than you can stop the water flowing over Niagara Falls.

God created us to worship him. Praise will be our activity when we gather around the throne in heaven. So practice now, with both structured and spontaneous worship.

## Do It Aloud

Praise gives words to our love for God. Speaking aloud while praying is important, and this is especially true with praise. We have no problem yelling at a ball game on Saturday. Why do we tend to stand like statues on Sunday morning during our songs of praise? Vocalize your love for God. He knows your deepest thoughts, but he loves it when we offer the "sacrifice of praise . . . the fruit of our lips" (Hebrews 13:15).

## Sing

One night I walked into my bathroom and wept from the depths of my soul in prayer. Suddenly, while sitting on the floor, leaning against the wall, and wondering what we would do regarding the problem, I began to sing a hymn. It didn't sound pretty to me, with my voice cracking and weak, but it did sound pretty to God. I know that. Praise helped me lift my eyes off the overwhelming circumstances to the One who was in control no matter what happened around us.

Not only have I hidden God's Word in my heart; I have songs hidden there too. Whether they're old hymns or contemporary choruses, I always find that something powerful happens when I praise God in song. Missionary and writer Amy Carmichael said, "I believe truly that Satan cannot endure it and so slips out of the room where there is a true song. . . . Prayer rises more easily, more spontaneously, after one has let those wings, words, and music carry one out of oneself into that upper air."[5]

Paul spoke of "making melody" in our hearts to the Lord and of singing spiritual songs (Ephesians 5:19; Colossians 3:16). Spiritual songs come from the heart. Sing a favorite portion of Scripture the next time you pray. Create the melody in your heart, and offer that song as a gift of praise to God. It will add a new dimension to your worship.

## Count Your Blessings

Joshua left us a great example for counting our blessings. We can make it a regular habit to think about the innumerable ways our heavenly Father has blessed us. Instead of focusing on your problems and undesirable circumstances, lift your eyes to the omnipotent, omnipresent God you serve. Remember the words of an old hymn by Johnson Oatman Jr.?

> *Count your blessings, name them one by one,*
> *Count your blessings, see what God has done!*[6]

There's always time for thanksgiving.

## Don't Ask

Worship is about loving God for his goodness. Worship doesn't involve begging. Instead, we lay aside our requests so we can fellowship with him. Dr. Harold Lindsell writes, "In adoration no promises are claimed, no long lists of answered prayers are recited; no proof is needed to reveal the power of God to hear and to answer prayer; no snares are attached to its practice. It has its own efficacious completeness, so that if adoration alone is engaged in, the aspiring soul needs nothing more. It has already found God. That is enough."[7]

I've already mentioned the words to several songs in this chapter, but allow me to refer to one more. Annie Herring, formerly of the group Second Chapter of Acts, sings this one, written by Dennis Jernigan:

> *And with our hands lifted high,*
> *We come before You and sing.*
> *With our hands lifted high,*
> *We come before You rejoicing.*
> *With our hands lifted high to the sky*
> *And the world wonders why,*
> *We'll just tell them we're loving our King.*
> *We'll just tell them we're loving our King.*[8]

Worship is just that, loving our King. Getting an audience with God by thanking him and going with him into his enclosed yard through praise. That's what worship is all about!

---

*DEAR LORD, I come into your gates with thanksgiving and into your courts with praise. I know that thanksgiving will get me an audience with you and praise will get me intimacy. How wonderful you are! I bow at your feet, O glorious Father. Let me live to worship you from this point on. Amen.*

# 14

## Understanding His Will

"God spoke to me. . . ." "I felt God direct me. . . ." "God impressed something on my heart. . . ."

When I was editor of Focus on the Family's *Single-Parent Family* magazine, I often published articles from writers who used words like these when referring to God's instructions to them. One day I received a stinging letter from a reader who wrote, "What? Do you all have a 1-800 number to hear directly from God? If you do, please pass it on so I can hear from God too."

Most of us have felt similar frustrations about not knowing God's will regarding decisions we face or crises we encounter. We may have felt envious of those who always appear to know what God wants them to do. And maybe we've felt disappointed after we've asked for God's guidance in a specific area and then not felt that we received it: "Where should I work?" "Whom should I marry?" "When should I make the move?" "Lord, what is your will?"

My children know me well, at times better than they would like to. They know me so well, in fact, that in most cases they could tell you what I would say about something even if I weren't there to answer for myself. This same privilege is available to us as children of God. One of the great benefits of really knowing God is getting to know his mind, too. That means understanding what his will is regarding issues we face, and it is a blessing God offers to those who really know him. Consider these promises from the Scriptures:

- "I will instruct you and teach you in the way you should go; I will guide you with My eye." (Psalm 32:8)
- "Your ears shall hear a word behind you, saying, 'This is the way, walk in it.'" (Isaiah 30:21)
- "I am the Lord your God, who teaches you to profit, who leads you by the way you should go." (Isaiah 48:17)
- "The steps of a good man are ordered by the Lord, and He delights in his way. Though he fall, he shall not be utterly cast down; for the Lord upholds him with His hand." (Psalm 37:23-24)
- "Do not remember the former things, nor consider the things of old. Behold, I will do a new thing, now it shall spring forth; shall you not know it? I will even make a road in the wilderness and rivers in the desert." (Isaiah 43:18-19)

Once when I was holding tenaciously to verses like these and seeking God's will for some important decisions, a wise man I know told me, "When you're seeking God's will, it's honestly easier to find it than not. God wants us to know his will more than we want to know it."

In the years since, I've found those words to be true. Our job in finding God's will is to seek; his part is to provide the direction.

## HEARING GOD'S VOICE

The Bible tells us that if we pray according to God's will, he hears us (1 John 5:14). Finding his will means discovering what God wants in a particular situation. Finding God's direction means we exchange our will and what we want for his will and what he wants. Finding God's will means hearing and understanding with clarity, as though he had called us on the phone. Finding God's will means talking things over with God, understanding his plans, and then carrying out those plans to the best of our ability.

Ever since Bible times God has spoken to his people. Paul told the Colossian church that he was continuing to pray that they would be "filled with the knowledge of [God's] will in all wisdom and spiritual understanding" (Colossians 1:9).

God loves seeing his people seek his will, and then he loves showing his will to his people. He loves making his voice known to those who want to hear it. He loves hearing from those who really want to know him more: "Speak, Lord. I'm listening." And each time he speaks to us, we learn to know him just a little more.

God speaks to us in three basic ways—through circumstances, through the Holy Spirit, and through his Word.

## God Speaks through Circumstances

God sometimes tells us what to do through unique situations and circumstances. These usually occur in relationship to specific prayers we have prayed about a matter.

I've learned to notice the circumstances of God's leading since I was a young woman. One time I especially remember was the summer of 1973. I had two quarters of school to go before finishing my bachelor's degree, and I was out of money. Spring student teaching had meant an end to the three jobs I'd carried to put myself through school. Now my choices were two: work through the summer, save my money, and graduate the following spring, or go to summer school, graduate in December, and then get a full-time teaching job.

I prayed about the decision along with my parents. When I didn't get any clear direction from God, my sister Connie and I drove to a neighboring town and applied at a factory that was paying a good salary for summer secretarial work. I must admit that I felt far more qualified than Connie. She was two years younger and a sophomore in college, and I was a senior. I could type faster than she could and could even hold my own in taking dictation.

A week passed, then two weeks, and we heard nothing from the factory. The first day of summer classes came and went. Crying, I called my mother from my part-time job with a car dealer: "I'm not going to find work *or* get to take summer classes. What am I going to do?"

I had barely hung up the phone and wiped my eyes when the phone rang. It was Connie. The factory had called to offer the job—not to me but to her! They had decided they'd hire someone who could come back trained the following summer too.

Through giant tears this time I ran through the usual litany of those who feel as if God has not come through for them. Just as I was at the peak of my pity party, the phone rang a second time. It was the dean of the school of education at the university, for whom I had done some earlier research. "Could you stop by the office?" he said.

I excused myself from work and drove to the campus. When I walked into the room, the dean asked me to sit down.

"I have some more research I would like for you to do for me this summer and fall if you're available, and my wife sent me these to give to you."

I opened the envelope and found certificates good for free classes at the university. She had received the certificates for hosting student teachers. I counted them—just enough to cover every class I needed in order to graduate in December.

As a summer secretary, nineteen-year-old Connie earned more money than she ever had before. I enrolled in summer classes, finished my degree at the end of the year, and became the first college graduate in my family's history. More important than the degree, however, was what I had learned once again about the trustworthiness of God's guidance.

God closes doors for his people that no one can open, but he opens windows that no one can close. Those windows are the circumstances through which he makes his will known.

## God Speaks through the Holy Spirit

In chapter 1 we read how Jesus told his disciples that he would leave us the Holy Spirit to guide and direct us (John 14:16-17). When he warned his disciples that they would face arrest for the sake of the gospel, he told them not to worry about what to say because the Holy Spirit would give them wisdom at that moment. The inner voice of the Holy Spirit would guide them (Matthew 10:19-20).

So it is for believers today. The Holy Spirit still guides and directs us, but it is important that we know how he works:

### God speaks from inside us.

Jesus said, "The kingdom of God is within you" (Luke 17:21). God dwells in human vessels, so that makes us temples of God (1 Corinthians 6:19). Since he lives inside us, he also speaks from inside us. This means we don't have to hear an audible voice to receive guidance. But when he speaks, our spirits will hear if we stay in tune with him and learn to recognize his leading.

### God's peace always accompanies his guidance.

We can distinguish the voice of God from counterfeits by the peace we feel and the confirmation we get. When I feel that God is telling me something, but I'm not sure about it, my mom tells me to put it "on the shelf" for a while. I've often asked God to confirm his will to me in one or two other ways. "The wisdom that comes from heaven is first of all pure and full of quiet gentleness" (James 3:17, TLB).

Peace is a reliable test of divine guidance.

*God speaks through various means.*

God always speaks through his Word, but Scripture tells us that sometimes he chooses to speak through visions, dreams, and prophecies. God spoke to Moses in a cloud (Numbers 11:25). He spoke to Elijah in a still, small voice (1 Kings 19:12). God speaks of his creative power through the wonders of his creation: "The heavens declare the glory of God; the skies proclaim the work of his hands. Day after day they pour forth speech; night after night they display knowledge. There is no speech or language where their voice is not heard" (Psalm 19:1-3, NIV).

God has often spoken to me through dreams. Most of them come early in the morning just after I begin to wake up. And when he's behind something I dream, I always know it. There's no mistaking God's urgency through dreams. The mistake we can make in hearing God's will through visions, dreams, or prophecies is to put all our stock in them to the exclusion of instruction from Scripture or other methods that confirm.

*God's guidance often comes unexpectedly.*

Sometimes I have heard from God when I least expected it. One Friday morning I stood in my kitchen fixing my lunch. I was teaching junior high English at the time while carrying fourteen graduate course hours, coaching girls' track, and studying for my oral exams, which would take place the next Monday. I prayed, "God, I can't teach in the condition I'm in. Please give me your peace." As I stood there, it was as though a sheet descended over me, and all the stress I had felt before was gone. I more than made it through the next few days. I passed my orals with peace in my heart. That event of answered prayer was so real that in the years to come, I would ask God to do it again. But it has never happened in the same way. God often meets us unexpectedly to get his point across.

*God's guidance does not show us the future.*

We learn to become content with a tiny view. God doesn't show us the whole future because knowing it would tend to weaken, not strengthen, our faith. We would dread every day before a heart attack came if we knew about it five years beforehand. Someday God may give us an aerial view, but for now we get the future one step at a time.

*God's Word is the final judge in all guidance.*

God never, ever tells his people something that runs contrary to his Word. Whatever method you use in seeking God's will, begin and end by looking to his Word for instruction: "Holy men of God spoke as they were moved by the Holy Spirit" (2 Peter 1:21), and "All Scripture is God-breathed and is useful for teaching, rebuking, correcting and training in righteousness" (2 Timothy 3:16, NIV).

You can't get it on higher authority than when you have God's Word on something!

## God Speaks through His Word

Some matters are clearly God's will, such as our salvation and our living a holy life (e.g., God forbids adultery in Exodus 20:14). Again, God's Word is the foundation of all guidance.

Recently our son-in-law, Doug, thought he had a job as minister of music pinned down in a particular place, so he declined an offer from another church. But when the "for sure" job fell through, Doug and our daughter Angie called us, disappointed and fearful about what they would do. Dave and I prayed for them and sent them an e-mail containing some of the Scripture verses found in this chapter. Within the month Doug received an invitation to check out a job near his mother's home. He was interviewed and accepted the job. God directed them through the words of Scripture and then through the peace and confirmation they found.

Here are some of the assurances we have from Scripture regarding knowing God's will:

*Rest in God. Don't be fearful.*

"Do not fear, for I am with you; do not be dismayed, for I am your God. I will strengthen you and help you; I will uphold you with my righteous right hand" (Isaiah 41:10, NIV). "You will keep in perfect peace him whose mind is steadfast, because he trusts in you" (Isaiah 26:3, NIV). As my wise friend told me, God wants us to know his will more than we want to know it. We can find that will with confidence, or we can find it with fear. The choice is ours, but we don't have to be afraid.

*Wait on God. Don't be in a hurry.*

"In repentance and rest is your salvation, in quietness and trust is your strength" (Isaiah 30:15, NIV). I once heard a sermon about a man who needed to buy a second car for his teenage children to drive. He felt God telling him to wait, but pressure from his family kept him looking. He went to the used-car lot, drove what he felt he could afford, and was walking around taking a last look while the salesman drew up the paperwork, when God spoke to him: *Do you want this, or do you want my best?*

The man didn't buy the car that day, and later someone gave him the keys to an automobile that was way above his price range. Why? Because he chose not to get in a hurry while he waited for God's direction.

*Seek God's guidance. Don't jump ahead.*

"Because the Sovereign Lord helps me, I will not be disgraced. Therefore have I set my face like flint, and I know I will not be put to shame" (Isaiah 50:7, NIV).

God's leading means just that—we follow his lead. When we jump ahead by failing to wait on his direction or go-ahead, we cease following his lead, and we can really mess up the plans that God has as we move forward.

My glue gun ran out of glue once when my children were young. Rather than wait to hear my instruction, Clint decided to go ahead and fix it, and fix it he did—by pouring Elmer's glue into the nozzle.

Going ahead with your will means going ahead of God's leading. It will never, ever be the best thing to do, so while you seek his guidance, be careful to wait on him.

### Trust God. Don't doubt his faithfulness.

"My word that goes out from my mouth . . . will not return to me empty, but will accomplish what I desire and achieve the purpose for which I sent it" (Isaiah 55:11, NIV).

When I was in college being trained as a teacher, I learned that young children need frequent reinforcement to keep them working hard. As they mature, however, the teacher makes the reinforcement less frequent and eventually withdraws it altogether. The teacher's goal is for the children's motivation to come from within themselves rather than from an outside source.

During my younger days in the Lord, he made his will more obvious because I needed that kind of reinforcement to keep me going. Maturity in the Lord means that we shouldn't need constant affirmation from him. We should keep trusting and cease doubting because we have experienced his faithfulness in the past. God is faithful for *his* name's sake, not ours.

### Rejoice in God. Don't focus on the problem.

"You will go out in joy and be led forth in peace; the mountains and hills will burst into song before you, and all the trees of the field will clap their hands. Instead of the thornbush will grow the pine tree, and instead of briers the myrtle will grow. This will be for the Lord's renown, for an everlasting sign, which will not be destroyed" (Isaiah 55:12-13, NIV).

I call this my lemonade-from-lemons verse. I found it in the early days of raising my children alone. It tells me that God will make good things out of bad. I sat in a board meeting recently with several people with whom I served in single-parent ministry. Many of them were or still are single parents themselves. Over dinner we compared stories of how our children are doing these days. I thought, *Did someone forget to tell these godly, accomplished children that they came from single-parent homes?* However, I couldn't help but think of two of my own children, who are still away from God. What I have is God's promises that he will bless my offspring. What I do is continue to trust in those promises and do what comes next for my children as God gives me wisdom.

An artist doesn't concentrate on the messy colors around her. She focuses instead on the finished picture. When I fix a large family dinner, I'm able to better handle the disheveled kitchen when I think more about the delicious dishes I'm creating.

## CONFIRM, CONFIRM, CONFIRM

As I was conducting research for my doctoral dissertation, I was taught to triangulate my data. That means that I had to be sure that the things I observed in one setting could be replicated in another. When I saw something happen in more than one time and place, I could be reasonably sure my observation was valid.

The same is true when it comes to seeking God's will. God guides us in all three ways: through circumstances, through the Holy Spirit, and through his Word, but our greatest assurance comes when we can triangulate the same answer from all three sources. If you are seeking God's will for a decision you are facing and the Holy Spirit seems to be speaking to your heart, be sure to confirm what you are sensing by looking at the circumstances and at God's Word as the ultimate source. All three aspects must function in harmony to assure true guidance. Only then should you move forward in a particular direction.

I would like to leave you with one more caution as you seek the will of God. Sometimes we can confuse God's wisdom with our own desires or even with deception from Satan. When you think God is speaking to you, be sure it's really God. Be sure it's not your flesh or, worse yet, Satan directing you in a certain way. Triangulate your data, be sure it lines up with God's Word, and talk honestly to God about your desire to find his perfect will for you.

Missionary and writer Amy Carmichael wrote, "Holy Spirit, think through me till Your ideas are my ideas." That should be our prayer as we seek God's will. Just as a child really knows his mother and knows just how she would feel about something, we can get to know our Father's mind too. Let it be our prayer that God will think through us until his ideas are ours.

---

*DEAR LORD, think through me until your ideas are my ideas. You said, "I am the good shepherd; I know my sheep and my sheep know me." You tell us in your Word that your sheep hear your voice and that they will not follow a stranger. If dumb sheep can hear, understand, and obey their shepherd's voice, so can I. Help me to listen to what you are saying through circumstances, through the Holy Spirit, and through your Word. Teach me to hear and follow your gentle leading. Amen.*

# PART THREE

# TAKING THE INSIDE OUT

The people who *know* their God shall
be strong, and carry out great exploits.*

*Daniel 11:32*

*emphasis added

# 15

# Moving from Knowing to Doing

We spent the first third of this book talking about an intimate, passionate, committed spiritual journey by examining Jesus' words to Philip: "Have I been with you so long, and yet you have not *known* Me?" (John 14:9, emphasis added).

After we unmasked our intimacy, ignited our passion, and renewed our commitment to God, we set out to know him as we took our place on the inside of a knowing relationship with Christ: "That I may *know* Him" (Philippians 3:10, emphasis added).

Through the difficult work of discipline, we sealed our commitment with a renewed devotion to prayer, study, fasting, being still, worshiping, and understanding his voice. That brings us to where we are now and the opportunity to take what we've learned on the inside *with* God to the outside, where we can share our knowing relationship with others. This is where the rubber meets the road.

Remember Much-Afraid? Once she had finally arrived on the High Places, the Shepherd changed her name to Grace and Glory. But it was not the Shepherd's plan to have her remain on the High Places forever. He let her know when it was time to take what she'd learned back down into the valley: "'The High Places,' answered the Shepherd, 'are the starting places for the journey down to the lowest place in the world. When you have hinds' feet and can go "leaping on the mountains and skipping on the hills," you will be able as I am, to run down from the heights in gladdest self-giving and then go up to the mountains again. You will be able to mount to the High Places swifter than eagles, for it is only up on the High Places of Love that anyone can receive the power to pour themselves down in an utter abandonment of self-giving.'"[1]

As long as no one is looking, it's easier to revel in the mountaintop experiences with God as we talk to him, read his love letters, and apply his Word to our lives. But "ministry in" should take place for only so long before we begin "ministry out." Our mountaintop experiences are preparatory "starting places," as Hannah Hurnard calls them, and they are designed to make us effective down in the valley, where our *knowing* manifests itself in *doing*. The goal of knowing God is to equip us to do the jobs he calls us to do: "The people who *know* their God shall be strong, and carry out great exploits" (Daniel 11:32, emphasis added).

We're not the first to make the trip up to the mountain, and we're not the first to need to bring the experience back down to the people below. We can look at examples from the Scriptures to see ways that others turned their knowing into doing.

## MOUNT HOREB: MOSES AND ELIJAH

"The Lord our God spoke to us in Horeb, saying: 'You have dwelt long enough at this mountain'" (Deuteronomy 1:6). On Mount Horeb, also called Sinai, Moses experienced his burning-bush encounter with God (Exodus 3). God also presented the Ten Commandments to Moses on Mount Horeb. And it became the point from which the Israelites set forth to conquer the Promised Land. Many years later on Mount Horeb, Elijah received a vision instructing him to anoint a successor (1 Kings 19:8, 16).

God had great encounters with his people on Mount Horeb. It became a place where people got to really know God. From there, men and women were filled, inspired, and instructed. The Israelites gathered at the foot of Mount Horeb while God spoke to them and gave them his law. Fire and smoke covered the mountain. Lightning flashed, and loud trumpet blasts pierced the air. The ground at the foot of the mountain shook, and the people trembled in fear (Exodus 19:16-25).

As important as it was for God's people to have this inspiring encounter with him, God had not rescued them from Egypt in order for them to settle around a mountain in the wilderness and grow fat on the sweet things of God. He had delivered them so that they could conquer the Promised Land. He wanted them to explore new places and share their new knowledge with others. He wanted them to whet others' appetites for knowing God. God wanted to demonstrate his power to the Israelites so that they would trust him in their conquest of Canaan. They had been long enough at Mount Horeb; now it was time to get to work.

## MOUNT HERMON: PETER, JAMES, AND JOHN

Peter, James, and John also had a mountaintop experience. Just before Jesus delivered the demon-possessed boy we talked about in chapter 11, he took a trip with his three closest disciples to what scholars believe was Mount Hermon, also called the Mount of Transfiguration. This inner-circle trio was so impressed with what they saw on the mountain that Peter was prepared to freeze the moment by building shelters and residing there forever. But the Lord knew that a demon-possessed boy and many others needed their assistance down below (Matthew 17:14-18). So he got them ready, then sent them out.

Why did Jesus take only Peter, James, and John with him and not all twelve disciples? I mentioned in chapter 3 that I thought their passion was part of what singled them out. Whatever it was, it exposed their desire to know Jesus in a more personal way. Peter, James, and John wanted a deeper walk. When these guys dared to make the extra effort and go an extra mile with Jesus, Jesus allowed them to see him transfigured: "His face shone like the sun, and His clothes became as white as the light" (Matthew 17:2). The terrified disciples fell on their faces. When the Lord told the disciples to get up, they saw no one except Jesus, for Moses and Elijah had departed.

*Transfigure* means to "change the form or appearance."[2] Jesus changed in form and showed a side of himself he had never revealed to anyone before. That's why we understand Peter's desire to freeze the moment and make it last by building booths or shelters.

I'm sure the two other supernatural attendees on Mount Hermon that day, prophets Moses and Elijah, understood because of similar struggles they had faced on their own mountain, Mount Horeb, hundreds of years before. Nothing had really changed. Humanity was still striving to find good things and hold on to them, but God was sending his people out to share these truly good things with others.

Not until they saw Jesus in this way were Peter, James, and John prepared to take the good news about Jesus to others. If they had only built a tabernacle to memorialize the experience up top, no one down below would have benefited. If Moses had framed the Ten Commandments he received high on Mount Horeb and had kept them there, the people down below never would have heard the message that the whole experience with Moses was designed to bring.

At times, God gives his people mountaintop experiences in which he reveals himself in a new way. He transfigures, or changes form, and shows us something more and better and bigger about himself than we have experienced before. We may wish we could spend the rest of our lives basking in the glow of our mountaintop experiences, but those encounters are God's way of preparing us for the battles and opportunities for ministry that await us. He teaches us, and then we teach others.

## YOUR MOUNT AND MINE

Like Peter, James, and John, we wandered into the realm of the inner circle with God the minute we decided we wanted to really know him. If we had lived in Jesus' day, he might have included us in his trip to Mount Hermon. We took a step toward knowing God, and he met us there. Now when we read his Word, he reveals new things to us. Our prayers can be more open and direct and rewarding. We can feel a closeness to God we've never felt before. We can enjoy a whole new depth in our Christian walk.

Yet all of us can grow fearful and uncertain when it's time to share what we've found with others. We suddenly begin to wonder whether what we've found is real and enduring or whether others will see us as having gone off the deep end when we talk about the supernatural things of God. Naysayers sometimes describe those who have just come down from the mountaintop as being "so heavenly minded that they're no earthly good."

So how do we become "earthly good"? We can avoid some of the obstacles that keep others from hearing our message by keeping at least three things in mind: our growth, our motives, and our opportunities.

### Our Growth

People watching us should see that we are different when we come down the mountain from the way we were when we went up. Let's say a mother finds a new relationship with Christ. Her going-through-the-motions faith has now become a vibrant, intimate one. Her business-as-usual encounters have turned passionate. Her sitting-on-the-fence involvement has transformed into solid commitment. Mom wants the children she loves to find the God she knows, but they don't respond—until Mom gets some bad news and responds differently from the way she did before. Without speaking a word, Mom has demonstrated that she's handling life in a new way, and her children are attracted to its source.

Mountaintop encounters should change us—not just parts of us but all of us. Close encounters with Jesus can't help but rub off some of his character onto who we are. Each time we see him for who he really is, we find opportunities to become more like him. As we become more like God, he uses the change in us to interest others when life doesn't turn out as they had planned.

The more time we spend on the mountain, the more God reveals new facets of who he is. The more we see these new facets of God, the more like him we become. The more we see of him, the more it should transform us. As a result, God uses us to reflect his character in reaching the world and to whet people's appetites to know him for themselves.

**Our Motives**
In chapter 2 we talked about the importance of checking our hands for sin and our hearts for wrong motives. Of course we want to keep sin out of our lives. But it's not always obvious to us whether our motives are right or not. It's easy to say we want God to get the glory from what we do, but it's not so easy to actually follow through with that. Again, the following questions and answers can help us focus on maintaining proper motives as we serve God.

- **Whom** do I want to be glorified from my journey to know God? God. I want him to be exalted, not me, so that people will be drawn to him.
- **What** is my goal for embarking on this journey to know God? I want to be changed, transformed more and more into God's likeness.
- **When** will I use this new information and experience? Only in those situations and for those people whom God brings across

my path. I don't have to make the opportunities. God provides them, and I simply need to respond.

- **Why** do I want to really know God? Because I love him and have discovered just how much and how unconditionally he loves me. I have "found the good part," and that can never be taken away from me.

When motives stay pure on the inside, they'll come across pure on the outside, and God will receive the glory.

## Our Opportunities

During the Transfiguration, Peter and the others were very sleepy. It wasn't until they were completely awake that they saw Jesus' glory and the two men with him (Luke 9:32).

On a recent airplane trip I sat in an aisle seat next to the bulkhead. After about thirty minutes, the young man in the window seat and I began to talk. He spoke of his faith, about his upcoming retirement as a physician in the military, and about how his wife and two children had moved ahead to their new home, where they would be near family. He went on to describe the challenges that separation had brought. He saw the four intervening months until they were all together again as a curse and drudgery, and he described all the negative impacts the decision to be apart could cause.

Unexpectedly I heard myself telling him things I hadn't prepared to say. I was surprised as I talked about the opportunity he would have in the silence of his home to grow in his faith and in his leadership abilities. On a piece of paper I listed books he could read and parts of the Bible he could study. I talked about the needs he would find once he rejoined his family and how rare it is to have the kind of opportunities for quiet growth he would have in the weeks ahead. The man appeared to awaken to an aspect of his faith that hadn't registered with him before. God wanted to prepare him in the quiet mountaintop experience for the public responsibilities he would face below. The man became emotional as he talked about this new revelation and the divine appointment the two of us had had together.

I learned something new from that experience too. After I returned home that night, I thanked God for the chance he had given me to speak truth to this man. I acknowledged the honor it was to be an ambassador for Christ and asked him to keep my eyes open to the opportunities the valley provides. Then I became bolder and talked to God about also opening the eyes of others and asked him to keep those people showing up for those divine appointments. As I prayed for my children, relatives, and friends, I said, "God, bring three intimate, passionate, committed Christians around them every day to witness about you and to proclaim your name."

## Our Power

It all comes back to that other Helper Jesus gave us, which we discussed in chapter 1: "I will pray the Father, and He will give you another Helper, that He may abide with you forever—the Spirit of truth, whom the world cannot receive, because it neither sees Him nor knows Him; but you know Him, for He dwells with you and will be in you" (John 14:16-17).

God's Holy Spirit resides in us every moment of the day and night, and that gives us new power. The Bible tells us about several Greek words that mean power: *ischus, kratos, dunamis,* and *exousia.*

- *Ischus* refers to great bodily strength or physical power.
- *Kratos* denotes dominion, authority, or controlling power.
- *Dunamis* refers to energy or great force. Words such as *dynamic* and *dynamite* come from this root. God exerted *dunamis* ("dynamite power") when he raised Christ from the dead. *Dunamis* is also the source of the mighty works ordinary people could do: "With great power the apostles gave witness to the resurrection of the Lord Jesus" (Acts 4:33).

- *Exousia* describes the right or authority to use *dunamis*. Jesus gave his followers *exousia* to preach, teach, heal, and deliver. Though *exousia* describes our right or authority to use the *dunamis,* if we are not aware of that right, we fail to exercise it and strip it of the very power it represents.

Our pastor's wife once told me a story about power. She and her family had just moved to Colorado from Texas. Unaccustomed to snow, her husband had purchased a Jeep. Joyce tells how she was driving home with her daughter one day in a snowstorm when they slid into a ditch. She said she pressed on the accelerator but the wheels only spun in the gathering snow. She rocked and pushed till her own energy gave out. Then she remembered that the vehicle had four-wheel drive. She reached down, engaged the lever, pressed on the gas, and felt the Jeep pull out of the ditch and onto the road home.

Such is the case with God's power. *Dunamis* becomes available to us through *exousia,* and it happens on our mountaintop experiences with God. Our souls become convinced of the power God has given us. When we become convinced, we engage the right levers, and the *dunamis,* or "dynamite," becomes ours for the greater works God has for us to do. Peter, James, and John found it on the mountain, and it was that power that sustained and empowered them for the post-Resurrection, greater-works ministry Jesus would leave behind.

*Exousia* is delegated authority, the right to use *dunamis* to forgive, heal, and deliver those in the "valley." God the Father gave it to Jesus, and Jesus gave it to us through the Holy Spirit, who lives in us. We find the power on the mountain, and we unleash it in the valley.

So pack a lunch and head back into the valley. There's much to do there. There are many people to reach, and you have lots of power to do it. They need what you have. Most of all, they are going to want what you have found because "the people who know their God shall be strong, and carry out great exploits" (Daniel 11:32).

---

*LORD, I want to know you. Shatter my present perspective. Open my eyes to who you are as you did for your disciples on the Mount of Transfiguration. Give me a sense of the power and authority you have placed at my disposal, and then show me how to take it effectively down into the valley. Amen.*

# 16

# Lifting and Drawing: Evangelism

I sat in a Sunday school class recently as we studied Acts 1:8: "You will receive power when the Holy Spirit comes on you; and you will be my witnesses in Jerusalem, and in all Judea and Samaria, and to the ends of the earth" (NIV).

Our teacher asked, "How many of you have led someone to Christ?"

Only a few raised their hands. In response to the question of why we don't evangelize more, an almost unanimous answer sounded around the room: fear. Class members went on to describe their fear of offending, being rejected, or being inadequate.

I believe that Sunday school class is a microcosm of the larger body of Christ. It certainly pinpointed much of the reason our church hadn't been growing like it should. Our leadership had been praying and working on some changes because we knew of only twenty people who had come to Christ in our services during the previous year. Our pastor had recently reminded us that if an automobile corporation with a half-million-dollar budget (which was comparable to the budget at our church) only turned out twenty cars in twelve months, it would soon go under. This truth also applies to producing converts through evangelism. In his book *Disciples Are Made—Not Born,* author Walter Henrichsen describes a quote from Dawson Trotman, founder of the Navigators: "Activity is no substitute for production. Production is no substitute for reproduction. whatever ministry we are engaged in, it ought to be reproductive."[1]

Though the word *evangelism* does not appear in the Bible, *evangelist* does, and it means one who proclaims the mercy and grace of God. Evangelism as the great commission is a command for all of us, not just for those in the pulpit. Evangelism is the method Jesus gave us for advancing and growing the kingdom: reaching out to another person and proclaiming the mercy and grace of God. New believers then grow and involve themselves in the work of evangelism too.

Scholars tell us that the first church prior to Pentecost had only a few hundred believers. Three decades later, evangelism had multiplied that number so that by the beginning of the fourth century, when Constantine was converted to Christianity, the number of believers may have reached ten to twelve million, or one-tenth of the population of the Roman Empire.

Regardless of that kind of "numerical success," ask evangelists down through the centuries, and they would probably tell you that the work of evangelism isn't easy. Charles H. Spurgeon wrote: "It is not at all an easy calling [to be a soul-winner]. He does not sit in the arm chair and catch a fish. He has to go out in rough weather. If he that regardeth clouds will not sow, I am sure he that regardeth clouds will never fish. If we never do any work for Christ except when we feel up to the mark, we shall not do much. We must be always at it, until we wear ourselves out, throwing our whole soul into the work in all weather, for Christ's sake."[2]

Although evangelism doesn't come naturally, really knowing Jesus demands it. Believing that knowing means doing, the Hebrews integrated their knowledge of God into their everyday lives. Their actions echoed their beliefs. They demonstrated their knowledge of God by obeying his commands and sharing their faith with others.

It's time to expand your *knowledge of* Christ to *doing for* him. And obeying the great commission to go into the world and share the gospel of Christ is part of that doing.

## POWER SOURCE

Courtney came home from basketball practice one day and told me about a girl she had witnessed to on the basketball court. "What if I didn't say the right things?" Courtney said.

I saw her relief as I explained John 12:32 (NIV): "I, when I am lifted up from the earth, will draw all men to myself." That verse reminds us that it's our job to do the lifting—that is, to exalt Christ—and it's his job to do the drawing. Because of that truth, we don't have to rely on our sufficiency; we rely on the sufficiency of God.

Before we look at how to evangelize, let's remember one more time the source of our power. It's the Holy Spirit. Acts 1:8 stresses the role of the Holy Spirit in evangelizing too: "You will receive power when the Holy Spirit comes on you; and you will be my witnesses in Jerusalem, and in all Judea and Samaria, and to the ends of the earth" (NIV).

The Greek word translated "power" in this passage is *dunamis*. As we discovered in chapter 15, *dunamis* means energy or great force. The power to reach out to others with the good news of Jesus comes not from us but from the Holy Spirit, and he is sufficient. Therefore, we don't have to be fearful.

Another thing we need to understand is that the movement of the Holy Spirit is a mystery: "The wind blows wherever it pleases. You hear its sound, but you cannot tell where it comes from or where it is going. So it is with everyone born of the Spirit" (John 3:8, NIV).

Though we don't understand the whys and wherefores of the Holy Spirit, we do know that the Spirit is the One who gives us the urge to do the lifting and he is the One who draws people to Christ. God begins the search, and he completes it. Os Guinness writes, "The secret of seeking is not in our human ascent to God, but in God's descent to us. We start searching, but we end up being discovered. We think we are looking for something; we realize we are found by Someone."[3]

The Holy Spirit does the drawing, but there's much we can do to improve our lifting, and we can do this by following Jesus' example.

## JESUS' STYLE OF EVANGELISM

In John 4 we read the story of Jesus' encounter with the Samaritan woman at the well. I mentioned her in chapter 3 as an example of someone who was intimate and passionate but was not yet a committed follower of Christ. Jesus was en route to Galilee from Judea, but he went out of his way to go through Samaria. When he arrived, he sat down at a well to rest, and a Samaritan woman came on what she thought was a routine errand to draw water. Far from routine, however, it was an errand that would change her life.

Jesus asked the woman for a drink. Jews normally hated Samaritans and avoided them at all cost because of their "half-breed" status. So it is not surprising that the woman said, "How is it that You, being a Jew, ask a drink from me, a Samaritan woman?" (v. 9).

Jesus responded to her question by saying, "If you knew the gift of God, and who it is who says to you, 'Give Me a drink,' you would have asked Him, and He would have given you living water" (v. 10).

### Jesus Cultivated a Burden for the Lost

Jesus felt compassion for the lost and reached out to them at every turn. Though he was tired, he took time to touch the heart of the woman at the well. I saw a drama once in which the audience walked through various scenes. One of them was hell. Though it was fiction, my walk through this experience reminded me that people going to hell have faces. Some of them are real, often lovely people in our grocery stores or living next door. Others, also real, are often unlovely people who do us wrong. We're to cultivate a burden for the lost whether they're lovely or unlovely, friend or foe.

Cultivating a burden for the lost helps us forgive those who hurt us while also seeing the deeper issue of that person's need for Jesus. But Jesus didn't just *feel* compassion for others; he also did something about it. He followed his feelings with action. We should too. Of course we want to pray that God will give us a deep burden for those who don't know him, but we also need to pray for wisdom about how to act on that burden.

### Jesus Understood the Plight of the Lost

Jesus told the woman, "If you knew . . ." (v. 10). His response to her tells us a great deal about those without Christ. Unbelievers often don't know about the gift of salvation God offers them. They don't know who Jesus really is. When they become convinced of the gift as well as the Giver, they will often come to faith.

Our role is to "lift," Jesus' role is to "draw." As lifters, our goal is to inform our listeners of the free gift of salvation that Jesus offers, and to tell them who Jesus is and how he gave his life for the lost— every single, individual lost person—especially the one sitting in front of you.

### Jesus Found Them Where They Were

Jesus needed to go through Samaria on his journey. He was tired and sat by the well to rest. The woman came to the well, and Jesus met her there.

If Jesus had held a service at the local park, the woman would not have come. So Jesus went to where she was. When he arrived at the well, his weariness could have kept him from doing the work his Father had sent him to do. When I get on an airplane, even when I see opportunities to talk about Christ, I find it easy to let my need for rest supersede those opportunities. Jesus, on the other hand, went about his normal day, always aware of opportunities in his path. He didn't let his own physical needs take priority over the needs of the souls he encountered. Jesus not only met where they were, he rallied when it was time to minister to them.

### Jesus Spoke Their Language

Jesus didn't start citing the laws of Moses or discussing great eschatological ideas. Instead, he spoke naturally to the woman: "Give Me a drink" (v. 7).

He engaged her in conversation, and the woman responded, "You have nothing to draw with, and the well is deep. Where then do you get that living water?" (v. 11).

The woman's question says she wasn't yet tracking with Jesus, but she was asking the right questions. We'll see that happen, too, as we share our faith with others. The Bible tells us to "be ready to give a defense to everyone who asks you a reason for the hope that is in you" (1 Peter 3:15). Being ready means recognizing when listeners are asking the right questions. Being ready also means knowing how to respond to the questions by speaking their "language." Talk in ways they understand, and introduce them to the Answer, who will meet their greatest need—for Christ—as well as their felt needs, such as loneliness, rejection, or fear. Tell people what coming to Christ has meant to you or someone you know. Jesus said, "Whoever drinks the water I give him will never thirst. Indeed, the water I give him will become in him a spring of water welling up to eternal life" (John 4:14, NIV). Give your listeners a taste of that water.

### Jesus Established a Relationship

Not only did Jesus speak the woman's language to elicit her

responses, he made the right comments and asked the right questions to keep the dialogue and self-analysis going. Jesus told the woman to go get her husband, and she replied, "I have no husband" (v. 17).

Jesus let the woman know that he knew she'd had five husbands and the man she was now living with was not her husband. He knew this information about her, but when he didn't bang her over the head with it, she saw him as legitimate and trustworthy: "You are a prophet" (v. 19).

## Jesus Moved the Conversation from Temporal Issues to Eternal Ones

Jesus told the woman, "A time is coming and has now come when the true worshipers will worship the Father in spirit and truth, for they are the kind of worshipers the Father seeks" (v. 23, NIV).

Jesus was letting the woman know that her trip to the well that day was no regular errand but a divine appointment, that God knew her and loved her and wanted to change her life. God was seeking her to become one of his worshipers.

As you transition to discussing eternal issues, you can direct your listeners to the Bible. Bill Fay, author of *Share Jesus without Fear*, suggests having listeners read the following verses out loud:

- All have sinned and fall short of the glory of God. (Romans 3:23)
- The wages of sin is death, but the gift of God is eternal life in Christ Jesus our Lord. (Romans 6:23)
- Jesus declared, "I tell you the truth, no one can see the kingdom of God unless he is born again." (John 3:3, NIV)
- Jesus answered, "I am the way and the truth and the life. No one comes to the Father except through me." (John 14:6, NIV)
- If you confess with your mouth, "Jesus is Lord," and believe in

your heart that God raised him from the dead, you will be saved. For it is with your heart that you believe and are justi-fied, and it is with your mouth that you confess and are saved. (Romans 10:9-10, NIV)

- Here I am! I stand at the door and knock. If anyone hears my voice and opens the door, I will come in and eat with him, and he with me. (Revelation 3:20, NIV)[4]

Whether you use these or other verses, such as Ephesians 2:8-9; Acts 4:12; Romans 6:8; 2 Corinthians 5:17, 21; and Hebrews 9:27-28, take your listeners to God's Word. Let them read it aloud. The Bible says, "Faith comes by hearing, and hearing by the word of God" (Romans 10:17).

Know the verses you want to share, and then direct your listeners to a small Bible you carry with you at all times. Let them hear the truth from the eternal Word of God.

### Jesus Told the Woman Who He Was

Jesus had the woman's ear and her trust, and he met her right where she was. The time had come to let her know *who* he was. The woman talked about the Messiah she had heard was coming, and Jesus said, "I who speak to you am He" (John 4:26).

Tears come to my eyes as I remember Mr. France, an antiques dealer whom I led to Christ before he died of black lung. I think about Kurt, whom my husband led in the sinner's prayer as they sat in first class on an airplane descending into Colorado Springs.

*I who speak to you am He.* It was no longer I who was loving and reaching out to Mr. France, it was Jesus speaking through me. It wasn't Dave who witnessed to Kurt on the plane but Jesus himself using Dave to let Kurt know about his deep love and knowledge of him.

These words of Jesus were enough for the woman at the well:

She "left her waterpot, went her way into the city, and said to the men, 'Come, see a Man who told me all things that I ever did. Could this be the Christ?'" (vv. 28-29).

Immediately upon coming to Christ herself, the woman was responsible for leading others to him: "Many of the Samaritans of that city believed in Him because of the word of the woman who testified, 'He told me all that I ever did'" (v. 39).

Kurt and his wife now help teach a Sunday school class for new believers. We do the lifting, and Christ does the drawing. "And many more believed because of His own word" (v. 41).

## SOME DON'TS FOR EVANGELISM

We've looked at some dos to use in evangelism. We can borrow these from Jesus' own ministry. Before we leave the topic, though, I want to alert you to four don'ts as well:

### Don't Let Others Distract You

Immediately after Jesus had his supernatural encounter with the Samaritan woman, the disciples—not exactly heathens themselves—wondered why Jesus had even bothered to talk to a woman, much less a Samaritan woman. Their question reminds me of something I once heard a pastor say. As he walked with another pastor in a downtown area, he handed some money to someone who was begging.

"Don't do that," the other pastor said. "Next thing you know, he'll be coming to your church!"

But isn't that what it's all about? Jesus sat down with sinners because they needed him, and they usually knew it. If we don't stay on our toes, even well-meaning Christians can distract us from our mission to evangelize. They can persuade us that other ministry tasks are more important. But Jesus knew he had an appointment with the woman *that* day, not later, and he didn't let naysayers or local customs or policies or laws keep him from being about his Father's business.

## Don't Fail to Convey the Big Picture

When the woman left her watering pot behind, she didn't for a minute suspect that her conversation with Jesus was about a dipper of water or about moral choices she was making. Instead, Jesus lifted her eyes to eternal matters.

As I was getting ready to board a plane recently, they announced mechanical problems that required them to switch all our flights. Later that day I ended up in a seat beside a woman I'll call Sandra, a professor at a major university. She proceeded to tell me about her painful past, including the sexual abuse she endured from age three to sixteen at the hands of her father. She talked as though she'd now figured life out through therapy. She also described the world religions she'd studied. "I think it's Taoism I'm leaning toward," she said.

I asked Sandra where she thought she'd end up if our plane didn't make it to Colorado. When she said she didn't know about heaven or hell, I told her the two-minute version of my journey with God. She watched tears fill my eyes as I described the specifics of how God came through in my life and how I'd found a relationship instead of mere religion. I told her Jesus loved her so much he had seen to it that my plane was rerouted and that I was seated beside her.

Sandra didn't pray with me that day to receive Christ, but I believe she got the bigger picture—the beginning, middle, and end of the salvation message. He created us, we sinned, he forgives those who ask, he gives abundant life here on earth, he gives eternal life in heaven. I assured Sandra that he had her number. "I'll be praying for you that you'll realize how loved you really are and give your life to him."

"I believe you will," were Sandra's parting words.

It wouldn't have been enough just to appeal to Sandra's emotions or scare her or help her address a painful issue she was facing. To have done so would have only given her the kind of "spiritual experience" that Gordon MacDonald wrote about in our discussion in chapter 1—and it would have been short lived. I don't know when or if Sandra will ultimately accept Christ, but I do know she will never forget our appointment on the plane, when from 33,000 feet up, she got the aerial view of God's loving plan for all of humankind—including her.

## Don't Fall into Legalism

Jesus didn't exactly follow the letter of the law when reaching the Samaritan woman. If he had done what the clerics said, he would have sat in a synagogue and waited for the men to come and ask the questions, and they would have gone and told the women. Instead, Jesus went out and did ministry where ministry was.

We, too, must avoid the trap of legalism, both in tone and in content. Yet we mustn't portray God as a distant *tsk-tsking* God who will have nothing to do with seekers until they get their act together. That leads only to despair. Speak the truth in love.

## Don't Become Discouraged If Nothing Appears to Happen

Bible scholars tell us that it takes a number of times of hearing about Christ before a person actually comes to him. I've heard an average of seven times, and I've heard an average of twelve. Whatever that elusive number of witnessing contacts is, we are to be faithful for the moment. In 1 Corinthians 3:6 Paul wrote, "I planted the seed, Apollos watered it, but God made it grow" (NIV).

Sometimes we'll be planters and sometimes we'll be waterers, but we will *never* make the seed grow. God and only God does that. We do the lifting, and he does the drawing.

I have a friend, Susan, who witnessed to an atheist friend, Nancy, for more than twelve years. She did everything she had learned to do during her years growing up in a Christian home. Nothing seemed to make an impact on Nancy.

One day, however, Susan called me.

"Guess what," she said. "Some stranger just led Nancy to the Lord!"

Nancy left her watering pot behind when a stranger became the voice of Jesus. Susan had planted the seed and others had watered it, but God caused it to grow and bear fruit in Nancy's life.

Nancy still serves God today, some twenty years later, and constantly watches for opportunities to introduce others to Christ. She, too, has learned that if she does the lifting, Jesus will do the drawing.

---

*DEAR LORD, help me to be an effective lifter as I speak to others about you. Remind me that you are working in ways only you can understand. Release me from the fear of being offensive or being rejected or inadequate. Thank you for your salvation, which is available to everyone, and thank you for allowing me to have a part in sharing that plan of salvation with others. Amen.*

# *17*

# Multiplying Disciples

Isabel and I spend the Thursday lunch hour gathered around an office conference table talking about life and God's Word.

Our time together began one day when I went to an appointment at the office where Isabel worked. Three years earlier I had arrived on the day she had prayed the sinner's prayer with her boss. Throughout the following months, I periodically checked in with her to see how she was doing.

When I arrived for my appointment that day, I asked her how things were going. "Not so good," she said, and she briefed me on what was happening in her life. I asked her to have lunch with me the following Wednesday.

As I arrived to pick her up for our time together, I called her on my cell phone to let her know I was in the parking lot. She took a while to come out, and when she did, she was wearing sunglasses. Once in my car, she removed her glasses and showed me her tear-swollen eyes. We decided to get lunch at a drive-thru and sit in the car and talk and pray. Isabel poured out her heart. I have never seen anyone cry from such depths. Suddenly I heard myself say, "Isabel, if you don't eat, what happens?"

"I get weak and can't do my work," she said.

I explained the same was true for us spiritually. We need to eat to stay strong. Since Isabel's new birth in Christ three years earlier, she had remained in her former church (which did not challenge her to grow), had not found any support or Bible study groups that worked for her, and had continued to shoulder life's challenges alone. I offered to start meeting with her once a week to help her find spiritual nourishment, and I assigned the book of Philippians to start.

We began meeting together over Isabel's lunch hour once a week. I didn't bring an agenda. Instead, Isabel would come with notes, underlinings, and thoughts regarding the Bible assignment I had made. Her depth, insight, and ability to apply Scripture could be explained only as an act of the Holy Spirit. As she talked, I took her to other parts of Scripture that would add to her understanding. She continued to marvel at the relevance of certain verses. She expressed wonder at Bible characters whose experiences were similar to her own.

I have loved the Lord for a long time and taken part in lots of things I knew he wanted me to do. But nothing in my whole life has compared to what I have discovered during those times with Isabel and now with another woman who has joined us. We have added Cynthia Heald's Bible study *Becoming a Woman Who Loves* to our study time. This takes us into the Scriptures with a specific focus. Every time I leave that lunch hour with these women, it takes me awhile to come down. We have seen prayers answered, burdens removed, joy and confidence restored, and hope recaptured. Almost every time I return from our study time together, I bend Dave's ear (without betraying the women's confidence), as I describe God's unmistakable presence.

Isabel grows at least an inch in the Lord every time I see her. She now goes to the Word on her own to handle problems. She's beginning to reach beyond her own needs and minister to others. She seeks direction from God for specific challenges she faces. She's like a sponge, soaking in everything she can learn about the Lord. Her childlike faith and desire to please God surpass those of people I know who have been Christians for a long time. I think my favorite thing of all is when Isabel says to me, "I am absolutely sure that Jesus loves me and has a plan for me."

I see greatness in Isabel, and every time I take the time to nurture that greatness, I also come away blessed.

## EVANGELISM AND DISCIPLESHIP

I have never been so absolutely certain that I'm doing God's will as when I'm spending time with these two women. It's called discipleship, and in Jesus' final words before he ascended into heaven, he gave instructions to his followers to make disciples of people like Isabel: "Go and make disciples of all nations, baptizing them in the name of the Father and of the Son and of the Holy Spirit" (Matthew 28:19, NIV).

Jesus was asking his followers to do what he had done while he was with them. Discipleship was the personal, hands-on work Jesus did to strengthen believers in their faith, to help them mature, to show them how to apply the truths of the Scriptures to real life, and then to enable them to pass it on to others. I've never been great at math, but I get excited thinking about the way God multiplies believers in the kingdom through evangelism and discipleship. Author Robert Coleman defines discipleship as "making learners of Christ."[1] We can see evangelism and discipleship modeled in the Bible, and God has commanded his children to be engaged in both of them. Again Robert Coleman writes, "The Great Commission is not a special calling or a gift of the Spirit, it is a command—incumbent upon the whole community of faith."[2]

But there are differences between evangelism and discipleship. Evangelism presents the Good News, defends the faith, and offers the salvation opportunity; discipleship teaches spiritual truths and disciplines. Numbers also differ between evangelism and discipleship. Billy Graham has led thousands to Christ, but he has no doubt discipled a much smaller number. While speaking to a group of ministers from Campus Crusade for Christ, author Bobb Biehl explained the quantity difference between evangelism and discipleship this way: In a year's time, you may see three hundred students come to Christ in your Campus Life program. Out of this three hundred probably thirty will become involved in a leadership program through which you will disciple them.[3]

Paul also evangelized lots of people but discipled only a few. His most well-known disciple was Timothy. Paul saw greatness in this young man from Asia Minor (modern-day Turkey) as I do in Isabel: "You therefore, my son, be strong in the grace that is in Christ Jesus. And the things that you have heard from me among many witnesses, commit these to faithful men who will be able to teach others also" (2 Timothy 2:1-2).

From this passage, *you* indicates the importance of individual people in discipleship. *Commit* means to transmit from one person to another. *Faithful men* refer to people whose hearts are tender toward the things of God, people who want to really know God: "The eyes of the Lord range throughout the earth to strengthen those whose hearts are fully committed to him" (2 Chronicles 16:9, NIV).

First Paul, then Timothy, then faithful men, then others also. That makes four generations of followers of Christ, and the multiplication of disciples continues. I like what Walter A. Henrichsen writes in *Disciples Are Made—Not Born:* "Implementing the vision of multiplying disciples constitutes the only way Christ's commission can ever ultimately be fulfilled. . . . Whatever ministry we are engaged in, it ought to be reproductive."[4]

As important as it was for Jesus to instruct his followers to go and make disciples before he left, I believe it could be even more important for us to make disciples before he returns. In chapter 2, we talked about Bruce Wilkinson's three-chair analogy, which represents how closely each of us walks with God. I compared it to the game of telephone, where someone whispers a message to someone else. The process continues around the room until each person has heard the whispered message. The last person reports a heard-it-through-the-grapevine message that typically bears little resemblance to the original.

Our job as disciplers today is to keep the message clear, pure, simple, and undecorated. Jesus said, "I tell you the truth, until heaven and earth disappear, not the smallest letter, not the least stroke of a pen, will by any means disappear from the Law until everything is accomplished" (Matthew 5:18, NIV).

I have loved passing on biblical truth to those I have discipled through the years, whether to my children, people I write or speak to, or Isabels I meet with one-on-one. The truths I show them today will still be true tomorrow. They always have been and always will be, and they provide the plumb line for living abundant lives. God's people need other people to help them, to teach them, to encourage them, and to hold them accountable to this plumb line. As each Isabel grows and passes on what she learns to others, discipling continues based on the pure Word of God.

Without discipleship, new believers are left to flounder and try to find their own way. Without discipleship, an intimate, passionate, committed relationship with Christ is much harder to achieve. Without discipleship, God's Word can become as fragmented and individually interpreted as the relativism we see in the world today. Without discipleship, the kingdom could forever consist of baby, nominal, compromising Christians who pass on the same lukewarm Christianity to others. Without discipleship, the "whatever" attitude we see in the world today can infiltrate our spiritual lives. And without discipleship, instead of God's Word being a lamp to our feet and a light to our path, as we read in Psalm 119:105, we're left to make our own road through the darkness.

When our daughter Ashley was about eleven, she was spending some time away from home when someone asked her to do something she knew was wrong. She always took her Bible with her when she traveled, and she went to her room and opened it to 2 Timothy 3, which talks about the last days and the fact that people will be searching in the wrong places. Then Ashley read Paul's discipling words to Timothy: "You must continue in the things which you have learned and been assured of, knowing from whom you have learned them, and that from childhood you have known the Holy Scriptures, which are able to make you wise for salvation through faith which is in Christ Jesus" (2 Timothy 3:14-15).

Paul discipled Timothy, Timothy discipled faithful men, and those men passed it on to others. Those "others" included my daughter. Discipling was the method Jesus gave us for growing his followers. It was true in Bible days, and it's still true today.

## NINE STEPS TO EFFECTIVE DISCIPLESHIP

I'm no expert on discipleship, but I know Jesus commanded me to disciple others, and I thoroughly enjoy doing it. Like many disciplines I try to build into my spiritual walk, the simpler I keep it, the more effective and enduring it tends to be. I recommend nine steps that will lead you to regularly fulfilling Jesus' command to disciple others:

### 1. Pray for Direction

Effective discipleship always begins with acknowledging Jesus' command to make disciples and our willingness to obey. God sometimes uses other disciplers to disciple us in discipling, but the Holy Spirit always has ways of making his will known and of answering our questions regarding:

- Who initiates a discipling relationship?
- How much time should we allow?

- What do we talk about when we meet?
- Can I disciple more than one person?
- Should I tell the one I'm discipling what to do?
- Can I ever get out of the relationship?

Pray for God's direction and wisdom about the people and methods he wants for your discipling life. Don't force the issue of finding someone to disciple, and don't overcommit yourself. As God opens a door of opportunity, walk through it. My discipling commitment to Isabel happened without warning, and it continues without accolades. Discipling affects one person at a time, not thousands, but sometimes as I drive away from our meetings, I just look up and smile at God and whisper, *Thank you.*

Discipling is so sweet and real and personal that I can't find words to adequately describe how it plays out. Recently Isabel described to me a relative who had repeatedly wronged her. Isabel prayed about it; then she and her husband invited the relative to stay in their home for a while when he was down and out. Isabel said, "I didn't feel like it. I just wanted to be obedient to God."

I went into our time together with the goal of helping Isabel grow and be obedient, but as a result of our time together I'm growing and becoming more obedient too.

## 2. Turn the Disciple On to Christ

I can talk until I'm blue in the face about how much I love Jesus and how wonderful it is to walk with him. But my words carry much less weight than my actions do. When I'm doing my discipling job well, my intimate, passionate, and committed walk with Christ reveals itself to those around me. Telling others that I really know Christ translates much more clearly when I demonstrate how I know him in the rubber-meets-the-road issues of my life.

## 3. Prepare for Disappointments

Not every attempt at discipleship will succeed, at least not in our
eyes. A woman whose husband was in ministry came to me and
asked me to disciple her in conjunction with a seminary class she was
taking. She filled me in on her background and some personal issues
she was working through. I tried the same methods that had worked
with Isabel and others, but they didn't work with this woman. We
had been meeting for only a short time when the woman told me she
felt a counselor in her program might suit her needs better.

If we keep remembering that everything is about God, not about
us, we can distance ourselves from having a sense of personal
ownership or from taking credit when things go well. As a result,
we don't have to own the "failures" either. Paul says that salvation is
not by our own works, so that no one can boast (Ephesians 2:8-9).
Emotions of defeat cannot overshadow our witness as long as we
remember that discipling is really God's work, not ours.

## 4. Don't Believe the Myths

I would have missed out on my time with Isabel if I had believed
some of the myths about being a discipler. I don't have to be eighty
years old and have sixty years of Christlike wisdom before I begin to
disciple others. Instead, as God teaches me new truths, I should teach
them to others. My children know this. When they were growing up,
instead of relying on the same simple Bible stories children often
hear, I would teach them what I had learned about how God talked
to his people through the Urim and the Thummim. I also didn't feel
that I needed to be perfect before I had something of value to teach
someone else. As a matter of fact, my times with Isabel and with my
listeners on the radio are greatly enhanced when I reveal a mistake
I've made or a correction or discipline through which God is teaching
me. Others find God's truths more refreshing and attainable as they
thank me for the transparency in my own Christian walk.

Having said that, I also need to say that my growth needs to be apparent to others and my mistakes need to be different and more "mature" than the ones I made last year. My role as a discipler should in every way portray me as a lifelong student of Christ as I show others how to be the same.

I also didn't buy the myth that I had to have all the answers. I have sat with my children or others I've discipled and answered frankly, "I don't know," three words that many find hard to say. I would then add, "Let's pray and go to the Word to find an answer." As I have modeled this search for direction, those looking on have learned it for themselves. This shows them how to fish for the answers themselves instead of relying on someone else to provide the answer every time they need one. In this way they mature in their faith.

Finally, I didn't believe that discipling happens in only one way. The process of discipling is as colorful and varied as the people who do it. The method I described above has worked beautifully for my Thursday-noon discipling appointment. Yours might be entirely different, and I might need to change some things as time goes on. Again, you'll find your structure as you follow God's leading. He will give you wisdom to make your discipling efforts as individualized as the unique people he puts in your path.

### 5. Make It Relevant

Jesus crafted his ministry to fit the individuals he addressed. He spoke their language and met their needs. It's important that we get to know our Isabels too, who they are and what they need. As we do that, we, like Jesus, can begin to speak their language and meet their needs. Choose the right materials, techniques, length, and location to make discipling work for the people in your life. Give bite-sized assignments. In addition to teaching them, let them talk, allow them to clarify their needs and the ways they are growing. I serve as the gatekeeper for our group, which involves keeping track of the time and keeping the study moving. Although I don't determine the content, I do try to keep us on track and on time so that we don't take advantage of employers or the women's other commitments.

Don't hesitate to alter your agenda as you see fit. That will be part of the Holy Spirit's guiding you and telling you the way to go.

## 6. Be Consistent and Available

I let my little group know they are a priority to me by keeping my appointment with them nearly every week. On a few occasions, illness or snow have kept us from meeting, but you'd better believe we rescheduled the meeting for a few days later. As I was finishing my work on this book, I had to pull out of the meetings temporarily, but the women continued to meet on their own. This showed me how much they valued the discipleship and also demonstrated their determination to keep growing.

Between meetings I keep myself available through e-mail and phone calls. When one of the women needs extra prayer, we join together in prayer and report the results at our next meeting. Discipling needs to be consistent, and the discipler needs to be available.

## 7. Demonstrate Honesty and Accountability

One day Isabel spoke honestly about one way she had struggled since we had met. Her words let us know that she had digressed a little in her faith. So although I was gentle with her, I was also firm, and I had her go back to some of the truths we had already learned. When our time was over, Isabel walked visibly straighter, and her confidence and joy moved her on to the next challenge.

As disciplers we need to be honest and to hold those we're discipling accountable by gently guiding them back to God's Word. It keeps the way clear and the disciples growing.

## 8. Find One and Be One

No matter how many people I disciple, I will always need regular discipling myself. I mentioned author Cynthia Heald earlier. I have humbly sat under her discipleship for several years. She always tells it like it is and challenges me to stay balanced and to become all I can be in Christ.

My mother continues to disciple me. She has been there through the years, not only as my mom but as a friend and a fellow "knower" of Christ. I stay malleable, correctable, and accountable as I continue to be discipled by these and other godly women.

The combination of having disciples and being disciples ourselves keeps us growing in a healthy way. Having and being keeps a good balance between ministry-in and ministry-out. Having and being keeps us under the authority of God's system of checks and balances.

We should also expose our children to discipleship early in their lives. Our son Clint grew up in a single-parent home. But God sent key men into Clint's life to disciple him. Coaches, youth leaders, pastors, teachers, family members, and friends have helped him grow into a godly young man. They have also shown him how to find and disciple others around him. Clint reached out to a boy in our neighborhood who had no knowledge of God. When Clint asked him what religion he was, he said, "Spanish."

Clint had his work cut out for him, but he continued to spend time with the boy until he moved away. How thankful I am as I watch my son take what he has learned and share it with nonbelievers and those who are learners of Christ.

## 9. Bathe Everything in Prayer

Finding God's direction for yourself isn't the only reason prayer is necessary; it's also necessary so that you can show your disciples how to personally pray about everything for themselves.

One Sunday morning was especially busy for me. I had stayed up the night before writing the narration for our Easter cantata. The next day I substituted for our children's pastor and taught my adult Sunday school class. At the end of my lesson, one woman asked if she could meet with me that afternoon. I arranged to meet the woman at the park. As she brought up the first problem she was dealing with, I showed her (with our eyes open while we walked) how to take it to God in prayer. I showed her how to come boldly to God's throne. Then we went on to the next issue. By the time we finished our walk, we had covered about five areas of struggle. Back at the car I pulled a deposit slip from my wallet and listed what we had prayed about. I drew a column where she could check an item off when she received an answer to that prayer. I moved some time later, and I haven't seen the woman since, but I'm hopeful that showing her how to pray rather than doing all the praying for her helped to equip her for the challenges she faces today.

The first time I took my children skiing after we moved to Colorado, I rode the chairlift to the top of Copper Mountain with Clint and Ashley. Courtney had stayed behind with a fever. As we stood on the crest, surveying the breathtaking scenery around us, Ashley expressed her impatience about wanting to hurry down the slope. Eight-year-old Clint, however, started to cry. This mountain was a far cry from the "bumps" we had skied on in the Midwest. There, after thirty minutes in lift lines, it took only thirty seconds for us to ski back down.

We made arrangements for Ashley to ski on ahead and meet us at the bottom. Clint and I started our move down the mountain, and I quickly understood what I needed to do for my son.

I *encouraged* Clint by convincing him that he had what it took to make the trip. I *instructed* him about how to use a technique called snowplowing to control his speed and about ways to get back up after falling. I *protected* him by keeping him away from trees and careless snowboarders. I *guided* him by skiing in front and showing him the way to go.

My most significant role, however, became clear at the bottom of the mountain. Clint skied past me confidently, making tracks of his own and calling over his shoulder, "Come on, Mom! Can't you go any faster?" At that point I realized that in addition to encouraging, instructing, protecting, and guiding my son, I also needed to let him go.

Such is the command to go and make disciples. God gives us the ability up high on the mountaintop with him so that we can show it to others along the way. Our discipling should include encouragement, instruction, protection, and guidance, while at the same time we should teach others how to make the journey on their own and how to disciple others.

That's it. Multiplication and discipleship. Two times two equals four. Four times four equals sixteen. Sixteen times sixteen equals 256, and on and on it goes. Jesus said it. Now let's do it!

> Go therefore and make disciples of all the nations,
> baptizing them in the name of the Father and
> of the Son and of the Holy Spirit.
>
> *Matthew 28:19*

---

*DEAR LORD, I'm amazed that your plan for growing your kingdom includes the participation of people just like me. Neither evangelism nor discipleship takes place through a computer program or only through well-known people. Both evangelism and discipleship are my responsibility. God, help me to do it well. Amen.*

# 18

# Plugging In to Ministry

When my children and I lived in Cincinnati, we attended a church we still remember with love today. As a single mom of three who was working as a teaching assistant while earning my doctorate, I didn't have much time to be involved in ministry. I had initially chosen the church because it stood close to our apartment and offered a thriving youth program. My children grew to love it there and thoroughly enjoyed going on Sunday mornings and Wednesday evenings.

I, however, struggled to find my place. I didn't fit in with singles because I had children, and I didn't fit in with couples because I had no husband. I wanted to be involved in ministry, so I prayed and then decided to customize a way to get involved.

As a family we began volunteering for an inner-city ministry. At least one Saturday each month the children and I drove downtown to a soup kitchen sponsored by our church. On Thanksgiving, Christmas, and Easter we helped with special events there. We brought food, set tables, washed dishes, and cleaned up. Sometimes we walked down the streets of this rough section of the city and witnessed to people we met and invited them in for a meal. One day two of my children and I prayed the sinner's prayer with three thirteen-year-old girls.

My children still talk about these experiences, and each of them has developed a soft spot in their hearts for the needy as a result of them. The ministry helped us in other ways too. Despite my marital status, we became part of a community. The people got to know us, and we got to know them, not out of our weaknesses but through our strengths. Our gifts floated to the surface, and over the years we found opportunities to plug them in, in other ways.

As I watch people in our churches today struggle to fit their strengths into some type of ministry, I often recall the simple way we discovered our place. Our activities allowed both for ministry-in to my family, which needed some healing in the aftermath of divorce, as well as ministry-out, which hastened that healing along as we nourished others.

The Bible calls the collective work Christians do through the church "body ministry." Scripture compares the different jobs we do with various functions of the parts of the body:

> The body is a unit, though it is made up of many parts; and though all its parts are many, they form one body. So it is with Christ. . . . Now the body is not made up of one part but of many. If the foot should say, "Because I am not a hand, I do not belong to the body," it would not for that reason cease to be part of the body. And if the ear should say, "Because I am not an eye, I do not belong to the body," it would not for that reason cease to be part of the body. If the whole body were an eye, where would the sense of hearing be? If the whole body were an ear, where would the sense of smell be? But in fact God has arranged the parts in the body, every one of them, just as he wanted them to be. (1 Corinthians 12:12-18, NIV)

In chapter 1 we talked about how Jesus told his disciples that they would do even greater works than he had done. This happens through the ministry of the church body, and you have a part in that body. The hand does not work in isolation but rather in concert with the arm, shoulder, and fingers. So it is with the spiritual body. Each individual member offers his or her strengths, and together we make up the whole body.

Whatever your function, are you where God wants you to be? Are you doing no more and no less than his perfect will calls you to do? Does your involvement in ministry excite you? Does it fit your talents and skills and the things you like to do?

God's desire for each of us is that we would be fruitful as we increase in our knowledge of him: "We . . . do not cease to pray for you, and to ask that you may be filled with the knowledge of His will in all wisdom and spiritual understanding; that you may walk worthy of the Lord, fully pleasing Him, being fruitful in every good work and increasing in the knowledge of God" (Colossians 1:9-10). Prayerfully take this issue before God before you read any further in this chapter. Ask God to show you how really knowing him can help you plug into your ministry.

## WHAT ARE YOUR BODY STRENGTHS?

Athletes capitalize on their body strength and structure and use them to excel in their field. Similarly, as members of the body of Christ, we can examine the ways we are created to help us discover the jobs we should do. As you consider your part in the body of Christ, take a look at several key areas of the "fearfully and wonderfully made" person God designed you to be (Psalm 139:14):

### Your Passions

Think back to chapter 5 and the things you discovered about passion. We saw that passion is "an intense . . . or overmastering feeling or conviction; a strong liking or desire for" something.[1]

Your passions are those things that turn your crank. Passions get you up in the morning. They touch your heart. They make you cry. Passions are the compass that can guide you to God's will for your life.

Rhonda's father sexually abused her when she was a child. God has brought a lot of healing to her, and the tears of other sexual-abuse victims touch her deeply. She prays for them, gathers information for them, and makes herself available. Most of all, she cares, and they know it. Her passions bring help to the body.

What is it that you feel most passionate about?

## Your Abilities

*Ability* is defined as "competence in doing; physical, mental, or legal power to perform."[2] Ability can be a natural talent or an acquired proficiency. Take a moment and brainstorm about your abilities. Broadly speaking, are you enterprising? social? investigative? artistic? realistic? conventional? Are your abilities mostly physical or mostly mental? In what skills or competencies do you feel the most sure of yourself?

## Your Personality

*Personality* could be defined as "the complex of characteristics that distinguishes an individual or a nation or group; . . . the totality of an individual's behavioral and emotional characteristics."[3] Our personalities make us distinct from other people.

Many good instruments exist for measuring our personalities. While the results obtained using these tools are not ironclad, nor is their function to pigeonhole us, personality tests do help us understand our strengths and weaknesses, as well as the strengths and weaknesses of those with whom we live and work.

Personalities play a big part in what a person's ministry work looks like. Peter was impulsive, the Pharisees went by the letter of the law, and John showed tenderness. These qualities helped determine the work they did.

Every personality also has its weakness. In *The Two Sides of Love,* authors Gary Smalley and John Trent explain that personalities have two sides: a hard side and a soft side. When we're a strong leader whose ministry work involves heading up a women's program, for example, our hard side is well-developed. But we need to be aware of the need to develop our soft side by working on things such as compassion and laughter. On the other hand, when we're naturally full of compassion, we're sometimes vulnerable to others' taking advantage of us, and we need to work on developing a harder side.[4]

My own leadership, type A, hard characteristics allowed me to successfully get my doctorate while raising my three babies alone. At the same time, I struggled with the soft side. I didn't allow the kids to get sick because it wasn't on my schedule. "Oh, you'll be okay," I would say. And although usually they *were* okay, my soft side and my compassion quotient dropped dramatically. So did my laughter.

One day I arranged to go to the zoo with Ashley's kindergarten class. Three times before we left that morning Ashley said, "Mom, laugh and tell jokes today. Laugh and tell jokes." Ashley was reminding me that I needed a softer side. I needed to lighten up.

Only Jesus possessed a perfectly balanced personality. He carefully organized the feeding of the five thousand, divided the crowd into smaller groups for food distribution, and arranged a cleanup committee (Matthew 14:13-21). He showed compassion for the crowds who followed him and cried at the tomb of Lazarus (John 11:1-44). He roared in the temple and drove the money changers out (Matthew 21:12-16), but he became the life of parties (John 2:2-10) and told wonderful stories (Matthew 13:1-52). Jesus also knew how to relate to the colorful personalities around him: to Peter, Jesus became direct and to the point; to the Pharisees, Jesus said, "If any one of you is without sin . . ." (John 8:3-11, NIV); and Jesus called John the beloved (John 13:23-25).

Your personality can become an asset to the ministry God has called you to. Be aware, though, that ministry starts at home and with the people you love. Practice your strengths with them, and work on your weaknesses as well. It's there you will come to know God more, and when you're ready, he'll put you where he wants you to be in the body of Christ.

## Your Experience

Often, the experiences we've been through create great opportunities for ministry. Where have we come from? What have we witnessed? How have our lives affected the ways we feel about things? How has God used what we've been through?

Experiences can affect us either positively or negatively. If you've been through divorce and witnessed God's healing, he might just use you to help others. But if you're still reeling and filled with bitterness, God may never be able to use you in this particular area of ministry; at the very least, your opportunity will be delayed.

Joseph had some pretty harrowing experiences. He was dropped in a hole to die, brought out and sold into slavery, unjustly accused and convicted, and thrown into jail. For sixteen years he endured unspeakable atrocities. Where was God when Joseph was sold into slavery in Egypt? "The Lord was with Joseph" (Genesis 39:2). Where was God when Joseph was in prison? "The Lord was with Joseph" (Genesis 39:21).

During those times when God was with Joseph, he was planning the ministry work he would use Joseph for in the future. Eventually Joseph's experiences equipped him to be second in command to Pharaoh and to bring his brothers—who along with Joseph would father the twelve tribes of Israel—to Egypt to escape the famine. Joseph's experiences became the foundation of his ministry.

## Your Spiritual Gifts

Believers and unbelievers alike possess talents, skills, and abilities. Spiritual gifts, on the other hand, are sovereignly and supernaturally bestowed on all believers by the Holy Spirit to enable them to build one another up spiritually and thus to honor God:

> Now concerning spiritual gifts, brethren, I do not want you to be ignorant: You know that you were Gentiles, carried away to these dumb idols, however you were led. Therefore I make known to you that no one speaking by the Spirit of God calls Jesus accursed, and no one can say that Jesus is Lord except by the Holy Spirit. There are diversities of gifts, but the same Spirit. There are differences of ministries, but the same Lord. And there are diversities of activities, but it is the same God who works all in all. But the manifestation of the Spirit is given to each one for the profit of all: for to one is given the word of wisdom through the Spirit, to another the word of knowledge through the same Spirit, to another faith by the same Spirit, to another gifts of healings by the same Spirit, to another the working of miracles, to another prophecy, to another discerning of spirits, to another different kinds of tongues, to another the interpretation of tongues. But one and the same Spirit works all these things, distributing to each one individually as He wills. (1 Corinthians 12:1-11)

The varieties of gifts fall into two general types: speaking and serving. The speaking, or verbal, gifts are prophecy, knowledge, wisdom, teaching, and exhortation. The serving, or nonverbal, gifts are leadership, helping, giving, mercy, faith, and discernment. All gifts are permanent, and their sole purpose is to strengthen and build up the church and to glorify God.

The Bible not only lists the gifts but provides instruction about how to determine what our gifts are:

- Believe you have gifts (1 Corinthians 12:7).
- Ask God to reveal your gifts (James 1:5).

- Explore possibilities (1 Corinthians 12:12).
- Receive teaching by other Christians (Colossians 3:16).
- Evaluate your effectiveness (John 15:8).
- Expect confirmation from the body (Galatians 2:9).
- Examine your feelings (Psalm 37:4).

Wisdom, knowledge, faith, healings, miracles, prophecy, discernment, tongues, and interpretation—these are God's gifts to us. Our gift to him is to accept those gifts and then give them back to him by using them for his purpose and glory.

**Your Fruit**

I realize that examining the fruit you are producing is not normally a part of determining your ministry work, but let me explain. Just as God wants us to use the gifts he has given us, he also wants us to develop the fruit. Here's what the Bible calls the fruit: "The fruit of the Spirit is love, joy, peace, longsuffering, kindness, goodness, faithfulness, gentleness, self-control. Against such there is no law" (Galatians 5:22-23).

In the Old Testament, mounted on the hem of the high priest's robe were alternating bells and pomegranates made of yarn and linen. The bells didn't strike each other but made their own distinct sound because of the cushioning of the fruit: "They made bells of pure gold and attached them around the hem between the pomegranates. The bells and pomegranates alternated around the hem of the robe to be worn for ministering, as the Lord commanded Moses" (Exodus 39:25-26, NIV).

Author Paul Willis compares the bells to our gifts and the pomegranates to our fruit. Just as the pomegranates keep the bells from clanging against each other, so the fruit that the Holy Spirit produces in us helps to keep our gifts from colliding with others' gifts.[5] The apostle Paul writes similar words: "If I speak in the tongues of men and of angels, but have not love, I am only a resounding gong or a clanging cymbal. If I have the gift of prophecy and can fathom all mysteries and all knowledge, and if I have a faith that can move mountains, but have not love, I am nothing. If I give all I possess to the poor and surrender my body to the flames, but have not love, I gain nothing" (1 Corinthians 13:1-3, NIV).

Willis goes so far as to match up the gifts in order with the fruits as they appear in Scripture:

- wisdom/joy
- knowledge/peace
- faith/long-suffering
- healing/gentleness
- miracles/goodness
- prophecy/faith
- discerning of spirits/meekness
- speaking in an unknown tongue/temperance
- interpretation of tongues/love

One morning during Sunday school at our church in Ohio many years ago, Brandy, a young woman and a new Christian, stood and asked to share something with the class. She talked about her trip the day before to help with our inner-city ministry. While on the street, speaking to a man about Christ, she had lit up a cigarette with him, thinking it might break the ice in their dialogue. But a woman helping in the kitchen had seen her and reprimanded her.

Brandy looked deeply into our faces that morning. With pleading and tearful eyes, she said, "Please be patient with me. I've only been a Christian for six months." She pointed to her hair. The ends were blonde, but she had about four inches of dark roots. "This new growth," she said, "is like the things that I have already over-come—drugs, alcohol, and sexual immorality. But this," she said, pointing to the blonde ends, "is where I still have to grow. Please be patient with me."

Brandy obviously had a desire to use her gifts to share the gospel, but she had not stopped to think about how her actions could weaken her Christian testimony. It became clear that she still needed to work on her fruit. We all do. Bells are made; fruit is formed. Gifts are made; fruit is formed. Even if we speak with the tongues of men and angels—or sing or teach or pray for the sick—if we don't demonstrate the fruit, we become a resounding gong or a clanging cymbal.

I want to mention just a few parting thoughts about your role in the body ministry. My family loves a certain kind of layered Mexican dip. Usually when I make it, I elicit help. Clint grates the cheese and cuts the tomatoes. Ashley chops the onions, avocado, and green pepper. I add the beans and sour cream, and we layer them all together. We all agree that it's the best dip around. We also agree that none of the ingredients by itself is as tasty and none of the ingredients is less or more important than the others.

Body ministry is similar. Many people with similar desires contribute to the whole, using what God has placed in their hands. It works best of all, however, when we keep several additional truths in mind from 1 Corinthians 12 (NIV):

- *It's God's deal:* "There are many parts, but one body" (v. 20).
- *No job is more or less important than another:* "The eye cannot say to the hand, 'I don't need you!' And the head cannot say to the feet, 'I don't need you!' On the contrary, those parts of the body that seem to be weaker are indispensable" (vv. 21-22).
- *All jobs should be acknowledged:* "The parts that we think are less honorable we treat with special honor. And the parts that are unpresentable are treated with special modesty, while our

presentable parts need no special treatment. But God has combined the members of the body and has given greater honor to the parts that lacked it" (vv. 23-24).

- *We should build each other up and encourage others in their ministries:* "There should be no division in the body, but . . . its parts should have equal concern for each other" (v. 25).
- *If one member suffers, we all suffer:* "If one part suffers, every part suffers with it; if one part is honored, every part rejoices with it" (v. 26).

Keep examining and developing your passions, abilities, personality, experience, and gifts, *and* keep growing your fruit, and God will plug you in. But always remember, your piece is but one part of the total picture of the puzzle called the body ministry. As we humbly surrender to God, you do your part, and I do mine. When we do, we accomplish God's work, and he receives the glory!

---

*DEAR LORD, I've struggled for a long time to know what I'm supposed to be doing in ministry. It feels as if everyone knows his or her place except me. If you have some more discovery and development you want me to do before you put me to work, help me do that with all my heart. Remind me that even if I learn to speak with the tongues of men and angels, it counts for nothing unless it is accompanied by mature fruit. Amen.*

# *19*

# Growing through Struggles

I once heard about a songwriter who went to church and heard a talented woman sing a song he had written about something he had suffered. Someone asked the writer what he felt about her version of his song. He answered, "She'll be really good when something happens to break her heart."

The songwriter was right: We won't be really good—good at being true ambassadors for Christ—until something happens to break our hearts. I would not have been able to write this chapter if I had not experienced my own measure of pain. You wouldn't be able to grasp its truth if you hadn't also seen your share of suffering.

John Claypool, a pastor whose young daughter died of leukemia, wrote in *Tracks of a Fellow Struggler:* "We do not first get all the answers and then live in light of our understanding. We must rather plunge into life—meeting what we have to meet and experiencing what we have to experience—and in the light of living try to understand. If insight comes at all, it will not be before, but only through and after experience."[1]

Pam McKnight found insight through her broken heart. She grew up in a military family and accepted Christ when she was in her early teens. After high school graduation, Pam enrolled at Abilene Christian University in Abilene, Texas, to major in psychology. It was there that Pam met Doug McKnight, the love of her life. They married, and Pam dropped out of college after her freshman year to help Doug become a CPA. Just before Doug's last two semesters, Pam gave birth to twin daughters, Tara and Shannon.

Doug graduated from college and immediately accepted a prestigious position with Arthur Andersen. His career took off, and by age twenty-nine Doug was the vice president of an oil company. Meetings with the Rockefellers and interviews with *Forbes* magazine became commonplace for Doug. With a beautiful family, an elegant home, and luxury cars, the McKnights found themselves living the American dream.

In February 1982, Pam and Doug enjoyed a weekend skiing in New Mexico. They had a wonderful time, but Doug grew unusually tired. When they returned home, he went to his doctor for a physical and discovered that, at age thirty-two, he had multiple sclerosis. The disease progressed rapidly. Doug began walking with a cane, and by April he was confined to a wheelchair, where he would spend the rest of his life. Doug's illustrious career ended as quickly as it had begun.

The McKnights sold their custom home and cars, dropped their country-club and petroleum-club memberships, and moved into a small house. In addition to being a mother and full-time caregiver, Pam went to work outside the home for the first time, selling artwork. When Doug nearly succeeded in taking his own life two years into the disease, Pam decided they should move closer to family in Fort Worth, Texas. Pam became a car salesperson so that they could have quality insurance and then went to work for a publishing company, selling curriculum.

Such is Pam's story of heartbreak. Yours is altogether different. Really knowing God does not exempt us from struggles and sadness. If it did, perhaps it would motivate us to seek an intimate, passionate, and committed walk with Christ only to escape troubles.

Although we may really know God, we still live in a fallen world. We get sick and face financial and relational setbacks, but

God is still in control. Poet and hymn writer Annie Johnson Flint once wrote: "Jesus Christ is no security against storms, but He is perfect security in storms. He has never promised you an easy passage, only a safe landing."

Struggles are a way of life for the Christian and the non-Christian alike. Author M. Scott Peck writes: "This is a difficult truth, one of the greatest truths. It is a great truth because once we truly see this truth, we transcend it. Once we truly know that life is difficult—once we truly understand and accept it—then life is no longer difficult. Because once it is accepted, the fact that life is difficult no longer matters."[2]

It was James the brother of Jesus who saw enough pain in his life to write: "Consider it pure joy, my brothers, whenever you face trials of many kinds, because you know that the testing of your faith develops perseverance. Perseverance must finish its work so that you may be mature and complete, not lacking anything" (James 1:2-4, NIV).

"*Whenever* you face trials," not *if* you face them. When trials do come, we can respond in one of several ways: We can curse them, nurse them, rehearse them, or reverse them. We can suffer and resist their intrusion, or we can count them pure joy and submit to the continued growth process God is doing in our lives. In *Disciples Are Made—Not Born,* Walter Henrichsen writes: "Every problem a person has is related to his concept of God. If we have a big God, we have small problems. If we have a small God, we have big problems."[3]

Paul recognized his choice of responses through trials, and he chose to count them all joy and reverse them by allowing them to further Jesus' message. Paul wrote: "I want you to know, brothers, that what has happened to me has really served to advance the gospel. As a result, it has become clear throughout the whole palace guard and to everyone else that I am in chains for Christ.

Because of my chains, most of the brothers in the Lord have been encouraged to speak the word of God more courageously and fearlessly" (Philippians 1:12-14, NIV). Paul rejoiced that his sufferings were contributing to the spread of the good news about Christ.

Knowing God in greater ways does not automatically result from difficult times, but the crises of life can become an ideal platform for seeing whole new aspects of God and walking with him in deeper ways.

## THE PURPOSE OF STRUGGLES

In chapter 8 I talked about the perfection process and the experience I had in the middle of the night several months before writing this book. God spoke two verses to my heart concerning perfection. I have already mentioned the first of these verses, Psalm 138:8: "The Lord will perfect that which concerns me." The second of the verses I received that night relates to perfection's role in suffering: "May the God of all grace, who called us to His eternal glory by Christ Jesus, after you have suffered a while, perfect, establish, strengthen, and settle you" (1 Peter 5:10).

The Bible leaves little doubt that the Christian will encounter hardship. *Strong's Concordance* tells us that *suffering* in this 1 Peter passage means "to experience a sensation or impression usually painful."[4]

Doug McKnight sat in his wheelchair for seventeen years before he died at age forty-nine. Pam would have given almost anything to escape the suffering she endured through her husband's illness. On the other hand, she would choose to go through it all over again to gain the growth she found in God. Pam is a living example of four of the benefits that accompany struggle. Through our hurt, God works to perfect, establish, strengthen, and settle us:

238

## God Perfects Us through Struggles

As we learned earlier, to *perfect* means to restore or repair, to complete, or to bring something into its final form.

God helped Pam ignore the statistics she had heard, that nine out of ten spouses divorce within the first two years of a long-term illness. She committed early on to the marriage vows she had made to Doug and to God. She told me, "I had had the health and riches, now it was time for sickness and leanness."

Pam saw her faith grow as she turned to God over and over again. She says, "I thought I had strong faith when I went into this thing. Now I know it was a baby faith. God perfects us by giving us things to bear. We don't grow when things are going along fine."

Doug matured in the Lord too. Before his illness, Pam explained, making money had become Doug's goal, and socializing had become his faith. Sometime during his illness, however, his heart changed. He counted up forty-nine thousand dollars, which he figured they owed in back tithes since they had been married. At his insistence, he and Pam gave every penny of that money back to God.

Pam also tells about Doug's love for pizza and how he ordered it often. One day he began to feel bad about not tipping the people who had delivered their pizzas through the years. So the next time Doug had a pizza delivered, he wrote the woman who delivered it a check for seventy-five dollars. As it turned out, the woman had just been released on parole. That check provided Doug an opportunity to talk to her about Christ.

Perfection restores or repairs. God takes the ways we're already strong, adds our adjusted weaknesses, and then fits them together in a whole new way.

## God Establishes Us through Struggles

To *establish* means to set fast or to turn something resolutely in a certain direction.

Doug attended church every Sunday morning, and after he had been ill for about eight years, Pam says, his prayers changed from "Heal me" to "Use me." As a result, God opened many doors for ministry. Doug lived in an attended-care facility for a time five years before he died. While there, Doug began holding Bible studies for many of the physically and mentally handicapped people who lived there. He also invited them to church. Pam made a rule, though, that Doug couldn't invite more people than their van could hold.

In February 1999, five months after Doug died, Pam's church approached her about heading up the new single-parent ministry at their large church in Fort Worth. Pam hesitated for a while; then she began to cry. Crying was something she had trained herself not to do because it had made Doug cry and that brought on paralysis. A counselor had told Pam to read sad books to help her learn to cry again.

But crying came naturally the day the church approached her about helping with moms and dads in the church who were raising their children alone. The following June, Pam joined the church staff as one of the nation's twelve full-time, single-parent pastors.

God used the hard places in Pam's life to turn her resolutely in a certain direction.

### God Strengthens Us through Struggles

In this verse from 1 Peter 5:10, to *strengthen* means "to confirm in spiritual knowledge and power."

My knowledge of Scripture began during the difficult years of my life. Pam's did too. She tells how she ran to the Word when things got really hard. It taught her Scripture and helped her better know God. At an airport recently I saw a man with just one leg. The other leg had been cut off above the knee, and a prosthetic limb extended to the floor. What I found myself noticing, however, was not the prosthesis. Instead, I looked at the leg that remained and the huge muscles that defined it. It was marked by strength and stability. Because of the work the remaining leg had to do to compensate for the pain and loss, it developed greater muscle, strength, and stability.

We often hear or read about the painful process a chrysalis goes through in becoming a butterfly. It's during the stretching time when the butterfly is struggling to break through to freedom that the body becomes strong and color forms in the wings.

That's what the 1 Peter passage means by *strengthening,* or "confirming in spiritual knowledge and power." When we surrender our hurtful losses and struggles to Christ, he will produce spiritual muscle, strength, and stability we never had before. As we submit to the painful process of waiting, God adds strength and color through our deep knowledge of him, and he develops those things into greater spiritual knowledge and power.

## God Settles Us through Struggles

To *settle* means to establish or secure permanently, to put something down or to lay a firm foundation.

Doug has been gone for more than five years. The lessons Pam learned, however, became foundational for everything else she would do for the rest of her life. When I asked her about the message she longs to share with people, she talked about two things: first, her absolute knowledge about how God provides. "I got hit with a thirteen-thousand-dollar back-tax bill last year. Other people were more upset than I was because I have learned that God provides."

Second, Pam talked about her changed perspective on life. "We fight so hard to prolong our days here," she said. "But one thing I know for sure, earth is not my home. Heaven is, and it's going to be wonderful to get there."

Pam's firm foundation was dug through suffering, and in the process, she's gotten to really know God.

## SO WHAT DO WE DO WHILE WE HURT?

Through our suffering, God perfects, establishes, strengthens, and settles us. God brings about his will in all circumstances of life, including the ones we see as bad. So what lessons does God teach us in the "prisons" of our lives?

### Rest

My father battled pancreatic cancer for about five years, the final days being the hardest of all. After we buried Dad in early March, my mother lay down on her bed to rest. She got up for brief periods to eat and do small chores and then rested again. This routine continued for some six months as Mom's body, soul, and spirit rebuilt from the long ordeal she'd been through. By the fall, Mom had enrolled in some college classes and eventually finished her degree in art and anthropology, but not until after she had rested.

The well-known words of Psalm 23 describe the process my mother went through: "He makes me lie down in green pastures, . . . he restores my soul" (vv. 2-3, NIV).

He *makes* us lie down in green pastures. We don't often do it voluntarily. But when health or financial issues creep up on us, we have no choice but to plunge headfirst into the difficulty. However, we have two choices about how to respond while we are there: We can fret about it, or we can rest in God's ability to see us through. Rest is God's gift to us:

- "Be still, and know that I am God." (Psalm 46:10)
- "There remains . . . a Sabbath-rest for the people of God; for anyone who enters God's rest also rests from his own work, just as God did from his." (Hebrews 4:9-10, NIV)
- "Ask for the ancient paths, ask where the good way is, and

walk in it, and you will find rest for your souls." (Jeremiah 6:16, NIV)

A plant that lies dormant in the ground when the winter brings its chill still lives but relies on the provision around it to sustain it. It's not the time to grow. The winter will come to an end, and the season for growing will come once again. But for now, continue to rest.

## Be Patient

I sat on a church pew early one Sunday morning. A wise elder of our church stopped by, shook my hand, and asked me how things were going. "Okay, I guess," I said, "but I'm not hearing from God on my direction."

"Could be," the elder replied, "he's not speaking because he doesn't have anything to say. He won't let you miss his will. He'll let you know when it's time to make a move."

I have spoken those same words to many I've counseled since. If God isn't speaking, just be patient.

## Trust

After I became a single mom, the University of Cincinnati offered me a scholarship and a position as a graduate assistant for the purpose of earning my doctorate. That fall I moved my five-, three-, and one-year-old babies and began the doctoral program. During the three years it took me to finish my work, I often questioned why God had me in this field. One day on the way to class I parked my car, rested my head on the steering wheel, and cried. What was God's will for my life? How would I find the sufficiency I needed to finish the course? I didn't like what I was doing, and on top of my huge responsibilities as a single mom, I was working like crazy to finish that degree.

In June 1991, I draped the red and black cap and gown over my car seat and headed toward the university for the hooding ceremony that would celebrate the completion of my doctorate. On the way I stopped at the house of a friend, who would go with me to the event. As I walked in, music filtered through the open windows, and I heard a song I had never heard before. It was called "Trust His Heart." On that day, as I got ready to take my next step without having any idea of what that next step would be, I soaked in the words of the song:

> He sees the master plan,
> He holds the future in His hand.
> Don't live as those who have no hope.
> All our hope is found in Him.
> We see the present clearly,
> He sees the first and the last.
> And like a tapestry
> He's weaving you and me
> To someday be just like Him.
>
> God is too wise to be mistaken.
> God is too good to be unkind.
> So when you don't understand,
> When you don't see His plan,
> When you can't trace His hand,
> Trust His heart.
>
> He alone is faithful and true.
> He alone knows what is best for you.
> So when you don't understand,
> When you don't see His plan,
> When you can't trace His hand,
> Trust His heart.[5]

On that June day I felt as if God spoke directly to me: *Do what comes next. Abide in me. I'll take care of you.* Over the next months and years, I could sometimes understand what he was doing, see his plan, and trace his hand. Most of the time, however, I could not. It was at those times that I sang this song over and over. My children heard it so often that Clint would try to beat me to the punch and say, "Trust his heart."

Pam told me about a trip she took to England before Doug died. The company she worked for had awarded her travel expenses in honor of ten years of service. Doug gave Pam three hundred dollars to buy a set of Spode Christmas china she had always wanted.

Pam arranged caregivers for Doug and then headed overseas for some much-needed time away. She prayed that she would find the china only if God would give her opportunities to use it. She did find it and was able to buy a whole set.

What Doug hadn't known before Pam left was that she was going to have to move him into a nursing home when she returned. After Tara and Shannon took the things they wanted, Pam would need to sell the house and its contents to pay for Doug's expenses.

Pam arrived home on a Saturday. She showed Doug her purchases and her quickly developed photos from the trip. The next day Doug became paralyzed and developed pneumonia. A few days later he was gone.

Doug is healed at last, and Pam will see him again someday. Maybe there's a way the two of them can even ski the heavenly slopes together. But while Pam waits, she continues more and more each day to know God—the God who sustained her through all her struggles and even saw to it that she got her china.

He who trusts in the Lord, mercy shall
surround him.

*Psalm 32:10*

---

*GOD, I realize you have a plan to grow us in and through our strug-*
*gles. Continue your work of teaching me through my hardships, but*
*show me, like James, how to "consider it pure joy." Take me out of*
*the way, and show me how to rest instead of fret, trust instead of*
*doubt. Through it all, perfect, establish, strengthen, and settle me for*
*eternity's purposes. Amen.*

# 20

# Leading in Disaster

Dave and I had hurried into the airport to catch an eight o'clock flight to Minnesota on the morning of Tuesday, September 11, 2001. Our oldest daughter, Angie, was to be married on Saturday, and we had arranged to go early and help with last-minute details. After checking in and receiving our boarding passes, I waited by the baggage screening area as Dave parked the car. Immediately I noticed people rushing to the TV monitors close by. Soon I knew why, and within minutes the first World Trade Center towers in New York City collapsed before our eyes. The evidence was clear: Our country had been attacked by terrorists.

We called the school and arranged for Courtney and Clint to get their homework by the end of the day; we would take off by car the next morning for Minnesota. Like most people, we were glued to the radio as we drove and while we prepared for Angie's wedding.

On Monday I received a call from Westar Media Group, which produces my radio show. They asked me to come by and record a three-minute message of hope and direction for listeners, which Westar would combine with those of twenty other radio personalities and distribute by CD to radio stations across the country.

I hope we never have to record that kind of message again. I also hope that experience woke us to the need to be there for people during a crisis, whether it's a national one as on 9/11 or the kind of personal crises we see every day. One thing became clear: When disaster strikes, people listen.

A recent AOL study reported that 80 percent of the population think we'll face another terrorist attack, yet only 7 percent have made any kind of preparation for such an event.[1] Add to that number a 100-percent chance that each of us will weekly encounter people involved in personal disasters, and our need to prepare is huge.

In the 1950s, theologian Richard Niebuhr wrote *Christ and Culture,* in which he discussed five different contemporary church views and their effectiveness in reaching the world for Christ:

- *Assimilating churches.* The culture ignores these churches because they have nothing to offer that people can't already find in the world; they've adopted the world's values.
- *Protecting churches.* These churches are culturally irrelevant because they have built walls around themselves in an effort to keep change and evil out.
- *Unchanging churches.* These churches are far removed from the culture because they ignore culture.
- *Battling churches.* These churches are annihilated by the culture after waging war against it with a them-against-us mentality.
- *Influencing churches.* These churches are involved and provide hope to the culture. They see the culture as a mission field and befriend it with the gospel.[2]

Because each of us is part of the body of Christ, as we discussed in chapter 18, when one person hurts, we all hurt. At the same time, when one person makes a difference, either individually or corporately, the entire body of Christ benefits.

## EIGHT WAYS TO LEAD

If we are to be Christians whom people going through personal or
global disaster will reach out to, we need to become part of the
influencing church that provides hope. What follows are things you
can do that will help you as you seek to lead others through
personal or global disaster.

### Realize That the God Void Exists inside Everyone

The hunger you have found in yourself for a deeper knowledge of
God resides in every man or woman, boy or girl. Regardless of age,
race, religion, or ethnicity, the absence of God in someone's life is
the most basic cause of all troubles, so the cure is God. When you
use that basic truth to guide your response to people in need,
everything you do should work toward the goal of eliminating that
"God void." You want the people you are leading to want what you
have. Be sure that your life conveys that desire. Ask yourself, *Is what
I'm doing directing people to God?*

### Provide for Them

Broadcaster and evangelist Mary Marr once joined me as a guest on
*The Lynda Hunter Show.* She works with the Christian Emergency
Network (CEN), whose goal it is to meet needs for the next "not if,
but when" disaster.[3] CEN's mission is summed up in the words
*prayer, care,* and *share.* In other words, *pray* now for what lies ahead,
and pray that God's people will respond. *Care* by letting others see
your compassion and by providing for people's physical needs. *Share*
by giving those you help the opportunity to learn about Christ.

Various Web sites and government agencies have suggestions
about what supplies to have on hand in the event of a national
disaster. These include duct tape and stored water. The Christian
Emergency Network recommends that we pay attention to these
suggestions and keep these items on hand in quantities sufficient
for our own families and at least one other.

People have physical needs, and when we meet those, often they will talk about their spiritual needs. I found this to be true in the inner-city ministry my family and I were involved in. Once we brought people inside and gave them food and shelter, we had their ear for the deeper issues of life. Just as Jesus fed the five thousand men plus women and children, we need to meet people's physical needs. Are we prepared to provide for at least one other person so that we may get the chance to talk with him or her about eternal issues?

## Watch for Opportunities

When I worked at Focus on the Family, I received a letter from a woman named Sarah, who lived in England, describing in detail the horrible atrocities her family had been through. "Can you help me?" she wrote.

I wrote back to Sarah, sent her some helpful materials, and as I planned a trip to the United Kingdom for Care for the Family, a ministry to those suffering from family breakups, I contacted Sarah to ask if we could meet. When I arrived at our meeting place, I spotted a downcast woman standing in the crowd. It was Sarah.

Over a lunch of lamb and mint jelly, Sarah recounted her plight. Venom seethed from her over the way her husband, a pastor, had betrayed her and their marriage. In England, if both parties don't agree to end a marriage, a five-year waiting period is required between the beginning of marital separation and the final divorce decree. Sarah had grown more and more bitter every day, and the five years were almost up.

Before I left for England, I had had an opportunity to talk with author Bruce Wilkinson at the Christian Booksellers Association meeting. Bruce had served as a mentor to me upon occasion. He had challenged me with the need to truly forgive my ex-husband. He had me name every yucky thing that had happened to me throughout the marriage and divorce, and he put objects on the table to represent each of them. Then he had me address them one by one by picking up each object and then letting it go, based on the words of Matthew 18:35 that tell us we must forgive from the heart.

Two weeks later, I was sitting in front of Sarah, who also needed to forgive. I tried to help her in ways similar to how Bruce had helped me. Though Sarah told me she wasn't ready to forgive, I felt that I had at least made some inroads with her.

When I returned home, I received a letter from Sarah that said, "You've learned to live life in color again, and I'm still living in black and white. Please don't go. Help me find a new life."

I received a lot of letters during my time at Focus on the Family, but something about Sarah's had alerted me to a ministry opportunity. Am I seeing opportunities when God brings them my way? Am I hearing his voice when he tells me to act?

## Be Ready by Really Knowing God

When disaster strikes, there won't be time to hurry up and get to know God in an intimate, passionate, committed way. Whether someone you know is gripped by sickness, financial struggles, or a terrorist attack, if you are to be of any spiritual help to that person, your relationship with God must be already under way. Knowing God should remain your preeminent passion. Then if disaster comes, you are prepared, and if it doesn't, you are still prepared. Am I concentrating on my knowing relationship with God so that on a moment's notice I can share with others what I know about the One I really know?

## Be Available

We live in a society where people change jobs and spouses often, so they search for solid alternatives. If we make ourselves available to people, either in person or by phone, they will respond. Dave is really good about sending people cards and notes to commemorate some difficult anniversary or crisis in their lives. Since he makes himself available during hard times, many gravitate toward him when conditions improve.

## Offer Networking

A single mom once told me that she needed a car. I couldn't help her, but I knew someone who could, and I was able to put those two people in touch with each other. If you don't know the answer, know how to get it. Then share that information with those who need it.

## Follow Through

I think that as Christians some of us dropped the ball when we didn't follow through on being there for people six months *after* the terrorist attacks. Offer the hope, provide the hope, and then follow up later to see whether the hope has taken hold. I'm constantly amazed at how touched people are when we come back to them later to see how they're doing.

## Help Them Stand on Their Own

The most important decision people can make is to accept Christ as Lord. Once they do, we need to help them pursue an intimate, knowing relationship with him. But our job isn't done at that point. Now we need to train them and help them stand on their own in Christ so that they, in turn, can do for others what we have done for them. Philippians 4:13 says, "I can do everything through [Christ] who gives me strength" (NIV). A very important part of our role as leaders is to instill in those we are leading the truth of this verse and to help them put it into practice.

Be there for those who need a drink of cold water. Be there for those who need to cry. Be there for those who fear the future. If you do, you will become Jesus with skin on. When they begin to experience that, they'll ask you to explain the hope that lies within you.

Be there, and be ready.

---

*DEAR LORD, you're coming back soon, and until you do, things will continue to get worse because of humanity's sinfulness. Whether I'm in the midst of a personal disaster or one on the scale of 9/11, turn my knowledge of you into prayer, care, and share opportunities for others. Help me to always be there to provide hope and answers to the questions others are asking. Amen.*

# 21

# Finishing Strong

The end of August had come much too quickly, and I filed into the giant cafeteria with the rest of the faculty from our school district. It was my first teaching job, so I still found the routine unfamiliar. I headed for a table and started to sit down, when I noticed that each chair held a white card with black letters that read "Neverflaginzeal."

I joined the other observers in the room, who prided themselves on their command of the English language, but we couldn't decipher its meaning.

Then the superintendent explained. "You won't remember all your students' names in the years to come, but every one of them will remember yours. The life you've chosen is meant to make a difference, so I'm here to remind you, 'Never flag in zeal.'"

The Bible also talks about the need for us to "neverflaginzeal":

- "Let us not become weary in doing good, for at the proper time we will reap a harvest if we do not give up." (Galatians 6:9, NIV)
- "Christ is faithful as a son over God's house. And we are his house, if we hold on to our courage and the hope of which we boast." (Hebrews 3:6, NIV)
- "We have come to share in Christ if we hold firmly till the end the confidence we had at first." (Hebrews 3:14, NIV)

- "Do not grow weary in doing good." (2 Thessalonians 3:13)
- "I have fought the good fight, I have finished the race, I have kept the faith." (2 Timothy 4:7)

Neverflaginzeal. Don't give up. Hold on to your courage and hope. Do not grow weary in doing good. The Bible is talking about not letting go of our passion for the deeper things of God. John accused the church in Ephesus of flagging in zeal. He called it leaving, or forsaking, their "first love" (Revelation 2:4). The fact that the writers of the Bible took such pains to tell us not to lose our enthusiasm for really knowing God warns us of the probability that it will happen. Yet as we read these words, many of us would probably deny that our faith could cool.

I wrote this chapter during the Easter season, so I can't help but think of the disciples as they celebrated the Passover with Jesus in the upper room. As they ate together, Jesus broke the time of celebration with somber words: "I tell you the truth, one of you will betray me—one who is eating with me" (Mark 14:18, NIV).

We can only guess what thoughts went through the disciples' minds. Their responses must have been similar to that of a waitress when my mother reported that she had found a fingernail in her drink. Instead of recoiling in disgust or trying to make amends, the waitress merely looked at her hands and said, "Ain't mine!"

As Jesus spoke the words, each of the disciples must have thought, *Not me! Ain't mine! I'll neverflaginzeal!* Only a few hours later Peter would say to Jesus, "Even if all fall away, I will not" (Mark 14:29, NIV).

Remember, Peter was one of Jesus' disciples, one of his best friends, an observer of Jesus' transfiguration on Mount Hermon. Peter had gotten to really know Jesus in a most intimate way. But Jesus told Peter without hesitation, "Assuredly, I say to you that today, even this night, before the rooster crows twice, you will deny Me three times" (v. 30).

Jesus realized that the surroundings of our lives can shift quickly from the security and tranquillity of the upper room to the harsh reality of Gethsemane and the Cross. We may experience an incredible, personal, life-changing transfiguration of Christ in our own time with him on the mountain, but how will we respond when "real life" hits?

## THE TREASURE YOU FIND

For my birthday one year Dave gave me pearl earrings with small diamonds mounted on the side. I had wanted pearl earrings for a while, but I had been wearing fake ones. Though observers didn't know the difference, I did, and I longed for the real thing.

Now, thanks to my husband, I owned them, and I wore them selectively. When I wasn't wearing them, I kept them in a small white box, tucked in the corner of a drawer. When I was traveling, I made sure I kept this treasure in my purse, just in case I got separated from my luggage.

But then I started getting careless. Instead of wearing my earrings only on special occasions, I put them on one day and wore them around the house. I enjoyed them all over again with every glance in a mirror; then I returned them to their safe place that night. The next morning I donned them again and enjoyed them all day long. That night I loved the way they looked with my nightgown, so I smiled confidently at Dave, hoping he noticed how pretty I looked before we switched off the light. Believe it or not, I checked my earrings at least once during the night to be sure they were still there.

This relaxed enjoyment of my pearls continued. Then one day my cleaning ladies arrived to do their thing. As I excused myself to continue my work at the computer, I unconsciously raised one hand to my ear to check my jewels again. One of them was gone. I shot out the door of my office and asked the cleaning ladies to help me find the earring before their sweeper did. We located the back of the earring, but not the pearl itself.

I continued my work that day with a certain sense of heaviness and alerted Dave to my loss. It wasn't until the following day that I found my earring in the laundry room. I was overjoyed.

Pearl earrings do not begin to compare with the treasure we found when we came to Christ. Having him forgive our sins and come to live inside us is the greatest prize a human being can ever have. But really getting to know Jesus in a deep and personal way adds pricelessness, brilliance, and lustre to our lives in ways we cannot measure. That's why Jesus told the parable of the pearl of great price: "The kingdom of heaven is like a merchant seeking beautiful pearls, who, when he had found one pearl of great price, went and sold all that he had and bought it" (Matthew 13:45-46).

We can compare this parable to our own quest to really know Christ. A merchant's goal is to make a profit, not through hard labor but through studying and gathering knowledge to help him make decisions that will cause him to prosper. Similarly, your salvation and mine were not a result of our works. We cannot earn the free gift God has given us. We depend on the things we learn about him, through which we can discover the wise things in which to invest. Relationship with Christ happens as we acquire knowledge and then make the decision that we must have him. What made it possible for the merchant to find the pearl of great price?

**He Looked for It**
The parable of the hidden treasure (Matthew 13:44) occurs just before the one about the pearl of great price. The earlier parable tells about a man who stumbles on a hidden treasure in a field, a treasure he didn't know existed, and he goes out and buys the field.

The parable of the pearl of great price (v. 45-46) is different, however, in that the merchant goes out for the *purpose* of finding the pearl of great price. Once he does, he sells everything he has to get it.

You were likely already a Christian when you opened this book. If so, you had previously discovered the hidden treasure of salvation. You could have stayed right where you were. Many believers do and still make heaven their home. But you wanted more. You longed for a deeper, more intimate knowledge of God, so you set out to get it. Like the merchant, you put your mind and efforts on pearly things. Pearl hunting became the goal of your life.

The merchant didn't seek ordinary pearls but "beautiful pearls." He put everything he had into finding them. He knew the difference between authentic, beautiful pearls and counterfeits, and he sought the real thing with diligence.

## He Didn't Stop until He Found It

The merchant set out with moderate expectations to find beautiful pearls, but he found something far more marvelous than he had ever envisioned. He discovered that one pearl of great price.

When my mother set out on her journey to "really know this Lord who would heal her little sister," she knew she was after something good. What she actually found, however, was better than she could have imagined. She found an intimate, personal, daily walk with Christ that has taken her on an adventure of hills and valleys where she continues to find him walking close to her.

My journey to really know him began when I was a desperate single mom, afraid to go forward without his help in raising my children. I have often said that God *had* to answer my prayers because he tripped over me every morning when he got up. I asked him to come into my life and use me for whatever he wanted. I knew I would find answered prayer, but I didn't know I would find

Someone who would instruct me, guide me, teach me in the most intimate ways. I didn't know that really knowing God would reveal the God who really knew me.

Like the merchant, we set out in this book to find the beautiful pearl of a personal, growing relationship with Christ. We searched with all our might to find it. My words, however, cannot do justice to what you actually find when you really get to know him.

My mom's journey has taken half a century, and mine has taken nearly twenty years so far. However long your journey has gone, you have found the pearl of great price. Every day that fellow knowers continue to pursue the treasure, the pearl shines brighter than the day before as we see yet another aspect of its brilliance.

## He Sold Everything to Get It

The merchant didn't stop to consult his accountant. He recognized a good thing and considered the cost; then he decided that the benefits of having the pearl far outweighed the sacrifice and inconvenience of getting it. He made a decision to go for it and never looked back. He sold everything he had, everything that stood between him and the pearl. Nothing would keep him from owning it.

You and I saw a good thing too. We took a look within ourselves and saw that we were living short of the relationship we could have in Christ. Then we set out to find it. Through much inward discipline, we shine the pearl within us and then take it outside to show it to others.

It's possible that you didn't think the pearl was worth the price and you didn't go after it. But if you have found it, be careful to keep it. Pearl snatchers abound, and we must take precautions to guard against them.

## THE TREASURE YOU KEEP

Peter did deny Jesus three times by the next morning, and you and I are only a rooster's crow away, too, if we don't keep watch to guard our treasure and neverflaginzeal. Before I leave you, let me suggest five ways to safeguard your intimate, passionate, committed walk with God.

### Be Honest

If Peter had realized his own propensity for not finishing strong in those early years, perhaps he would have been more careful to guard against it. One afternoon in the hospital during Dad's final days of battling pancreatic cancer, he described to my mother some people that God had laid on his heart to pray for. He also talked about how God was challenging him in his own life with the words of 1 Corinthians 9:27: "I discipline my body and bring it into subjection, lest, when I have preached to others, I myself should become disqualified."

That night, Dad died. Dad knew that though he had walked with the Lord for a long time, every child of God has to guard against laying down his arms. God was still working in my dad just hours before he died.

Finishing weak became possible for the first disciples, and it's possible for you, too. Be honest about that and take whatever steps are necessary to guard your commitment.

### Be Accountable

After we moved to Colorado, the wife of a young Christian family we knew called and told me that her husband had had an affair. His mistake threatened to destroy that beautiful family. I talked to them often and recommended a Christian counselor I knew.

Inside, however, I felt angry. Where were the men in her husband's life to hold him accountable? Were men he'd grown to trust regularly meeting with him, giving him the chance to tell them about the temptation he was facing? Where were the men who could show him how to overcome temptation?

Make yourself accountable to at least one mature believer that you trust, and accept at least one invitation from someone else to hold that person accountable too. When we have such a support system, we have help in keeping our Christian commitment and our walk strong.

## Be Aware

Keep your eyes on the potential pearl thieves in your life. Remember your own weaknesses, which left unchecked could destroy your growth and enthusiasm for the Lord. Maybe you have trouble praying regularly. Perhaps you're holding on to some sin, a damaging habit, or a wishy-washy commitment. You can still be a Christian and live side by side with these thieves for a time, but if you do, they are sure to rob you of the pearl of a real, knowing relationship with God. This, by the way, is a good argument for the importance of accountability partners, who can speak the truth to you in love when they see an area in which you may be at risk.

## Be On Fire

Victor Hugo wrote about love's duration in *Les Miserables:* "The power of a glance has been so much abused in love stories that it has come to be disbelieved in. Few people dare now to say that two beings have fallen in love because they have looked at each other. Yet it is in this way that love begins, and in this way only. The rest is only the rest, and comes afterwards. Nothing is more real than those great shocks which two souls give each other in exchanging this spark."[1]

Though Hugo's romantic thunderbolt sounds appealing, for many men and women, falling in love takes a slower course. Whether love grows from one passionate glance or takes its time, enduring love takes work. Psychologists have identified a number of factors that increase the chances that a love relationship will last:

- *Alikeness:* The more alike two romantic partners are, the more apt they are to stay together. Relationships in which the partners are well matched for age, intelligence, education, and physical attractiveness have a better-than-average chance of surviving.
- *Closeness:* Couples who stay together tend to spend a lot of time together, to engage in many shared activities, and to consider each other when making everyday plans and decisions. For such couples, the enjoyment of being together tends to increase with time.
- *Personality:* Certain personality traits can affect how people behave toward a romantic partner, how they perceive themselves and are perceived by that person, and their partner's satisfaction with the relationship. Among the traits most important to maintaining a relationship is empathy, a feeling of compassion and sympathy for the other person.[2]

Qualities similar to those above will also help your intimacy, passion, and commitment in your relationship with God to last over the long haul, if you work at staying close to him through the disciplines of prayer, study, and fasting. You know your personality and your history related to consistency, perseverance, and commitment. What does it take for you to be on fire with passion for God? What will it take for you to stay on fire for God? Find out what does it for you, and then do those things.

**Be Focused on Eternity**
Every time I start to get distracted in my quest to know and love God more, I realize that I am not keeping my eyes on eternity. K. P.

Yohannan, author of *Living in the Light of Eternity,* calls it horizontal instead of vertical thinking. He writes: "You're horizontally oriented, thinking about the here-and-now—your tired and dusty feet, your growling stomachs, your parched throats. But pull your attention away for a minute. Lift up your eyes! Look into eternity and see what I see. You say there are still four months before harvest arrives. But I tell you, look right now to the souls of men and women around you. The fields are already ripe and ready to be harvested. If you wait a little longer, the crop will be gone—destroyed."[3]

Focusing on eternity requires that we keep our eyes on what is ahead, not on what is behind us. The great heroes of the faith described in Hebrews 11 lived in the light of eternity. They didn't look back:

> These people were still living by faith when they died.
> They did not receive the things promised; they only saw
> them and welcomed them from a distance. And they
> admitted that they were aliens and strangers on earth.
> People who say such things show that they are looking
> for a country of their own. If they had been thinking of the
> country they had left, they would have had opportunity to
> return. Instead, they were longing for a better country—
> a heavenly one. Therefore God is not ashamed to be called
> their God, for he has prepared a city for them. (Hebrews
> 11:13-16, NIV)

Again Yohannan writes: "We need to retrain our minds to interpret everything we do, everything we see, everything we spend in light of eternity—in the light of souls that are dying without Jesus."[4]

Whenever you face a choice between doing or not doing a task, ask yourself, *Does it matter for eternity?* Whenever you need to make a call between spending your efforts on building your career or building your walk with God, ask yourself, *Which of them matters for eternity?*

If you use this as a filter for every decision you make, you'll be able to make right decisions consistently.

Recently our pastor told a story about his father, Andy, who as a high school student in Kansas in the late forties set all kinds of records in the one-mile race. When it came time for the state meet, everyone had Andy picked to win first place.

The day came, and the gun sounded. Andy immediately jumped out in front and carried his usual, comfortable lead. Spectators cheered as his momentum grew. At last the finish line was in sight. Andy glanced over his shoulder and didn't see anyone close, so instead of finishing those last few yards with a kick, he relaxed as he envisioned holding the blue ribbon. Then the crowd started going wild. Andy smiled with confidence at the fans cheering him on. But just as he was about to cross the finish line, a runner who had been in sixth place bolted past him and won by a nose. Andy came in second.

Our pastor says his dad has replayed that race in his mind hundreds of times. Each time he stays strong to the end and actually wins. But only one race counted—the one in the record books, and it's the one Andy didn't win.

You've been running the race, and you've chosen to run it well through discipline and regular workouts with God. But unless you stay with it and don't let up, unless you sprint to the finish, you won't end strong. That's why the apostle Paul made up his mind to neverflaginzeal: "I consider my life worth nothing to me, if only I may finish the race and complete the task the Lord Jesus has given me—the task of testifying to the gospel of God's grace" (Acts 20:24, NIV).

Just before Paul was executed, he again affirmed his commitment to neverflaginzeal: "I have fought the good fight, I have finished the race, I have kept the faith. Now there is in store for me the crown of righteousness, which the Lord, the righteous Judge, will award to me on that day—and not only to me, but also to all who have longed for his appearing" (2 Timothy 4:7-8, NIV).

The closer we get to the end, the more we will have to fight the desire to relax. Lots of things will try to distract us, lots of people will try to discourage us. But resist the urge, and finish strong: It is the last step that wins. It is when heaven's heights are in full view that hell's gate is most persistent and full of deadly peril. Let us not be weary in well-doing, for in due season we shall reap, if we faint not. So run that ye may obtain.[5]

Don't get careless now. Finish the race. Protect your pearl. Keep the faith and your intimate, passionate, committed walk with Christ the most cherished treasure of your life. Neverflaginzeal.

And if you do these things, then you will really know him as he is. Amen and amen.

# NOTES

## Introduction

1. John Stallings, "Learning to Lean," copyright © 1976 (Bridge Building Music, Inc. [BMI], a division of Brentwood-Benson Music Publishing, Inc., 1976).
2. Emphasis was added in all three verses.

## Chapter 1

1. J. I. Packer, *Knowing God* (Downers Grove, Ill.: InterVarsity, 1993), 34.
2. Packer, *Knowing God,* 34.
3. *Roget's II: The New Thesaurus* (Boston: Houghton Mifflin, 1980), 545.
4. Gordon MacDonald, *The Life God Blesses* (Nashville: Nelson, 1997), 61.
5. David Gates, "Living a New Normal," *Newsweek,* 8 October 2001, 54–59.
6. Gates, "Living a New Normal."
7. Calvin Miller, *Into the Depths of God* (Minneapolis: Bethany, 2000), 13.
8. Packer, *Knowing God,* 26.
9. Packer, *Knowing God,* 41.

## Chapter 2

1. A. W. Tozer, *That Incredible Christian* (Harrisburg, Pa.: Christian Publications, 1964), 64.
2. Bruce Wilkinson, *First Hand Faith* (Santa Ana, Calif.: Vision House, 1996), 13–20.
3. A. W. Tozer, *Faith beyond Reason* (Camp Hill, Pa.: Christian Publications, 1989), 102.
4. Calvin Miller, *Into the Depths of God* (Minneapolis: Bethany, 2000), 16.
5. Miller, *Into the Depths of God,* 17.
6. Dietrich Bonhoeffer, *The Cost of Discipleship* (New York: Collier, 1949), 105.
7. C. S. Lewis, *The Problem of Pain* (New York: Macmillan, 1962), 92–93.
8. Miller, *Into the Depths of God,* 17.
9. Henry Blackaby, *Experiencing God* (Nashville: Broadman and Holman, 1997), 217.
10. J. I. Packer, *Knowing God* (Downers Grove, Ill.: InterVarsity, 1993), 22.
11. Packer, *Knowing God,* 19.

## Chapter 3

1. Brennan Manning, *The Ragamuffin Gospel: Good News for the Bedraggled, Beat-Up, and Burnt Out* (Portland, Ore.: Multnomah, 1990), 165.

2. Robert J. Sternberg, *Psychology: Contexts of Behavior* (Guilford, Conn.: Brown and Benchmark, 1996), 666–667.

3. Gary Chapman, *The Five Love Languages* (Chicago: Northfield, 1995).

**Chapter 4**

1. Joni Eareckson Tada, *A Quiet Place in a Crazy World* (Sisters, Ore.: Multnomah, 1994), 9.

2. Tada, *A Quiet Place,* 11.

3. *Psychology Today,*

4. John Eldredge, *The Sacred Romance: Drawing Closer to the Heart of God* (Nashville: Nelson, 1997), 19.

5. Joseph M. Stowell, *Far from Home* (Chicago: Moody, 1998), 165–173.

6. Stowell, *Far from Home,* 39–40.

7. Hank Hanegraaff, *The Prayer of Jesus* (Nashville: Word, 2000), 10.

8. Frederick Buechner, *Telling Secrets,* (San Francisco: HarperSanFrancisco, 1991), 45.

9. Eldredge, *The Sacred Romance,* 4–5.

10. Connie Neal, *Dancing in the Arms of God: Finding Intimacy and Fulfillment by Following His Lead* (Grand Rapids: Zondervan, 1995), 21.

11. Stowell, *Far from Home,* 14.

**Chapter 5**

1. *Merriam-Webster's Collegiate Dictionary,* 10th ed., s.v. "passion."

2. Bill and Kathy Peel, *Discover Your Destiny: Finding the Courage to Follow Your Dreams* (Colorado Springs: NavPress, 1996), 78.

3. Calvin Miller, *Into the Depths of God* (Minneapolis: Bethany, 2000), 23.

4. Gerald May, *The Awakened Heart: Opening Yourself to the Love You Need* (San Francisco: HarperSanFrancisco, 1991), 1.

5. John Eldredge, *The Journey of Desire: Searching for the Life We've Only Dreamed Of* (Nashville: Nelson, 2000), 13–15.

6. Langston Hughes, "Dreams," in *The Random House Book of Poetry for Children* (New York: Random House, 1983), 225.

7. Gordon MacDonald, *Renewing Your Spiritual Passion* (Nashville: Nelson, 1989), 37–68.

8. *Braveheart,* Paramount Pictures, 1995.

9. Miller, *Into the Depths of God,* 81–87.

10. A. W. Tozer, *Tozer on Christian Leadership* (Camp Hill, Pa.: Christian Publications, 2001).

11. MacDonald, *Renewing Your Spiritual Passion,* 56–68.

12. Miller, *Into the Depths of God,* 25.

## Chapter 6
1. *Merriam-Webster's Collegiate Dictionary,* 10th ed., s.v. "commitment."
2. Jerry White, *The Power of Commitment* (Colorado Springs: NavPress, 1985), 13.
3. White, *The Power of Commitment,* 14.
4. Joni Eareckson Tada, *Holiness in Hidden Places* (Nashville: Countryman, 1999), 53.
5. A. W. Tozer, *Jesus Is Victor,* comp. Gerald B. Smith (Camp Hill, Pa.: Christian Publications, 1989), 116–117.

## Chapter 7
1. Hannah Hurnard, *Hinds' Feet on High Places* (Wheaton, Ill.: Tyndale, 1976), 52–53.
2. *The Confessions of Saint Augustine* (New York: Collier, 1961), 129.
3. C. S. Lewis, *The Great Divorce* (New York: Macmillan, 1946), 98–103.
4. Henry Blackaby, *Experiencing God* (Nashville: Broadman and Holman, 1997), 155.
5. A. W. Tozer, *The Pursuit of God* (Camp Hill, Pa.: Christian Publications, 1993), 27.
6. Frances J. Roberts, *Come Away My Beloved* (Palos Verdes Estates, Calif.: King's Press, 1970), 74.
7. Hurnard, *Hinds' Feet on High Places,* 44.

## Chapter 8
1. *Merriam-Webster's Collegiate Dictionary,* 10th ed., s.v. "epiphany."
2. Gordon MacDonald, *The Life God Blesses* (Nashville: Nelson, 1997), xxii–xxiii.
3. Mrs. Charles E. Cowman, *Streams in the Desert* (Grand Rapids: Zondervan, 1965), 53.

## Chapter 9
1. François Fénelon, *Christian Counsel on Divers Matters Pertaining to the Inner Life* (Philadelphia: G. W. McCalla, 1899).
2. A. B. Simpson, *The Quotable Christian,* comp. Helen Hosier (Uhrichsville, Ohio: Barbour, 1998), 179.
3. Hank Hanegraaff, *The Prayer of Jesus* (Nashville: Word, 2000), 20.
4. Samuel Chadwick, *The Path of Prayer* (Kansas City, Mo.: Beacon Hill, 1931).
5. Henry Blackaby, *Experiencing God* (Nashville: Broadman and Holman, 1997), 146.
6. John Allan Lavendar, *Why Prayers Are Unanswered* (Valley Forge, Pa.: Judson Press, 1967), 21.

7. R. A. Torrey, *How to Pray* (Chicago; New York: Revell, 1900).

8. *Merriam-Webster's Collegiate Dictionary,* 10th ed., s.v. "fervent."

9. Oswald Chambers, *My Utmost for His Highest* (New York: Dodd, Mead, 1935), October 17.

10. *Merriam-Webster's Collegiate Dictionary,* 10th ed., s.v. "tarry."

11. Henri Nouwen, *The Way of the Heart.*

12. Gary Smalley, *Secrets to Lasting Love: Uncovering the Keys to Lifelong Intimacy* (New York: Simon and Schuster, 2000), 28.

13. Smalley, *Secrets to Lasting Love,* 28.

14. Hanegraaff, *The Prayer of Jesus,* 21.

## Chapter 10

1. Ralph S. Cushman, *Spiritual Hilltops* (New York; Cincinnati: Abingdon-Cokesbury, 1932).

## Chapter 11

1. Ole Hallesby, *Prayer* (Minneapolis: Augsburg, 1959), 117.

2. For more information about these seven important things to consider in fasting, you can order a copy of the late Bill Bright's pamphlet "Seven Basic Steps to Successful Fasting and Prayer" by writing Campus Crusade for Christ, P.O. Box 593684, Orlando, FL 32859.

## Chapter 12

1. Calvin Miller, *Into the Depths of God* (Minneapolis: Bethany, 2000), 54.

2. Miller, *Into the Depths of God,* 54.

3. Miller, *Into the Depths of God,* 48.

4. Richard J. Foster, *Celebration of Discipline* (San Francisco: Harper & Row, 1978), 84–89.

5. Foster, *Celebration of Discipline,* 93–95.

6. Dick Eastman, *Change the World School of Prayer* (Studio City, Calif.: World Literature Crusade, 1976), C62–64.

## Chapter 13

1. John Calvin, *Devotions and Prayers of John Calvin,* comp. Charles E. Edwards (Grand Rapids, Mich.: Baker, 1976).

2. Virginia Whitman, *Mustard: The Excitement of Prayer Answered* (Wheaton, Ill.: Tyndale, 1973), 100.

3. E. M. Bounds, *The Essentials of Prayer* (Minneapolis: Bethany, 1961), 38.

4. Miller, *Into the Depths of God,* (Minneapolis: Bethany, 2000), 55.

5. Amy Carmichael, quoted in Donald E. Demaray, *Alive to God through Prayer* (Grand Rapids: Baker, 1965), 27.

6. Johnson Oatman Jr., "Count Your Blessings" in *Songs for Young People* (Chicago, 1897).
7. Harold Lindsell, *When You Pray* (Wheaton, Ill.: Tyndale, 1969), 30.
8. Dennis Jernigan, "We Will Worship the Lamb of Glory," copyright © 1989, Shepherd's Heart Music, Inc. (Nashville: Word, 1989).

## Chapter 15

1. Hannah Hurnard, *Hinds' Feet on High Places* (Wheaton, Ill.: Tyndale, 1976), 49–50.
2. *Webster's Third New International Dictionary of the English Language Unabridged,* s.v. "transfigure."

## Chapter 16

1. Walter A. Henrichsen, *Disciples Are Made—Not Born* (Wheaton, Ill.: Victor, 1988), 11.
2. Charles Haddon Spurgeon, *The Soul-Winner* (Grand Rapids: Zondervan, 1948), 140.
3. Os Guinness, *The Call: Finding and Fulfilling the Purpose of Your Life* (Nashville: Word, 1998), 14.
4. William Fay, *Share Jesus without Fear* (Nashville: Broadman and Holman, 1999).

## Chapter 17

1. Robert Coleman, *The Master Plan of Discipleship* (Grand Rapids: Revell, 1998), 9.
2. Coleman, *The Master Plan of Discipleship,* 10.
3. Bobb Biehl, *Mentoring* (Nashville: Broadman and Holman, 1996), 31.
4. Walter A. Henrichsen, *Disciples Are Made—Not Born* (Wheaton, Ill.: Victor, 1988), 11–12.

## Chapter 18

1. *Merriam-Webster's Collegiate Dictionary,* 10th ed., s.v. "passion."
2. *Merriam-Webster's Collegiate Dictionary,* 10th ed., s.v. "ability."
3. *Merriam-Webster's Collegiate Dictionary,* 10th ed., s.v. "personality."
4. Gary Smalley and John Trent, *The Two Sides of Love* (Colorado Springs: Focus on the Family, 1992).
5. C. Paul Willis, *Bells and Pomegranates* (Shippensburg, Pa.: Destiny Image, 1991), 10–17.

## Chapter 19

1. John Claypool, *Tracks of a Fellow Struggler: How to Handle Grief* (Waco, Tex.: Word, 1974), 30.

2. M. Scott Peck, *The Road Less Traveled* (New York: Simon and Schuster, 1978), 1.

3. Walter A. Henrichsen, *Disciples Are Made—Not Born* (Wheaton, Ill.: Victor, 1988), 42.

4. James Strong, *Strong's Concordance*

5. Eddie Carswell and Babbie Mason, "Trust His Heart," copyright © 1989, May Sun Music (Nashville: Word, 1989).

**Chapter 20**

1. AOL national on-line study, spring 2003.

2. H. Richard Niebuhr, *Christ and Culture* (New York: Harper, 1975).

3. For additional information about Mary Marr's ministry, Outreach Alert and Christian Emergency Network, please visit the Web site www.ChristianEmergencyNetwork.com.

**Chapter 21**

1. Victor Hugo, *Les Misérables,* quoted in K. P. Yohannan, *Living in the Light of Eternity: Your Life Can Make a Difference* (Grand Rapids: Chosen Books, 1995), 19.

2. Camille B. Wortman and Elizabeth F. Loftus, eds., *Psychology* (New York: McGraw-Hill, 1992), 578–579.

3. Yohannan, *Light of Eternity,* 22.

4. Yohannan, *Light of Eternity,* 22.

5. Mrs. Charles E. Cowman, *Streams in the Desert* (Grand Rapids, Mich.: Zondervan, 1925), 81.